# MANAGING PRODUCT MANAGEMENT

**EMPOWERING YOUR ORGANIZATION TO PRODUCE COMPETITIVE PRODUCTS AND BRANDS**

## STEVEN HAINES

New York  Chicago  San Francisco  Lisbon  London  Madrid  Mexico City
Milan  New Delhi  San Juan  Seoul  Singapore  Sydney  Toronto

The **McGraw·Hill** Companies

1 2 3 4 5 6 7 8 9 10   DOC/DOC   1 9 8 7 6 5 4 3 2 1

ISBN 978-0-07-176997-6
MHID 0-07-176997-8

e-ISBN 978-0-07-177005-7
e-MHID 0-07-177005-4

McGraw-Hill books are available at special quantity discounts to use as premiums and sales promotions, or for use in corporate training programs. To contact a representative, please e-mail us at bulksales@mcgraw-hill.com.

This book is printed on acid-free paper.

*I dedicate this book to three important people in my life who serve as my inspiration:*

To my wife, Debra. There is no other human being on the planet who demonstrates more of a zest for life and an uncanny knack to connect with people; she inspires me to believe in possibilities by always asking the simple question, "Why not?"

To my daughter, Alex. Although Alex is not a product manager or a corporate leader, she inspires me because she is passionate, creative, determined, and undeterred by adversity.

To my mom. When I was 17, she sat with me and inspired me to be a better writer, especially when I had to dissect *A Portrait of the Artist as a Young Man*; and she's still a brilliant editor, beyond what she may even acknowledge herself.

# CONTENTS

Prologue      ix

Introduction: Why Product Management      1
Matters to Your Company

## MODULE I      15
## CONTEXT

### CHAPTER 1      17
### REINVENTING THE WHEEL—FOR THE LAST TIME

### CHAPTER 2      36
### DESIGNING AN ORGANIZATIONAL STRATEGY
### FOR PRODUCT MANAGEMENT

*Case Study I*      61

Spotlight on Product Management Excellence:
Thomas & Betts, by Bob Caporale

## MODULE II      67
## CLARIFY

### CHAPTER 3      69
### EVERYONE IS IN THE PRODUCT MANAGEMENT SANDBOX

**CHAPTER 4**                                              **83**
**SOLVING THE PUZZLE OF THE PRODUCT MANAGEMENT
ORGANIZATION**

    *Case Study II*                                        III

    Spotlight on Product Management Excellence:
    TD Canada Trust, by Thomas Dyck


**MODULE III**                                            **117**
**CULTIVATE**

**CHAPTER 5**                                             **119**
**CLARIFYING THE ROLE OF THE PRODUCT MANAGER
TO IMPROVE STAFFING STRATEGIES**

**CHAPTER 6**                                             **147**
**CULTIVATING AND SHAPING PRODUCT MANAGERS**

    *Case Study III*                                      175

    Spotlight on Product Management Excellence:
    FedEx Services, by David K. Payton


**MODULE IV**                                             **181**
**CONTINUITY**

**CHAPTER 7**                                             **185**
**BUILDING A KNOWLEDGE-BASED COMMUNITY OF PRACTICE
FOR PRODUCT MANAGEMENT**

## CHAPTER 8                                      199
### DESIGNING AND SPONSORING CROSS-FUNCTIONAL PRODUCT TEAMS

## CHAPTER 9                                      217
### EMBEDDING A GOVERNING MODEL FOR SUSTAINING PRODUCT MANAGEMENT

*Case Study IV*                                  251

Spotlight on Product Management Excellence:
JetBlue Airways, by Rachel McCarthy


Epilogue                                         255
Bibliography                                     257
Index                                            259

# PROLOGUE

*The longest journey begins with the first step.*

—OLD CHINESE SAYING

About a year before I started writing this book, my editor at McGraw-Hill urged me to write a supplement to my first book, *The Product Manager's Desk Reference* (PMDR), since that book had surpassed everyone's expectations. The PMDR established *the* definitive body of knowledge for Product Management. In fact, it has become a standard reference for product managers, Product Management leaders, marketers, and others who help create, develop, launch, and manage products and services.

After considering his suggestion, I admitted to my editor that I could not visualize what I'd want to write about in a supplement. And for me, visualization is critical to anything I undertake.

Sometime later, after delivering an organizational diagnostic presentation to a client, I wondered whether the executive team of that client firm would actually follow through on the recommendations since there was so much work to do. In a parallel thought stream, I wondered about how other firms achieved success in their transformations. Thoughts about them led me to think about other client firms and the struggles they also faced. For instance, our transformational recommendations for some companies included work that would better align roles between Product Management and other areas. However, several of those firms had achieved only mixed success because there was resistance from leaders in other functions.

To clarify these concerns, I consulted with other leaders and started a project to assess the present state of Product Management by assembling some definitive, formalized data. To make it more relevant to those for whom it would have the most significance, the research would be performed from the vantage points of senior leaders, and it would reach across a vast and varied landscape of organizations, industries, and geographies. I wanted

to know what these leaders thought about many aspects of their own organizations regarding structure, strategy, market insight development, innovation, and portfolio management.

With that goal in mind, I decided to create a survey, and in my usual
overzealous style, I came up with no less than 211 questions! Furthermore,
I wanted answers to all of them, not only for my research but also because
I thought, "What leader wouldn't want to know the answers?"

It mushroomed into a monumental task: I had to ask, cajole, and plead
with people to spend a precious hour or two of their time on my survey
and then to spend more time on the phone with me. Some told me, "If you
weren't the person asking me to take this survey, I would have given up!"
Thankfully, they all came through. What I learned resulted in a 34-page
report (in a small font) entitled *The State of Product Management*. But that
was just the beginning. Now that I had some research, what should I do
with the information garnered? (This sort of situation reminds me I'm still
a product manager at heart—because I am compelled to ask the "What's
next?" question.)

The next questions were, "How do we tell people about it?" And "What
do I want them to do with it?" I decided to set up a meeting, and I determined
it should be a *big* meeting. How about gathering a few dozen executives in
a room to talk about Product Management? It would not be a gripe session
about what was *wrong*. I wanted to create a forum of senior leaders who
could talk about what was *right*. As a result, 51 leaders (of very estimable and
distinguished companies) gathered in a meeting room in New York City, in
mid-May 2010, for the first ever Product Management Leadership Summit.

The guiding principle of the meeting was that a group of people who
share a common interest in high-performance Product Management would
discuss their ideas and concerns. First on the agenda: My team and I presented a short summary of important findings from our research. Then
five senior leaders of eminent companies representing differing industries
presented their showcase examples. These examples were aligned with the
various segments of the research project. After each presentation segment, a
highly interactive discussion followed. As I led the wrap-up discussion at the
end of the summit, I asked for a show of hands: "How many people feel that
we would all benefit from a senior leadership community that would focus
on Product Management excellence?" All the participants raised their hands.

About a month after the summit, my editor from McGraw-Hill came to my office. Once again he wanted to discuss a possible supplement. Instead, I talked to him about my research and diagnostic work and about the insights I had gained from the summit. I also told him I had decided we needed to work more with senior leaders to help them in organizational planning and design with respect to the function and practice of Product Management. After all, leaders are responsible for the results of Product Management's endeavors—and they are the ones who know if they are succeeding or falling short.

The editor asked me, "How would you do that?" I replied that I wasn't sure, but maybe he could find an answer by reading my 34-page research report. He did read it. A week later he asked me to create an outline for a book that would expand on the results of the report. A few weeks after I sent him the finished outline, he asked me to write a brief paragraph on each chapter. It took me a month because once I started to delve into the issues, I couldn't limit my ideas to only one paragraph; the paragraphs ended up as two or three pages for each. And so the journey for this book began.

In the following months, my firm carried out another research project. This one focused on issues associated with organizational design and effectiveness as they related to Product Management. These efforts led to the formation of the Product Management Executive Board (PMEB). The mission of the PMEB is to create a community of senior leaders whose common desire is to effectively ingrain a *durable, repeatable, flexible, and scalable Product Management structure* within their firms, while sharing what they've learned along the way. The PMEB will carry out annual benchmark research projects that track trends in Product Management organizational design and effectiveness. The plan is that PMEB members also will participate by having annual assessments made in their own organizations. By doing so, they can not only compare their performance year over year but they can also track their position with respect to other member firms.

## THE JOURNEY WE ARE ABOUT TO TAKE

We are awash with comments in books, articles, and many consultants' websites telling the readers how complex the business world is. When I read these observations, I feel that the writers are belaboring the obvious. The more *important* discussions should be focused on:

- What do we do to support shrinking staffs and expanding markets?
- How do we adjust our organizational strengths and make intelligent adjustments to our staffing models to support our strategic imperatives?

The key to unlocking the door to this challenge is to do a more exacting and in-depth job of diagnosing our Product Management structures and then taking purposeful steps to allow us to fortify this function. The Product Management function is, in many cases, poorly understood within companies, and it is improperly and inconsistently placed on the organization chart.

Ideally, Product Management should be the heart and soul of an organization, instead of merely an adjunct. When it operates properly, this function can represent a unified source of competitive advantage and provide greater motivation to people who must work together, and in harmony, to produce competitive, innovative products and brands.

## MOVING FROM ORGANIZATIONAL ADOLESCENCE TO ORGANIZATIONAL MATURITY

When my daughter was an adolescent, going through her transformative times (need I say more?), in a fit of upset, I had to admit that parenting didn't come with a manual. I am fallible. We are all doing the best we can. That's where I think we are in our organizational evolution with respect to Product Management. Many firms are doing a great job and have reached Product Management adulthood. However, many, many more need to move the needle. And I'd like to help all who want to do so.

*I wrote this book for organizational leaders* because, as my research has shown me, it is the leaders who are best equipped to inspire, catalyze, and motivate people to move in the right direction. My desire is to provide you with the information necessary to make the substance of Product Management more meaningful, thus improving your Product Management assets and adding more value to your companies.

## SMALL STEPS ON THE JOURNEY

There may be areas where you find some significant challenges for you and your organization. You may be concerned that you will encounter resistance from people who lead major functions like engineering or manufacturing or operations. However, we can at least make a start. I want this book to equip you with the ideas and the tools you'll need to help you along your own journey. Even if you take only one small step or attempt only a gradual change, you may find that there are some rewards for doing so. And one step can lead to another because, as they say, "Nothing succeeds like success."

## INTRODUCTION

# WHY PRODUCT MANAGEMENT MATTERS TO YOUR COMPANY

In the business climate of the twenty-first century, companies must hone their operations to become more strategic, agile competitors. I firmly believe that the best approach to achieving this goal is through an enhanced utilization of the function of Product Management. My definition of this function is this: *Product Management is the systemic, holistic business management of products and services.*

With this simple definition, in the nine chapters of this book, I will provide a complete holistic guide to the improvement of Product Management in your company.

During the many years I have carried out practical research and worked with clients, I have learned that there are broad variances in how companies utilize Product Management. To give credit where credit is due: *Approximately one-quarter of the companies studied have done and continue to do a stellar job in managing Product Management!* These firms serve as the true benchmarks; they are enviable examples. If you are with one of these best-in-class companies, it might seem I am preaching to the converted. In that case, please use this book as a source of validation or reference.

Another third of the companies studied have begun to assemble the pieces of what I call the "Product Management puzzle": they are making some progress, but they are aware that they have some work to do.

That leaves the remainder of firms that have yet to begin their Product Management journey. The ancient saying "The longest journey begins with the first step" would seem to be apt. Whether you are in the segment of those who have yet to take that first step or you are among those who have already begun this journey, it is my hope that you will find this book to be a valuable and worthwhile source of material you can use.

I am greatly concerned about the degree to which the key skills and competencies of product managers have been allowed to erode. This erosion undermines the core capabilities of an organization, and thus, its competitive edge. To rectify this situation, it falls to the senior leaders to strengthen the Product Management function of their organization.

Most of you have an extensive background of corporate experiences and perspectives, all of which have contributed to your own unique understanding of Product Management and organizational dynamics. You have witnessed the effects of new strategies, leadership changes, organizational realignments, and other structural adjustments. Therefore, you know that many corporate changes and reorganizations are fraught with challenges and unfulfilled expectations. In such cases, the changes have detrimental impacts that include the following:

- *A domino effect that leads to more changes:* This compounds the challenges for employees (including product managers) as they struggle to understand their roles and responsibilities to carry out their work.
- *A static effect that leaves day-to-day work activities largely unchanged, due to fewer available resources:* As a result, many product managers and others tend to see radically increased workloads.
- *A degradation of continuous learning, coupled with a lack of acknowledgement of past mistakes:* By not fully understanding and appreciating how an organization arrived at its present state, current executive leadership teams may repeat mistakes they could have learned from.

In the face of all this, I believe senior leaders can be a force for positive change, by properly aligning and strengthening the function of Product Management of the organization.

## PRODUCT MANAGEMENT IS A VITAL *FUNCTION*

Although the Product Management function is included on the organization chart in many companies, the roles and expectations relegated to product managers tend to vary widely. From my experience in the field, I've found that companies often confuse the functions of Product Development, Project Management, and Product Management.

Organizational structures also differ. In some companies, product managers work directly in the business functions; in other organizations, they work in geographic regions. How you perceive Product Management is likely affected by the procedures you're most familiar with. No matter how you view it, the important thing to keep in mind is that within the organization, *Product Management is a function*, not a job title.

When Product Management isn't properly chartered, aligned, or scoped, you may encounter many challenges in the process of integrating the discipline of Product Management into an organization as a core capability. Therefore, organizational models need to be altered to best support the function of Product Management and the capabilities of product managers.

## THIS IS A BOOK FOR SENIOR LEADERS AND MANAGERS

I believe this book will be of particular interest to senior leaders and managers in every type of organization, regardless of size, structure, industry, or geography. The reason is that it presents and explains *the most important best practices that impact the effectiveness of Product Management*—including those that affect the creation and management of products and portfolios.

Since I'm part realist and part idealist, I will explain my ideal vision of vibrant organizational models; then I will show you how, in practical ways, these models can be fortified when you enhance the capabilities of those who perform Product Management. Doing so helps to ensure that the products, services, and portfolios will provide the desired competitive advantage.

## HOW THIS BOOK IS POSITIONED

There are a multitude of truly first-rate resources available to senior leaders. These resources provide focused insight into singular topics such as organizational design and development, business process improvement, business transformation, corporate maturity models, business excellence, and change management. Although each of these resources is excellent in its own right, *no single resource provides a comprehensive discussion about the vital role Product Management can play in corporate transformation*. This book is intended to fill that void.

Since the launch of my company, Sequent Learning Networks, I have been in continuous collaboration with hundreds of companies and thousands of people. This cast of thousands includes executives, managers, and individual contributors; and most of them work in Product Management and marketing organizations. Aside from giving me a position in which to conduct business, this situation has provided me with a genuine—and unique—learning laboratory in which a wide scope of ongoing practical research takes place.

Through various corporate assessments and diagnostics performed, I have found common characteristics and weak areas in Product Management implementations—namely, these:

- Product Management is deeply misunderstood, grossly marginalized, and vastly underutilized. For example, some companies create independent, deal-driven organizations in geographic regions. This structure does not provide fertile ground for product innovation. In such an environment, product managers are the fragile glue that works tirelessly to keep this function performing to meet the needs of the business.
- *Product* Management is treated like *project* management. This is common in industries with mature product portfolios, in firms with IT- or software-based products, and others. In this model, individuals with the title of "product manager" handle inbound requests from Sales and outside customers. In such circumstances, these product managers are forced by the circumstances to focus on the prioritization of features and other requests based mainly on available resources or customers' insistence that their requests are the most important. I refer to this as an *Insource-Outsource Model* because development is effectively "outsourced" using internal resources. Such a model prevents the product portfolio from being optimized.
- Product Management is considered to be another organizational silo. This model is best described as an impenetrable "City of

Silos" where functional agendas trump rational holistic business decision making. Furthermore, independent sanctions of diverse, incompatible goals typically result in ill-conceived activities and poor decision making. This can lead to products that do not contribute to the firm's bottom line.

- In many cases, senior leaders expect a product to come to market at breakneck speed. Some expectations are unrealistic. In the past few years, I have witnessed the spread of rapid, technical product development techniques used to meet the perceived need for speed. This is especially prevalent in firms with technology products or large technology infrastructures. Unfortunately, such methods outpace the actual work that is required to defend strategic product line investments. This means corporate gears spin at different speeds. As a result, products (complete or incomplete) are made available to the marketplace before they can be operationally absorbed or effectively sold. This model also undermines good business decision making and results in poor portfolio performance.

By learning to recognize these and other related issues, leaders can effectively discern the common denominators that impact product portfolios. Application of this knowledge to the Product Management organization will help the company become a more active competitor in chosen markets.

## WHO SHOULD CARE ABOUT PRODUCT MANAGEMENT?

Leaders in all functions need to understand the purpose and importance of the Product Management function. They also need to know how much it can contribute to the ways a company creates and sustains profitable products and portfolios. Who's included? It's a long list, but at minimum, it consists of leaders and managers in the following areas:

- The C Suite
- Product Strategy
- Product Management

- Innovation and Discovery
- Research and Development
- Engineering
- Information Technology
- Marketing
- Product Marketing
- Human Resources Management
- Organizational Development and Effectiveness
- Finance
- Legal
- Compliance
- Manufacturing and Production
- Supply Chain

At first glance, this probably looks like everyone in the company. Yes, you're right! I truly believe leaders who work in *each of these functional areas of the company* will benefit from a clear understanding of Product Management, as presented and discussed in this book.


## THE MAIN PLAYERS IN THE PRODUCT MANAGEMENT SANDBOX

In a typical organization, there are many different job titles and levels used within the Product Management function. Since this can be confusing, I will use the term *product manager* as a general term for those people who typically carry out all aspects of Product Management work.

Although I may simplify things by using a single title, your company probably segments the population of product managers in a variety of ways. These would include the product managers' perceived levels of competence and experience, as well as the maturity of the products. In Chapter 5, I will discuss the benefits of segmenting the population of product managers and guidelines to help you improve your staffing strategy. In the meantime, it is appropriate to restate my position that Product Management *does not refer to a job title*. Product Management *refers to the business management of products and services in a systemic and holistic manner.*

## HOW THIS BOOK IS ORGANIZED

This book is written in a linear fashion and organized into four modules and nine chapters that together can help you create or fortify a robust, successful Product Management organization. This allows me to present Product Management as a dynamic, interconnected living system that reaches into every branch of the organization. As you read the material, it is vital for you to keep in mind that *the function of Product Management is not necessarily a linear set of actions and work flows. Rather, it is a dynamic system that depends on the work of various people and many interconnected processes across the lives of many products and portfolios.*

The book provides a variety of helpful tools, suggestions, and guidelines. Many are shown as lists, tables, or templates. As you read the material, and as you identify with areas that are unique to your own situation, you may feel that there is just too much to do, or you may feel overwhelmed by the enormity of it all. To avoid these frustrations, keep in mind that the complete implementation of Product Management is not something accomplished in a day, a month, or even a year. Think about how you consider a variety of strategies for your product lines and, based on a set of decision criteria, how you prioritize each move. I suggest a similar approach to Product Management—that is, move forward in gradual steps. Try to break down your opportunities for improvement into small pieces. That way, you can accrue a few solid victories that will effectively help you plant and cultivate Product Management roots that will survive for the long term.

### MODULE I. CONTEXT

You cannot set any type of strategy in place if you don't understand the road you've traveled and how you got to where you are. This module serves to provide a broad perspective on the path that an organization may have taken and what its current state actually looks like. Knowing where you are and how you got there will allow you to plot an astute path forward that puts Product Management in a much more advantageous position within the organization.

## Chapter 1. Reinventing the Wheel—for the Last Time

In today's business environment, most firms reorganize with some degree of regularity. Many of these organizational changes fail to consider the impact on the function of Product Management. This is mainly because *there is no universal approach to the function and purpose of Product Management.*

While it is true that people in the organization are actually managing various aspects of the product's business, this work is not being performed consistently. This lack of consistency makes it difficult to attain predictable results. When there is a lack of consistency and predictability in any organization, it may be a challenge to establish the proper strategic focus and direction. Unfortunately, many senior leaders who assume their new roles do not look at prior transformational efforts, and they may repeat the mistakes of the past.

In this chapter, I suggest how to evaluate prior transformative efforts, and I describe how you can better situate Product Management in the firm. I describe my rationale for making this happen, and I offer important suggestions for you to consider so that you don't have to reinvent the wheel when it comes to Product Management.

## Chapter 2. Designing an Organizational Strategy for Product Management

Although companies strive to be more efficient and operate more effectively, transformative efforts for the organization should strongly consider the impact of those efforts on Product Management and the optimal organizational structure for Product Management. This chapter suggests that leaders create the structure of Product Management in much the same manner as they formulate strategies.

A Baseline Competency Model and a Reference Model for Product Management must be agreed upon and implemented consistently. This will yield a fair measurement of the knowledge, skills, and experience of the product managers. Organizational gaps can be analyzed against the standardized model, and relevant options can be considered for the future direction of Product Management. *The importance of measuring against a consistent model cannot be overemphasized.* This is one part of the formula that creates a standard foundation for effective Product Management. Furthermore, this foundation, when put into place, helps Product Management to survive future transformative reorganizations. Otherwise, you're just starting from scratch every time the organization chart is redrawn.

## MODULE II. CLARIFY

It is impossible to secure a vision for the future if you don't have clarity around the potential in front of you. For Product Management to take root and to thrive in any organization, leaders need to provide a central theme for Product Management that addresses how Product Management should fit within the organization, regardless of corporate architecture. The chapters in this module can help your organization attain a clarity of purpose so that you can fulfill the vision for Product Management as a corporate function.

### Chapter 3. Everyone Is in the Product Management Sandbox

The basic precept for this chapter is that everyone in the organization is, to some extent, involved in Product Management. While each function contributes in varying degrees, everyone contributes to the overall success of the firm. Unfortunately, people who work in different functions do not always operate with this mindset because they feel their particular functions are more important than others. Such a functional "silo mindset" is unproductive.

This chapter focuses on getting everyone into the Product Management sandbox. It achieves this through the use of a common definition and Reference Model for Product Management (established in Chapter 2). It also sets the stage to ensure that product managers can establish their credentials as dependable businesspeople. Finally, it will put a stake in the ground for everyone across the organization who should understand the processes, tools, and documents used to plan, develop, launch, and manage products and portfolios.

### Chapter 4. Solving the Puzzle of the Product Management Organization

Product Management is a holistic business methodology that can be compared to the structure of a human body. The analogy suggests a vibrant living entity that is composed of overlapping, interlocking systems and functions that influence each other in very complex ways. Relationships between the "players" in the body are dynamic and situational, and they are motivated by a fluid array of decisions that arise from changing circumstances. As a result, these interactions and decisions are driven by finely tuned protocols and methods. This chapter lays out the pieces of this systemic organizational puzzle, enabling leaders to fortify the structure of Product Management within the organization.

## MODULE III. CULTIVATE

With the proper context set and a clear vision in place, it's time to make sure that you have the right people on staff. Once you get them on staff, you have to cultivate and shape them for success. This module introduces business leaders to usable methods, tools, and techniques that can be easily adopted in any organization.

### Chapter 5. Clarifying the Role of the Product Manager to Improve Staffing Strategies

Whether a company flourishes, merely survives, or fails depends on the effectiveness of its overall staffing strategy. This is especially true for product managers. With this perspective, the case for the sustainability of Product Management is closely coupled with how a firm hires, situates, and enables product managers to excel as strategy-minded, critical thinking business managers.

An efficacious staff of product managers can equip the firm with great potential to achieve competitive advantage. This chapter helps leaders understand how to clarify the role of the product managers based on the most common set of competencies required for the job. The methods set forth in this chapter serve to guide leaders to select, hire, and deploy product managers in the most optimal ways.

### Chapter 6. Cultivating and Shaping Product Managers

Jim Collins, a noted contemporary author, suggests in his book *Good to Great* that a company cannot ascend to greatness without the right people in the right jobs at the right times. Therefore, companies that consistently classify and evaluate product managers will ensure that, in fact, they have the right product managers in the right jobs. This is *vital* if the managers are to fulfill the responsibilities and commitments that have been envisioned by their leaders.

Chapter 6 provides comprehensive guidelines that include several key ideas to help leaders establish job levels and progression plans using a unique Product Manager Scorecard. It also provides suggestions to help product managers think more holistically about their products and to use performance management techniques. The chapter concludes with suggestions and methods that help leaders create targeted development programs for product managers. Readers will learn that, in the final analysis, companies that cultivate and shape product managers can expect better human performance and better business results—in other words, better yields.

## MODULE IV. CONTINUITY

Effective organizational strategies have to be implemented, verified, and sustained. This module provides the building blocks to ensure that Product Management can become an embedded, long-lived structure in the organization.

### Chapter 7. Building a Knowledge-Based Community of Practice for Product Management

Many companies realize that some sort of community is needed to draw people together. In fact, they utilize electronic repositories for posting templates, procedures, and documents. However, posting documents and information on shared or central websites may be popular, but there's no really good substitute for face-to-face interactions and communication. Such interactions serve to draw product managers and others together to collaborate and share knowledge and experience. Doing so can fortify and improve their competencies and thus the organization's competitive capability. The value derived from the formation of this type of community cannot be overestimated.

However, deciding to build community is one thing. *Continuing and sustaining the community is another.* Community building in Product Management is at best a work in progress. My hope is that this chapter will call out the need to pivot in your thinking about this important topic and provide some powerful recommendations.

### Chapter 8. Designing and Sponsoring Cross-Functional Product Teams

A cross-functional *product team* is totally *different* from a cross-functional *project team.* The cross-functional product team is actually a microcosm of an executive leadership team, and it consists of members delegated from each of the relevant functional organizations that represent their primary function's interests.

The cross-functional product team's purpose is to steer a product line or small portfolio and deliver agreed-upon business results. In companies where this structure is already loosely in place, it most likely needs to be bolstered. Thus, in these companies the cross-functional product team needs to be formally chartered, more deeply ingrained, and *more widely used*.

This chapter offers suggestions to help leaders agree on the cross-functional product team's work structure, as embodied in a well-thought-out set of guidelines. This chapter also describes the benefits of utilizing this team configuration within the organization, and it suggests ways to implement this powerful method.

### Chapter 9. Embedding a Governing Model for Sustaining Product Management

Performed correctly, Product Management will serve as a *unifying function that spans all functions*. Unlike the functions of Finance or Human Resources Management, a firmly entrenched and chartered Product Management function must have a direct stake in guiding and directing the corporation's product portfolios. Therefore, Product Management itself must be governed—and governed in a sustainable way—for the long term.

This chapter introduces a governance model for Product Management. The model provides a structure such that policies and procedures, processes and methods, protocols, and general rules of engagement are clearly spelled out and flexibly adopted. Understand that I do not advocate for heavy-handed governance. Rather, this model reveals important benefits to senior leaders, of a durable governing model that embeds Product Management into the firm's DNA.

## MY PERSONAL VISION (A MISSION STATEMENT)

My own personal aspirations for this book are quite ambitious. I want to inspire senior leaders to care more about the optimal utilization of Product Management than they do now. I want to impel senior leaders to nurture and develop this vital structure as part of a strategic corporate framework that is robust, durable, sustainable, interconnected, and easily governable. My vision extends to the creation of a community of senior leaders who work collectively, across industries and around the world, to fortify the practices and methods used for Product Management.

During the writing of this book, I surveyed and interviewed more than 120 senior leaders of product organizations. Each survey and interview revealed remarkable insights that are woven throughout the fabric of this book. My commitment was to ensure that their identities would not be uncovered due to the sensitive nature of what they revealed. However, you will also find embedded within the book a series of *spotlight case studies* that are written by senior leaders of noted companies who have a story to share about their own Product Management journey. These companies are FedEx Services, Thomas & Betts, TD Canada Trust, and JetBlue Airways.

Overall, what I hope, deep in my heart, is to propel Product Management to having a recognized "seat at the table." This in turn, will allow Product Management to lead in a way that makes visible, recognized contributions to the firm in the form of a robust portfolio of products that sustain and profit the firm for the long term.

I hope you will join me on this exciting journey!

# MODULE

## CONTEXT

All companies strive to be better and more efficient. As business leaders seek greater efficiencies, they make adjustments to the firm's structure. In other words, they reorganize.

Reorganizations are now so commonplace that it seems they are expected to take place once or twice a year. A well-thought-out realignment is a reflection of solid leadership, but often the ideal structure is not easily attained. There are many issues that result from reorganizations, issues I have come to understand quite thoroughly. For instance, when leaders move in and out of the organization, they rarely consult past records of justifications that were made during previous organizational transformations. Therefore, newer leaders may not have a sufficient appreciation for the paths already taken. In addition, an unintended side-effect of some organizational adjustments is a distinct lack of clarity about the roles of those people who work in various business functions.

Imagine a football game during which the coaches and players are changed in the middle of the game, but there is no hand-off of the play plans or role assignments to the new "staff." It seems unthinkable in sports. However, this "unthinkable change in midgame" does happen in many organizations.

No matter how well leaders think through these organizational realignments, many do not give a whole lot of consideration to the impacts on the Product Management processes or on the people who plan, manage, and market the firm's products and services—the product managers.

It is a well-known fact of strategy formulation that you cannot plot your path forward if you don't know the road you've traveled. Once you know the paths already taken and you've acknowledged what's been learned along the way, it's easier to motivate and inspire others to go forward. The same is true for Product Management.

That's why this module is entitled "Context"—the idea being to help you put many of the past and current Product Management organizational issues on the table for evaluation. When you can more completely understand these perspectives, the senior executive leadership team in your organization may not have to keep reinventing the wheel and will be able to construct a more durable organizational strategy built around Product Management. Therefore, the two chapters in this module are aptly named:

*Chapter 1. Reinventing the Wheel—for the Last Time:* This chapter provides suggestions that allow you to appraise prior transformative efforts and discusses how to properly situate Product Management in the firm.

*Chapter 2. Designing an Organizational Strategy for Product Management:* This chapter builds on the first so that you can incorporate Product Management into the firm's organizational strategy. It also provides suggestions to help establish a constant and definitive Product Management structure that acts as the stable underpinning of the company.

CHAPTER 1

# REINVENTING THE WHEEL— FOR THE LAST TIME

**EXECUTIVE SUMMARY**

- A *universal approach* to the function of Product Management can serve as a powerful organizational model.
- An assessment of the impact of prior transformational efforts offers vital clues that help effective Product Management take root in an organization.
- Every organizational adjustment must take into account the impact on the firm's ability to plan, develop, launch, and manage products and product lines.

*If your actions inspire others to dream more, learn more, do more, and become more, you are a leader.*

—ANDREW JACKSON,
SEVENTH PRESIDENT OF THE UNITED STATES

Years ago, when I worked as a product manager in large corporations, they seemed to reorganize every six months. I could always count on getting a new boss every year—and once, I had three bosses in two years. Each new manager had new methods and ideas—and quirks—to contend with. Each reorganization brought new leadership teams who complained about past leadership teams—and promised things would be *different* under *their* management.

We product managers found it hard to get our minds around the changes because what senior leaders showed us on their PowerPoint slides had no relevance to the work that we, as product managers, were actually doing! While their new strategies cascaded and evolved, we still had to wrestle with the ever-present, day-to-day tactical and product-related issues of our product manager duties. There was a huge disconnect. To our teams, it seemed like the senior leaders worked in one place, while the rest of us worked somewhere else, and the leaders were totally oblivious to our everyday challenges.

In time, some aspects of the organization would begin to morph. However, there was little resemblance between the resulting structures laid out by one senior leadership team to the next. I believe one cause of the problem was that they couldn't adequately describe their desired end state (read: "couldn't communicate their vision"). Further, they failed to anticipate, with enough detail or clarity, how the changes would impact the function of Product Management and the role of the product managers. The result? Product managers and the managers of the product managers could not effectively adapt behaviors and actions to achieve the hoped-for results.

I began to suspect that most of the leaders couldn't imagine how and where each piece of the "organizational puzzle" was supposed to fit into the whole picture. To me, this situation was comparable to doing a jigsaw puzzle where the disparate pieces could not be properly arranged because there was no illustration on the box to show the finished puzzle.

I see all such issues as a *phenomenon of dysfunctional change.* The dilemma has been the subject of books, research projects, and consultant engagements for decades. What's more, the function and structure of Product Management has suffered greatly as a result of these many dysfunctional changes. *Note:* This also applies to brand management, market segment management, or product category management, if you're in industries with these embedded structures.

Based on all my experience in this field, I believe the cause of this dysfunctional change phenomenon is that there is *no universal approach to the function and purpose of Product Management.* It's not that Product Management is not being carried out. In fact, it is being performed everywhere—but in myriad different ways. With so much variation in *how* Product Management is performed and with *no paradigms for improvement,* there can be negative impacts on the organization, such as role confusion and poor interpretation or misalignment of key business processes. All in all, these dysfunctions act like heavy boat anchors, dragging down corporate efficiency.

## PRODUCT MANAGEMENT: A VITAL ELEMENT OF ANY ORGANIZATION

No one before has actually put a stake in the ground to recommend the establishment of a transformational framework for Product Management. In my first book, *The Product Manager's Desk Reference*, I set forth the body of knowledge clarifying the basic elements needed for doing the work involved in Product Management. Based on that foundation, and on what I have since learned from the years I've spent in research and benchmarking, I feel strongly that *now* is the time to focus attention on the creation of a *solid organizational structure to enable better Product Management*. It is the logical next step.

Every time a reorganization takes place and a new management is in charge, companies have to "reinvent" how Product Management is performed. To prove my point: At a client firm, the leader of Organizational Development was charged with guiding the firm's Product Management transformation. However, that action was delayed because, as the leader explained: "We have to put things on hold until our new chief marketing officer (CMO) arrives— we're not sure of her philosophy about Product Management."

I want to change the state of the art. I believe that in the current business world, when a reorganization occurs with a new management in place, *companies shouldn't have to reinvent the wheel once again* to deal with the Product Management function.

For the balance of this chapter, I will discuss my observations about some past transformational efforts and their impact on Product Management, and I'll comment on what I've learned from them.

## APPRAISING PRIOR TRANSFORMATIVE EFFORTS

If we are going to work out how to *reinvent the wheel for the last time*, the first thing to do is appraise some Product Management situations involved in past reorganizations (or transformations). Think of it this way: When you want to craft a strategy for the future (e.g., an organizational strategy), you should have a good picture, first, of where you were and, second, how you got to where you are. As I explain the details of my appraisals, I will note some significant factors for you to consider. As you will see, these notes will contribute greatly to the areas of work I lay out as the book unfolds.

The appraisal process starts by asking six basic questions. It's not rocket science, and I'm not trying to oversimplify their importance. I have personally encountered so many of these situations in my research and in my work with clients that I believe it's a good idea to resurface these fundamentals. As you read the questions and some of the brief anecdotes, you may find you can identify with some of them. In turn, your ability to ask and answer these questions may prove to be of help as you think about options for organizational design and change. First, I'll list the questions, and then I'll expound upon on each one.

1. What prompted the reorganization in the first place, and what was the vision for the new organizational structure as it related to Product Management?
2. How did the envisioned transformation impact the Product Management population?
3. How much time was allowed for the Product Management transformation to take place?
4. How well did senior leaders communicate their vision and the path forward, especially to the product managers and other stakeholders?
5. How clearly did management explain the roles, responsibilities, and future rules for cross-functional engagement?
6. What measurements and milestones were established for the initiative, and what evidence was sought to validate that those objectives were being met?

*Question 1. What prompted the reorganization in the first place, and what was the vision for the new organizational structure as it related to Product Management?*

A few years ago, I worked with a division of a major media firm that published textbooks for the primary and secondary public education sectors. I was called in because they were reorganizing the company. In our meetings, I asked the senior leaders, "What prompted this reorganization?" They said their leaders were getting too many complaints from people on the curriculum teams of many school districts and state education departments. Apparently, a lot of salespeople were bombarding these curriculum planners with their sales pitches. The administrators were suffering cutbacks, and they didn't have the bandwidth to deal with so many salespeople.

The CEO and his team decided to restructure the firm and organize it into product groups. Since they believed their imperative was to be more focused on their products, they created an organizational structure with product lines based on the various academic subjects (math, English, and so on). The CEO appointed a leader to be the executive vice president (EVP) of Products, and four VPs of Product Management were appointed as head of each subject (product) area. The EVP of Product Management was to serve as the portfolio leader for the product line areas.

At another senior leadership meeting, I talked frankly about the phases of transformation and the work required. The leader of one operational area asked, "How long should this transformation take?" My answer was, "Plan on spending two or three years to achieve the end state, . . . and plan on some midcourse corrections along the way." I added the caveat that some companies could take longer.

As the project got underway, we interviewed many people in the product organization. After our data analysis, we held another meeting with the leadership team. Our proposal was that we select a pilot group of higher-potential types (who showed some ability) and run them through a basic Product Management workshop. This step would serve as a point of discovery because we believed it would show these pilot participants the scope of the work for which they would ultimately be responsible. I also recommended a go-slow approach because there was a lot of work needed to define the extent and reach of the required changes. We also wanted to develop a more detailed plan that would take into account staffing, processes, methods, tools, and other "infrastructure" areas to align before proceeding.

A few years after this organizational transformation, I had occasion to follow up with the same EVP of Product Management. She told me that once they really began peeling back the layers, they came to understand just how sales driven the company really was. This helped them to more purposefully implement Product Management. What's most important to note is that the transformation did take two to three years.

What you can take away from this anecdote is this: Even if you know the *theoretical* constructs for the organizational change, there are always unexpected *reality* problems and experiences that arise during the time of change. The "blessing in disguise" is that these events can help you realign your expectations and reset your vision for future adjustments in the Product Management function. Some of the other lessons learned are outlined below (a few of these items are referred to in other areas of the book):

1.  Throughout any corporate transition, you must retain a clear vision of how Product Management will be embedded into the organization's structure. Further, you will need just as clear a vision about how Product Management should operate when it is set in place. As you encounter unanticipated challenges, it is important to remember that if you can stay true to that vision, it will help you achieve the end state originally envisioned, even though it may take several years.

2.  The corporate culture is an important construct that must be considered when the future shape of the Product Management organization is envisioned.

3.  Roles and responsibilities must be clearly spelled out in order to minimize confusion. To this end, functional leaders need to understand and buy into their roles instead of clinging to the "life rafts" of their current or past professional paradigms.

4.  Longer-term planning is important. Senior leaders must analyze and work out all the details of how the pieces of the organizational puzzle will fit together and how the organization will function at least a year or more into the future.

*Question 2. How did the envisioned transformation impact the Product Management population?*

A divisional president of one of my client firms lamented about how his company, typically number 2 or 3 in the company's chosen markets, had been losing market share. The company's plan of action, based on the prior year's reorganization, had diverted centralized control of many of its business units to Sales and Marketing functions in international geographic centers. The rationale was that when Sales and Marketing people were closer to the local markets, they would influence the creation of localized, higher-value solutions. In turn, that would improve customer relationships, deliver better products, and reverse the erosion in market share overall.

In this firm, a high degree of domain understanding was required to support the products. The product line managers (PLMs) were, without a doubt, experts in their respective domains. Their level of business acumen needed some improvement, but I firmly believed this was still doable.

However, there were some issues with the reorganization. As explained to me, the people in the local geographies did not possess a sufficient level of domain expertise (though they believed they did). As a result, they were feeding back product requirements that were not validated, were often unclear, or in some cases, were not at all feasible. Further, no one was scrutinizing all of the requests across those geographies to rationalize the requirements. The pipeline of requests overwhelmed the product line managers, and they were drinking from the proverbial fire hose. To make matters worse, product development resources were cut due to other economic factors.

The PLMs were being squeezed from all sides. First, there was the increased flow of unsubstantiated demand; second, there were limited development resources; third, senior leaders were pushing the PLMs to take a more decisive role in leading these dysfunctional constituencies—not just at corporate headquarters but in the geographic regions as well. But the money for travel was seriously limited. Also, Sales and Marketing leaders who worked in the geographies advised the PLMs that they could no longer reach out to customers directly. Instead, the beleaguered home team was supposed to depend on the available local resources in order to gain context and achieve insights. It's not surprising that the PLMs felt totally disempowered and just succumbed to the structure.

We discovered an *additional factor* that created a lot more problems. When the PLMs (understandably!) weren't able to deliver on regional requests, people in the regions created their own solutions by reaching out to local vendors—who, in some instances, were actually competitors! Moreover, many leaders in the regions were hiring local product managers. Since each region held its own P&L and was solely accountable for results, these regional leaders had virtual carte blanche. Thus, they could do whatever they wanted, without regard for global product portfolio decisions or the impact on the entire company. As if that weren't enough, the senior leaders did not have a formal product portfolio council that actively rationalized market insights and other data in order to direct product portfolio investments more efficiently.

After I interviewed about three dozen PLMs and some of the senior leaders, it became clear to me that the envisioned transformation wasn't properly elucidated to all major stakeholders. Maybe the senior leaders *believed* their organizational strategy was clearly explained, but the actual communications did not lay out enough details to ensure that the changes were easily understood by the PLMs and the other key stakeholders.

We traced back to the root causes of these misconceptions. What we found was that the leaders who embarked on this plan did not fully realize what such a complex reorganization really entailed. They failed to consider all the interconnected systemic interfaces and all the cross-organizational impacts that should have been more carefully taken into account.

Here are some of the points I took away:

1.  Any reorganization that impacts planning, execution, and management of products must be completely understood by all major constituencies in the firm in order for positive, realistic outcomes to be achieved.
2.  Close connections between product managers and customers are mandatory. This is also important in order to validate needs and requests, and it is especially important when a high degree of domain expertise is needed.
3.  Methods need to be instituted that *rationalize requirements across disparate inputs.* Whether sales and marketing types are in local markets or in a centralized (geographic) location, the myriad inbound requests call for a *robust product portfolio process* to effectively allocate funds across product lines and to aid in decision making.

*Question 3. How much time was allowed for the Project Management transformation to take place?*

Many leaders seem to expect that the metamorphosis will take place within a couple of quarters. Without equivocation, I can safely say that if you believe this is all the time you can allow for the effort, or if you think longer-term vision is not possible or effective, then it might be wise to consider other options. To focus in on the issue of the time needed for successful change, let me share a story with you about a company that did a spectacular job with its Product Management transformation. Yes, there can be bright spots!

Several years ago, I began to work with a European-based multinational firm in the transportation services sector. We carried out a number of interviews and assessments and provided recommendations for a multiphase series of changes to the structure of Product Management. These changes included, among others, adjusting staffing models and process changes.

Despite many organizational changes in the intervening years, the company's leadership team stayed true to the Product Management organizational development program.

This firm first established a *Product Management Council of Executives* who focused on the governing model, established the core competencies needed, and firmly embedded the new product development process within the organization. They then catalyzed and improved cross-functional and cross-organizational communication through the use of specific key performance indicators. This increased transparency, enhanced product quality, and improved launch performance. Along with these, they reinforced the roles and responsibilities of the product managers and built a *vibrant community of practice.*

What's interesting about this case is that there were a variety of pivot points during this transformation. There were some economic cycle changes, some leadership changes, and some acquisitions and other growth pains during this period of time. I will be talking about most of these areas throughout this book, but for now there is an important takeaway from this story: *This transformation took over five years to achieve!* At a recent Product Management Leadership Summit,* one of the senior leaders who presided over the entire transformation presented a description of the process. At the end of the summit, every attendee sought to talk to this speaker and each expressed his or her overwhelming interest in this firm's success!

---

* The Product Management Leadership Summit is carried out several times in the period of a year and is organized by the Product Management Executive Board (www.productmanagementexecboard.com).

This company was successful in its transformational endeavor because of several factors:

1. Each step along the way had relevant, achievable, and realistic objectives.
2. All objectives were clearly stated and effectively shared across the organization. Thus, everyone could "digest" the changes as envisioned by the leadership team, and each person involved could see the benefits of the evolving structure.
3. Despite the fact that the leaders had to make several adjustments along the way, they stayed true to objectives of their Product Management evolution plan.

*Question 4. How well did senior leaders communicate their vision and the path forward, especially to the product managers and other stakeholders?*

Some years ago, I worked with a communications firm based in North America. The company was under extreme competitive pressure, margins were eroding, and it was being acquired by a larger firm. Senior leaders told me that a population of 50 product managers needed to change some of their behaviors in order to turn the business around. The senior vice president of Product Management complained to me that the product managers were not performing their jobs in a manner consistent with his own beliefs and expectations. He also indicated that the product managers were not taking steps to differentiate their products in the market (which, as you know, can be difficult when the products are seen as commodities!). He wanted all the product managers to lead, innovate, and deliver results, yet he did not realize that many were ill equipped to do so.

In this environment, the product managers were relegated to acting more like project managers. The products were mainly mature, and staff members were running on fumes in their efforts to keep up with immediate customer requests while they tried to respond to competitive threats. It's no surprise that the senior vice president was frustrated since, aside from the unrealistic expectations of his people, he was trying to plan the Product Management organizational evolution entirely on his own.

Before I agreed to deliver a workshop for the product managers in his group, I coached him about the messages he should deliver. He agreed to work under my tutelage and adopt the strategy necessary to deliver the message.

However, at the outset of our first workshop, he forgot what he was to communicate. He also wandered off topic as he emphasized all the competitive pressures the company was experiencing. Finally, he made a very strong statement to the participants (in his "training will cover it" mode) saying, "You are in charge of your products. I want you to participate fully because afterward, you will all be empowered." He added that he was expecting good things to come, wished them luck, and left the room.

The people in the workshop looked far from encouraged. One of the directors I had worked with on some structural aspects of the program actually put his hands over his eyes in despair. There were several lessons to be learned from this experience.

1. Communication is a cornerstone for successful Product Management transformation. The changes to come should be clearly explained and should convey the rationale for these changes, the steps to be taken, and the outcomes that will be produced. Merely stating that product managers will be taking on new responsibilities or that their roles may be redefined is not enough; it will surely engender unsatisfactory reactions. Communication to and with the product managers must never lag or be overlooked; it should be crafted carefully such that the product managers know what is expected, how they are supported, and how they will be evaluated.

2. Product managers and their teams deserve to know that a cohesive, supportive executive leadership team stands behind them and has a plan of action that can be digested by both product managers and their managers.

3. Along with this implicit transparency, leaders need to earn the respect of the product managers through their own actions.

4. Product managers need to feel connected to the bigger picture. They are not "orphans" in the organization, and if senior leaders do not shepherd their cause, product managers will not be able to take their rightful roles as stewards of the products for which they are responsible.

*Question 5. How clearly did management explain the roles, responsibilities, and future rules for cross-functional engagement?*

I have carried out many organizational diagnostic projects and competency assessments over a number of years. At the end of these projects, I always provide additional recommendations, guidelines, and suggestions to ensure that the processes and work flows are in place. These key competency areas (such as Developing Market Insights, Strategic Planning, Performance Management, and so on) must be supported and should be linked upward to explicit organizational objectives. I also provide these companies with guidance in aligning work activities and deliverables that, again, should be clearly defined both horizontally and vertically within the organization.

While working with a software and technology client, I learned some valuable lessons about the ability of leaders to assimilate and buy into a series of Product Management organizational change recommendations. The assessments and associated diagnostics made note of many areas for potential improvements, and it became obvious that one area needed the utmost priority.

That challenge was to fortify the abilities of product managers so they could better articulate clear, actionable strategies for their products and product lines. This would enable the collaborative efforts from Product Management, Marketing, and Finance to take place. Certain general precepts were decided upon to facilitate application of these situations and capabilities.

We recommended the following: The Marketing role would be responsible for carrying out research and deriving customer insights; the Finance role would be held responsible for producing historical data and analyzing future state scenarios for the product lines; and the role of Product Management would be to coordinate and synchronize the "gears" to align with future-state product line visions and ultimate objectives. These are fairly common connections that "functional" (as opposed to "dysfunctional") organizations would usually carry out.

However, in this instance, what was recommended could not be realized. The reason these stumbling blocks existed in the organization was quite obvious. The company operated in a "silo-ized" mode. The work was done within "silos" without regard for the customer or the user of information. Despite the stated objectives about changes to Product Management, the leaders from each discrete function favored their own agendas. For example: Even though senior leaders acknowledged that specific hand-offs were required, the work products from key functions were not synchronized around a common set of goals. Because management did not align the functions, clarify the roles, and ensure that the assigned people could actually carry out the work, nothing could really change. In fact, this misalignment resulted in more role confusion and in duplication of efforts.

The important lessons from this experience included these:

1. Leaders of Product Management and leaders in all the other key business functions need to have an agreed-upon and unified plan of action to describe expected outcomes, clarify the roles of stakeholders, and guide the work of all constituencies.
2. The CEO's position should be to serve as the corporation's guide and role model. If a CEO does *not* build a shared view that agrees on what the function of Product Management should be, then every business line and portfolio group will resort to creating versions of the Product Management function that are based on their own previously understood paradigms—or even their *own* versions of the function.

*Question 6. What measurements and milestones were established for the initiative, and what evidence was sought to validate that those objectives were being met?*

Change initiatives involving Product Management are too often allotted *too little time than would actually be required* to mature and deliver results. What's more, many of these initiatives fail to include accurate milestones and thresholds and at which points to evaluate the various aspects of such change initiatives.

This was exemplified when we worked with a large software company. At an all-hands meeting, the CEO set forth a *one-year plan* for a Product Management transformation. The proposed strategy was that the company's product managers would become more market focused. They would then be better equipped to hunt for opportunities in adjacent markets. As a result, innovation would be stimulated. However, there was another angle to this firm's venture. The company sought to make substantive changes such that it could achieve CMMI Level 3 maturity within the subsequent three years.

In case you're not familiar with the abbreviation CMMI, it stands for Capability Maturity Model Integration, and it was created by the Software Engineering Institute at Carnegie Mellon University. To sum up its purpose, this is a process improvement methodology. A CMMI maturity level of 3 is achieved when processes are managed with a high degree of predictable consistency.

What was particularly problematic was that the firm's 150 product managers were unaware of how the CMMI work program factored into their own jobs. The vital linkage between the grand plan, the timing, and the actual work involved made most product managers feel a lack of confidence in their own senior leaders.

Another factor, unrelated to timing, was that due to the composition of the portfolio, the company's reorganization planning was unrealistic. The majority of the product lines were mature; therefore, the role envisioned for the product managers was *inconsistent* with the needs of the business of those mature products. Moreover, provisions had not been made for the work involved to identify new opportunities. Based on my experience with this firm and many others who had broad plans for a Product Management transformation, here is what I learned:

- The introduction of a maturity model like CMMI or any other Product Management reference model in an organization may overwhelm people if they do not understand how it impacts their jobs.
- Any company that contemplates a restructuring should take into account the composition of the product portfolio and the staffing model. Further, if leaders expect the same product managers presently responsible for mature products to also be responsible for new products and new product revenue, this change should call for a thorough organizational evaluation.

## MOVING FROM APPRAISAL TO ACTION

I have shared some relevant anecdotes to illustrate the reasons this appraisal process is so important. Having read these accounts, many of you may think, "These stories merely point out commonsense business ideals. Besides, most companies probably do these things as a matter of course." However, based on my experience with Product Management assessments and diagnostics, I believe it's always productive to revisit the foundations that will effectively guide organizational evolution.

From these six questions and illustrative anecdotes, I've distilled some important information for you to consider while you are laying the foundation for a more durable and long-lasting Product Management organization. These suggestions, outlined below, will also help to set the stage for what I will discuss in Chapter 2 (which deals with stable foundations), and they will also align with content in other chapters of the book.

1. Like any winning game plan, the organizational strategy for Product Management requires a clear vision for a desired end state, with a solid rationale, and a linkage to the overarching strategy for the organization. Though most senior leaders are usually adept at crafting vision statements, I believe you should have some additional ideas that can help you derive a clearer vision for the "function" of Product Management. This vision would have the following *fundamental* business elements:
   a. How market insights are to be derived
   b. How the company wishes to be competitively positioned in the market
   c. How all business functions (and associated roles) should align around clearly planned work flows and work processes
2. Since Product Management serves as a horizontal function, all senior leaders should be obliged to demonstrate, through their commitment and behavior, that they are working more closely and collectively on behalf of product portfolio strategies and that they are focusing less on the specific agendas of their own functions.
3. The initiative should be based on a reasonable, achievable, and managed timeline so that realistic thresholds can be set and met. It is also important to document exactly what is to happen, with whom, and when. Passing any decision milestone without adequate appraisal and analysis can lead to potholes in the organizational road map.
4. Set in place a *governance board* to guide the execution and sustenance of Product Management. This topic is so significant that I have

dedicated an entire chapter to it later in the book. For now, keep in mind that product leaders cannot lead and product managers cannot manage if there is no clarity around the objectives.

5. Since there may be changes to the company's business model, it is necessary that the day-to-day work activities of product managers, as well as those they work with, be well documented and understood. Doing so will ensure that current methods of operation and current work flows can be matched to future methods of operation and future work flows. Many of the disruptions in Product Management processes and work flows occur when these current and future methods are not fully understood or implemented. When I dissected Product Management at an industrial company, I found that product managers were preparing customer quotes and Operations people were writing requirements. You can imagine the conflicts that arose when the leaders realigned work activities that were out of the usual paradigms of those accustomed to doing those jobs.

6. Change management protocols should be carefully crafted. A large number of academics and consultants who have studied change initiatives believe that most employees don't like change because they don't know what's in it for them and how any change will impact their current or future jobs. Product managers are no different. In fact, because the roles and responsibilities of product managers tend to vary based on product line maturities, industry focus, and other variables, they may feel particularly vulnerable.

## CARRYING OUT YOUR OWN APPRAISAL

As I suggested earlier in the chapter, you may want to review the six basic questions and appraise your organization's results from any prior programs. Consider conducting a brief appraisal exercise with your colleagues from other functions and/or your leadership team members. The exercise results may change how you think about your future direction. As you read other chapters in this book, you may come up with other ideas as well. You can refer to the table in Figure 1.1 to guide your work in this appraisal.

**Figure 1.1 Questions for the Appraisal Process**

| | What Was the Desired or Envisioned Outcome? | How Did the Outcome Compare to the Desired Result, and Why? | What Do You Believe Was the Root Cause for the Variance against the Plan? | What Could You Have Done Differently? |
|---|---|---|---|---|
| 1. What prompted the reorganization in the first place, and what was the vision for the new organizational structure as it related to Product Management? | | | | |
| 2. How did the envisioned transformation impact the Product Management population? | | | | |
| 3. How much time was allowed for the Product Management transformation to take place? | | | | |
| 4. How well did senior leaders communicate their vision and the path forward, especially to the product managers and other stakeholders? | | | | |
| 5. How clearly did management explain the roles, responsibilities, and future rules for cross-functional engagement? | | | | |
| 6. What measurements and milestones were established for the initiative, and what evidence was sought to validate that those objectives were being met? | | | | |

An appraisal of this sort can take on the characteristics of an operational audit. Don't be daunted by the term *audit*. An audit merely seeks to compare an actual situation with a formerly planned outcome.

What this audit seeks to uncover is this: What was the objective? What actually happened? Why? And so on. Again, refer to the six basic appraisal questions.

Review again how these questions are posed, and how the outcomes are listed in the *comparison of the outcome to the original plan*. It is quite possible that you will begin to uncover some of the key root causes of problems encountered, and you will be able to describe what you might have done differently. This may help you or your successors to realign as you continue your journey toward best-in-class Product Management.

As you list and evaluate some of the root causes of the troublesome areas, you may feel motivated to examine your thoughts and ask yourself some questions. I have prepared a few of these questions for you to consider.

By maintaining a record of what you discovered, you will likely avoid some the mistakes of the past. You may want to ask the following:

- Who developed the plan for the communications directed to the employees?
- How was the plan communicated? (Hopefully, not in e-mail!)
- What were the reactions of the product managers and their managers?
- Did you observe any objections or other behaviors that indicated to you that there might be serious negative reactions?
- What was the original timing for the program?
- Who were the leaders providing oversight of the program?
- Did all the people involved completely understand and agree on how the program was to be carried out and managed over the agreed-upon time frames?
- How were interim results to be tracked?
- How were remedial course corrections to be processed?
- Did you conduct any pre- and postprogram surveys to gauge employee satisfaction as it relates to the program?
- What altered behaviors did you observe?
- What failed to happen that you believe should have happened, and why?
- How did people in other functions participate?
- Given their current work and responsibilities, were the product managers and their managers equipped to make the transition?

## SUMMARY

Improving the effectiveness of any organization remains a high priority for senior leaders.

On the positive side: Excellent efforts have been undertaken within various areas of many companies, and these have served to improve organizational performance. Many firms have improved processes and work flows. Others have admirably improved their strategic market posture. Still others have notably improved systems and methods to effectively drive corporate performance.

However, on the negative side: Many issues still remain that are perhaps rooted in the realm of Product Management. Why is this the case? The reason lies in the fact that there is no standardized plan or accommodation to situate Product Management within the organization.

One explanation is that Product Management is rarely at the top of the list for firms in relation to how they reorganize or adjust their focus and priorities from time to time. This happens despite the fact that, bottom line, *Product Management is the crucial mechanism through which products and portfolios are planned, developed, launched, and managed.*

Product Management should not be thought of as just one or more linear work flows. Rather, it is a critical organizational function that is composed of many functional participants, acting together as a unified whole. In a nutshell, Product Management at the product line or portfolio level is a microcosm for the macrocosm of the entire organization, much the way a General Management function serves to bring the disparate pieces of a company or a division together.

If leaders will make the decision to view Product Management in this way, they will be able to better integrate it into their organization's structure, design, and evolution. In turn, product managers and others who work together on behalf of the product line or product portfolio will be able to better align their efforts at being formidable competitors.

CHAPTER 2

# DESIGNING AN ORGANIZATIONAL STRATEGY FOR PRODUCT MANAGEMENT

**EXECUTIVE SUMMARY**

- Product Management is a vital foundational organizational structure that can contribute greatly to the firm's success.
- A capable, competent Product Management organization should be designed to survive the test of time *and* allow the firm's business model to evolve in lockstep with markets and customers.
- Greater levels of consistency and predictability in Product Management process execution will result in the evolution of robust, profitable product portfolios.

*There is nothing more difficult to take in hand, more perilous to conduct, or more uncertain in its success than to take the lead in the introduction of a new order of things.*

—MACHIAVELLI

A *mantra* is a word that is considered capable of "creating transformation," and *change* seems to be the mantra for our times. Company leaders are constantly seeking ways to change, by aiming to transform organizational architecture, create greater value, improve efficiency, and, of course, deliver better profits.

One thing I know: There is no silver bullet, no philosopher's stone, no panacea for curing what ails an organization. The good news is there *are* changes that can create improved performance and greater success for any company. I believe that the most effective of these is to *establish a constant and definitive Product Management structure that acts as the stable underpinning of the company.*

At least half the companies I work with do not have a clear perspective about how to get their organizations to work more effectively. One problem is that many leaders assume the behaviors that have created good results cannot be precisely captured, written down, replicated, and taught to others. They also assume that no coherent paradigm already exists. Or they believe that the complexity of the necessary skill set cannot be codified into a body of knowledge or a repeatable sequence of activities. These nonbelievers are wrong.

Such beliefs may have been justified years ago when Product Management was an emerging, yet undefined, structure—an "Accidental Profession" as noted in *The Product Manager's Desk Reference*. My mission in this book (as in all my work) is to inform you that there *is* a universal set of Product Management paradigms, methods, and tools that can be instituted that will ensure more predictable business outcomes.

It's been said that the only thing we learn from history is that we never learn from history. Before shifting into "change" mode and moving on to improve the present and the future, I believe leaders need to refer to past history to avoid or rectify mistakes and erroneous ideas, and they need to adopt (or adapt) what has worked well to meet present and future needs.

As senior leaders move in and out of organizations, new leaders take little interest in the lessons of the past, which leads to a sort of "organizational amnesia." Recently, I watched a documentary about the Ford Motor Company where one of the Ford descendants was being interviewed. He was asked why the company's fortunes had ebbed and flowed so dramatically over the decades. Ford explained that leadership teams who were in place at various points along the way *forgot the lessons of the past*. He believed that his role was to act as a steward (the word is my interpretation) and that his job was to make sure *someone serves as the institution's memory in order that the lessons of the past will not be forgotten.*

## CHANGING YOUR PERSPECTIVES AND PARADIGMS

No matter how things are presently organized in your company, presumably the work of gathering market insights, strategizing, executing, and managing organizational performance is getting done. The real questions are these:

- Do you have a clear *perspective* about what is actually making this happen? Have you captured this knowledge as a repeatable set of processes to ensure that it is done consistently?
- Can you shift the *paradigm* as you adapt it to your particular situation? Do you know how it can be accomplished?

For too many companies, the answer to one or both of these questions is no.

To help adjust your viewpoint, think of Figure 2.1 as a representation of how Product Management is typically incorporated into an organization. Business functions are shown vertically, like a picket fence with no back brace. In this illustration (as in many companies), Product Management is treated as just another responsibility that fills gaps in the work carried out by the various functions. Though few can define the function, everyone knows the product managers are supposed to be doing *something* that is *somehow* related to making their products a success. What's missing is that there is no *consistent* level of cross-functional guidance taking place. As a result, individual functions can interpret Product Management in the way that's most convenient and beneficial to their discrete interests. However, these functions have a hard time standing on their own, so product managers must (figuratively) run hither and yon, constantly propping up whichever board seems ready to fall over next.

Even if these functions do manage to hold themselves up, they are very seldom well aligned. They need constant reorganization to keep them in good alignment. As a result, the organization falls out of balance, as evidenced by missed market signals and the introduction of uncompetitive products. The side-effect, in some cases, is that Product Management devolves into *project* management; in other cases, Product Management

**Figure 2.1  How Product Management Is Typically Incorporated into an Organization**

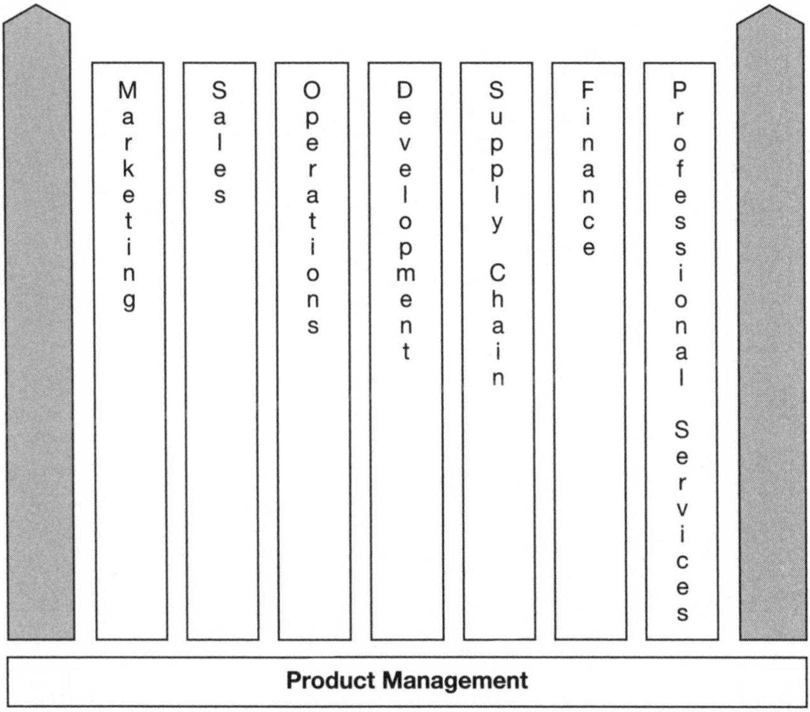

| Marketing | Sales | Operations | Development | Supply Chain | Finance | Professional Services |
|---|---|---|---|---|---|---|

**Product Management**

"activities" are distributed across business divisions with no uniform governance or coordination.

Now, contrast this "plate spinning" with Figure 2.2, wherein Product Management becomes an active, well-staffed, supportive *horizontal* structure that serves as the organization's backbone, orchestrating the activities of all business functions in tune with the achievement of the current strategy for the company or business unit. In effect, it functions as a microcosm within the macrocosm of the entire business—where each product line is a business within the business and where great ideas are generated, captured, and translated into meaningful actions, projects, and initiatives.

**Figure 2.2 How Product Management Can Serve as the Organization's Backbone**

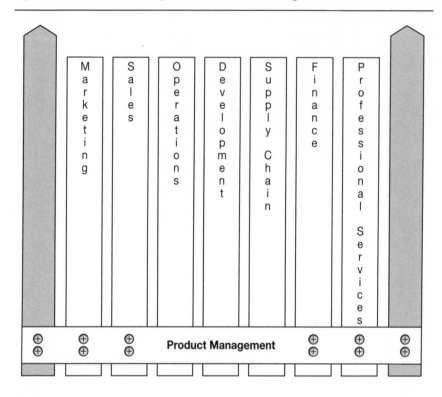

## BUILDING A STABLE FOUNDATION

The Product Management function requires a stable foundation of processes, systems, and people. When applied consistently, many aspects used to create, deliver, and manage products produce better outcomes. Such stability can also be a "shelter from the storm" if your company is in flux for any reason or is experiencing the side-effects of change. When Product Management processes are codified, you can pivot more quickly, allowing you to swiftly monitor and implement your directional shifts. In turn, it will help you track markets and competitors with much greater speed and precision than you might have previously thought possible.

A stable Product Management function effectively utilizes the product managers to think and act strategically. As a result they are able to skillfully execute, in order to produce and manage great products. Even when corporate strategy needs to shift, Product Management serves as the consistent, pliant, and capable "connective tissue" that implements the changes across the organization and across its functions. You may even find that product managers can catalyze a major strategic change! This can be possible because competent, capable product managers, working within the stable system, have a clear view of the "big picture" of everything that relates to their products and product lines.

If you want the winning combinations of stability and agility, productivity and creativity, you'll need to establish Product Management as a dedicated, well-staffed, cross-functional leadership role, chartered with a specific set of mandates and measured at a specific level of competence.

## A MASTER PLAN FOR THE PRODUCT MANAGEMENT ORGANIZATION

In Chapter 2 of *The Product Manager's Desk Reference*, I recommend that product managers use a Product Master Plan as a "holding document" or plan of record for everything related to the product's business. The Product Master Plan captures the product's history and decisions, and it stores bodies of evidence for those decisions just as the judicial system uses precedents to keep track of prior decisions. Having a properly maintained Product Master Plan also allows future product managers and/or product leaders to better understand what was done before, and why. This archive can also help them see the historic record of how various strategies or objectives were affected, which in turn can help them project how they might affect product performance, changes in markets, and other major forces.

Corporate leaders can leverage this technique by creating a Product Management Organization Master Plan. This plan or repository would serve two purposes:

- It would be the *charter* documentation for the Product Management organization.
- It would create a repository for all actions related to the structure and governance of Product Management.

Among other things (depending on the type of business), this repository could include the following:

- Competency management program information
- Human resources programs for product managers
- Product Management processes
- Work flows, systems, templates, and other similar tools
- Any method or system used to plan, execute, measure, or manage the overall performance of the Product Management organization

By definition, it must contain all of the documents, artifacts, and pertinent records necessary to allow leaders to track the overall maturity of the Product Management organization. And just like the Product Master Plan, the Product Management Organization Master Plan can serve as an active archive to establish precedents, minimize confusion, and foster communication among key constituencies in the organization.

To establish an effective Product Management Organization Master Plan, it must, at minimum, encompass the following four building blocks:

1. A Competency Model to assess and evaluate the knowledge, skills, and experience of your Product Management staff, based on a reliable Reference Model for effective Product Management
2. A method to assess and evaluate gaps between competency measurements and desired performance levels
3. An optimized, strategically aligned organizational design that encourages the various functions to work collectively on behalf of the product
4. A method to periodically evaluate the maturity of the Product Management organization so that it will evolve and progress over time

These four components, visualized in Figure 2.3, form a good foundation, but they will need to be tracked and updated to make sure that they remain relevant. There will be other items you'll probably want to add to the Master Plan as you read through the book.

Figure 2.3  Product Management Organization Master Plan

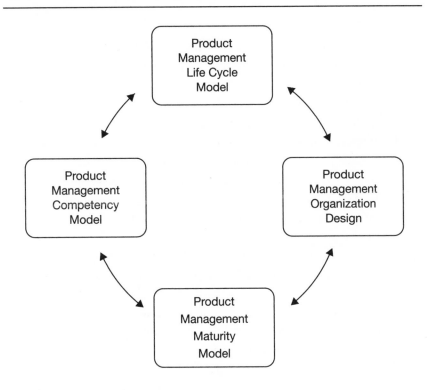

## A BASELINE COMPETENCY MODEL

The universal first step to a achieving vibrant Product Management organization is to use a *relevant* Competency Model. This Competency Model is used to assess the knowledge, skills, and experiences of product managers.

**Definitions**

A **competency** is generally recognized as the combined knowledge, skills, and experiences of an employee, expressed through work behaviors that lead to desired outcomes.

A **Competency Model** is a collection of competencies that characterize a complete body of knowledge, according to a relevant reference point, in a given professional area, such as Product Management.

This Competency Model for Product Management serves four primary purposes:

1.  It describes how product, product line, and product portfolio managers are expected to utilize knowledge, skills, and experiences to carry out their jobs.
2.  It defines the processes, work flows, and documents that must be utilized in order for people to get their jobs done.
3.  It underscores the mindset needed to translate vast pools of dynamic data into a unified set of actions for others to follow.
4.  It delineates the underlying substrate of interpersonal skills needed by product managers to engage the attention of and to influence people in other corporate functions.

The reasons for using a Competency Model to routinely assess product managers, product line, and product portfolio managers are as follows:

- The model allows the leadership to gauge the organization's Product Management capability at any time.
- Such an assessment will serve to identify what's needed to raise competency levels.
- It will contribute to your organization's ability to measure progress over time.
- It yields an essential correlation between maturity levels and key metrics like profitability or market share.

When you can take the organization's pulse from time to time, you are better equipped to (a) segment the population of product managers at all levels, (b) determine the areas where you might wish to invest in professional development efforts, and (c) identify any needed changes to the organization based on business conditions.

However, a Competency Model has no essential value unless it serves to build core capabilities within the organization. In other words, *it must help to promote those activities and actions that make positive contributions to the business*. At this point, I will summarize the major components of the product managers' Competency Model. Later, in Chapter 5, I will expand the discussion within the context of your product manager staffing strategy.

I usually refer to competency groupings as *meta-level competencies* because they are broad groupings that describe the high-level work flows or major processes within the product life cycle context. The seven broad groupings in this Competency Model provide for the following:

1. Developing market insights
2. Crafting effective strategies
3. Planning and carrying out effective, timely product launches
4. Managing the financial and market performance of products and portfolios
5. Translating information from many sources into cohesive decisions
6. Driving action throughout the organization
7. Using basic work management skills

## A REFERENCE MODEL

The Competency Model can provide a good anchor for Product Management, but only if it's linked to a logical point of reference. I use the Product Management Life Cycle Model (PMLCM), shown in Figure 2.4 and as used in *The Product Manager's Desk Reference*. This is the *primary vehicle* to situate the major Areas of Work and the fundamental processes that support the model. The Reference Model is integral to the organizational strategy for Product Management because *it portrays the life of a product, from start to finish.*

Within the model, there are three Areas of Work:

- New Product Planning (NPP) serves as a backdrop for the actions of exploration, discovery, and the creative process. It is also the guide to decision making and project selection.
- New Product Introduction (NPI) looks at the agreed-upon plans and focuses on getting the necessary work done for building and launching products—in other words, executing.
- Post-Launch Product Management (PLPM) covers the strategic and tactical management of existing products and portfolios.

**Figure 2.4 Product Management Life Cycle Model (PMLCM)**

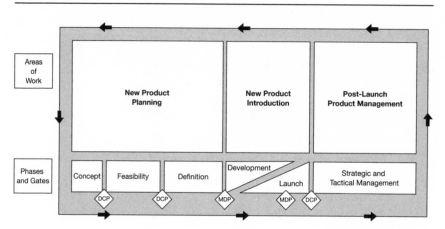

Source: Copyright Sequent Learning Networks.

Although I will provide greater detail about these Areas of Work in Chapter 3, you can see how the Product Management Life Cycle Model sets the right backdrop for identifying product manager competencies.

## EVALUATING THE COMPETENCIES

As discussed earlier, a Competency Model will not be worthwhile if it's not used to evaluate job performance on a regular basis and to see where improvement is needed. The data derived can be applied to programs that enhance the knowledge, skills, and experience of all those who should be contributing to the organization's overall Product Management capability.

In addition, some sort of assessment instrument is needed to determine where the product managers are situated vis-à-vis the model and to compare what has been learned with the performance expectations placed on them. It will help to clarify the responsibilities of the product manager and associated individuals, and it will serve to determine the type of intervention needed to improve the performance of specific product managers. I take this further in Chapter 5.

In my practice, I utilize a robust competency assessment as a diagnostic tool. It will be useful to summarize it here. The assessment refers to the meta-level competency groupings that contain subgroups called *competency clusters*. These clusters contain an array of relevant questions (or statements) that, when responded to, help to evaluate the knowledge and experience of a product manager. This diagnostic tool also provides a relevant rating scale to capture the responses.

For example, within the grouping "developing market insights," a statement about market segmentation might be presented in this way:

"I have an up-to-date market segmentation model."

That statement is relevant because all product managers should know the market segments within their purview. Sounds simple, right? When I reviewed the data from prior client assessments, captured in my company's assessment system, I found that *only half* of the product managers we've assessed over the years actually *have* a formal market segmentation model—a model that must be used to create market size and market share estimates. That's a huge disconnect and a significant handicap.

Here is another sample statement within the cluster that relates to the derivation of market insight:

"I routinely analyze competitors and the products they sell, and I share the findings with members of my team."

What makes that statement (and its associated response) important is that it captures at least two dimensions of facts in its breadth and depth. One is *competitor analysis* (analyzing companies with whom you compete), and the second is *competitive product analysis* (discussing and analyzing the products of each competitor in relation to your own products).

*Competitive positioning*, in turn, is linked to two of the other clusters: (1) strategic planning and mindset and (2) critical thinking. To help you visualize these interrelated elements, please refer to Figure 2.5.

As another example, product managers sometimes have trouble prioritizing their work, especially in planning possible attributes or features. They may consider timing, resource availability, technical complexity, and

**Figure 2.5 Competitive Positioning as Linked to (1) Strategic Planning and Mindset and (2) Critical Thinking**

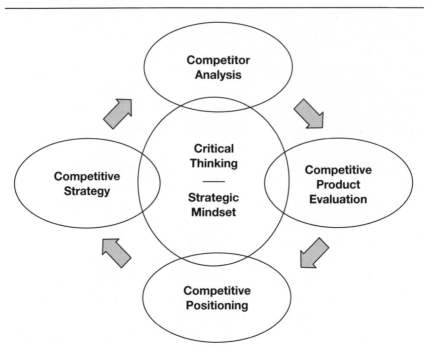

other tactical or project aspects because they work with Engineering or Development to rationalize these priorities. However, they may *neglect* to consider the strategic or market impact of the decision as part of their criteria—and their team members usually don't think of these aspects either. Appropriate parts of the competency assessment could pinpoint these deficiencies and lead to suggested ways to broaden their focus.

One more example: You will most probably agree that product managers should be able to analyze a product's performance to make sure it is delivering the intended business results. With this in mind, a relevant competency statement might be worded like this:

> "I routinely analyze the financial results of my product and compare those results to established plans—and I report these results to my leadership team."

Another dimension of the prior statement might include this statement:

> "I work with my (product) team to analyze aspects of the product's financial contribution to the business."

These assessments ensure that product managers not only have a performance-oriented mindset but they also create and enforce shared accountability for the product within their cross-functional team.

To sum up, the evaluative instrument or competency assessment should identify the grouping or cluster; it should use relevant statements or questions designed to uncover the individual's ability to carry out the work; and it should provide a means to evaluate responses so that remedial actions can be considered.

## EVALUATING THE COMPETENCY GAPS

After the Competency Model is agreed upon, you will need a method to assess and evaluate gaps between the competency measurements and the desired performance levels. This is an important *variable* as you solve your unique organizational strategy *equation*. Once assessments have been carried out, the results need to be analyzed against a common point of comparison. In most cases, a simple yes or no answer isn't going to produce a usable measurement. Many companies use standard competency analysis tools that ask questions and measure responses on a *Likert scale*, which is a bipolar statistical range. You've no doubt seen this type of scale before; it uses common headings like "strongly agree," "agree," "neutral," "disagree," and "strongly disagree."

Unfortunately, these tools tend to produce *belief-based responses*, so they may introduce higher levels of bias than are preferable. It's possible to limit bias if we design responses that more accurately uncover issues. Then you can more easily point to some type of remedial action. There should be obvious linkages between the actual responses and some desired future states. The linkages will make the rating scale more actionable. There are two possible paths:

1. We could change the selections on the rating scale from words that inspire "agreement" or "disagreement" to those that indicate

*work frequency* (which would still be a form of the Likert scale). The choices would then appear as "to a very great extent," "to a great extent," "somewhat," "to a small extent," and "to a very small extent."

2.  Alternatively, we could use an *experiential scale*, which is the technique I use in my diagnostic work. It isn't perfect—the responses reflect the perspective of individuals evaluating themselves—but at least this scale helps us get closer to responses that will establish the foundation for a viable work plan.

Here's how this might work. Let's go back to one of the statements posed earlier:

> "I routinely analyze the financial results of my product and compare those results to established plans—and I report these results to my leadership team."

Suppose the product manager responds with "somewhat" on the generic rating scale. What can be done with that piece of data? From my vantage point, it would require a more detailed investigation by an evaluator to get to the heart of what that person actually does in this regard. However, if you have a lot of product managers, it would be difficult and time-consuming to do this. Instead, why not have an option that indicates the degree to which they actually carry out the work and the degree of independence they exhibit in doing that work? We want product managers to indicate their actual current level of experience or proficiency rather than their *beliefs* about whether they know how to do the work.

To achieve a response closer to the truth, I recommend that the instrument set the response scale according to various levels of experience, with a concrete definition of what that means. Would such an instrument give us absolutely accurate information? No. There is no instrument that is 100 percent perfect. Would such an instrument get us closer to a good diagnostic? I believe it would.

In Chapter 22 of *The Product Manager's Desk Reference*, "Charting Your Career," I included a basic do-it-yourself test as a tool for product managers that helps them carry out their own self-evaluation. The rating scale looks like this:

- A score of 1 means that the respondent *has no knowledge of or experience with this work*. (This is not a negative attribute. It may just indicate that the person has never had the opportunity to do this work.)
- A score of 2 means that the respondent *has a fundamental awareness of and can explain the work*. The respondent may have demonstrated this work on a limited basis and carried it out under the guidance of a manager.
- A score of 3 means the respondent *consistently demonstrates his or her proficiency because he or she carries out this type of work as needed, with little or no management support*. This response shows that the person tends to continuously try to improve his or her proficiency in this area.
- A score of 4 means that the respondent *is an expert (or a role model) and can transfer his or her knowledge to others*.

Once you have a rating scale that suits your purposes, you're almost there. However, the real objective is to use the outcomes to inspire action. *Action* in this sense means "reading" from the assessment: asking yourself what it means and, most important, what you should do about it.

Suppose the product manager scores himself or herself a 2 in response to the statement about analyzing competitors. In this case, you can consider one of two possible gaps:

1. The first would be the difference between 2 and 3.
2. The second would be the difference between 2 and 4.

You might want this person to either be proficient (3) or an expert (4). Depending on what you require, you may want to devise work plans that will bridge the single gap, if that's enough, or bridge both gaps at the same time.

However, you may be disappointed in the results if both you and the product manager do not have a common understanding of these areas:

- Work involved in improving that proficiency
- Other work activities for which that product manager is responsible

- Financial resources that can be applied to this effort
- Cross-functional collaboration that might be needed to carry out the work

### THE VALUE OF A SECOND OPINION

Sometimes it's a good idea to have the *manager of the product manager* take the same assessment to evaluate his or her product manager employee. This will transform it into a 180-degree evaluation. Any gaps between those two scores can help pave the way for additional conversations between employees and their managers. It's also a good idea to interview some or all of the product managers in the population. *Interviews, when carried out correctly, can probe deeply into a work area or competency to determine the depth of the employee's experience and uncover any inconsistencies or biased responses in the assessment.* These techniques are very effective tools and important considerations if you want to fine-tune or validate the responses.

## ORGANIZATIONAL DESIGN CONSIDERATIONS

After you have a Competency Model and you've carried out an analysis, what's the next step?

It's very likely you'll need to make adjustments to elements of the organization's design—in order to clarify roles and responsibilities. *Role confusion* in Product Management is often cited as one of the biggest obstacles to efficiency. While the next logical step would be to improve the knowledge, skills, and experience of your staff, there's a caveat: Education and skills improvement programs carried out in the environment of a poorly designed Product Management organization generally yield unsatisfactory outcomes. Many organizational changes fail because of fundamental flaws in the design of the Product Management organization.

A successful design must consider the following:

1. *The strategy and direction of the company or business division in which the product managers work*: This requires a specific focus on the product portfolio strategy and what it takes to attain the objectives established by senior leadership. Such objectives

might include the organization's ability to develop newer, innovative products, expand the scope of the product line, and/ or expand the sales of current products in newer geographies or market areas.

2. *The most important outcomes that are expected in order to help achieve those strategies:* These could be improved product line strategic planning documents, realistic Business Cases for product investments, or improved Launch Plans and protocols. Outcomes might also include explicit market share numbers or more efficient project prioritization.

3. *The designation of the most important roles:* In other words, the people who carry out the work and the outcomes they are responsible for producing must be identified. In many cases, there will be a number people who are responsible for individual tasks. People fulfilling the role will most likely need to work together— which leads me to the next item.

4. *The clear identification of role interdependencies:* The questions "Who does what?" "With whom?" and "When?" must be answered.

These are the main ingredients in an effective Product Management organization, and they are depicted in Figure 2.6.

However, there may be some challenges within the context of the organization's design. Roles, responsibilities, and cross-functional interdependencies are rarely simple pairwise constructs. What looks like an uncomplicated diagram depicts a very complex reality. The nature of that reality depends on the makeup of the processes or work flows stemming from or producing the desired outcomes.

As an example, let's look at a subprocess used to secure market insights: the customer visit process. When you construct a *customer visit process*, you need to delegate resources (assign roles and funding) and make sure the product managers and others know what they are responsible for. I've provided a diagram in Figure 2.7 to show this customer visit process as a high-level work flow. For simplicity, I assumed that the assigned roles have the requisite knowledge and competency to do the work.

**Figure 2.6  Elements of the Product Management Organizational Design**

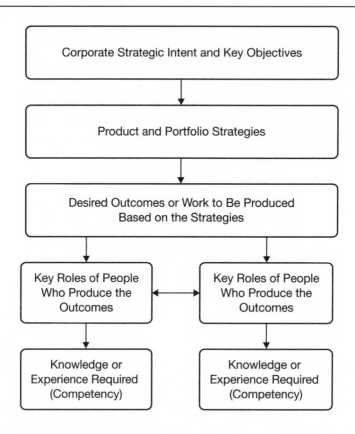

Here's the general cadence of work:

Step 1. The product manager needs additional customer information to complete a Business Case. The marketing manager also has to validate some work for a sales training program.

Step 2. They meet, talk it over informally, and decide they want to design and carry out a customer visit program. Now they have a lot to coordinate.

Step 3. They have to create clarity around the activities. Notice I said, "create" clarity. Clarity can be created through the negotiations of the people serving in different roles or through their managers' setting boundaries.

**Figure 2.7  High-Level Work Flow for a Customer Visit Process**

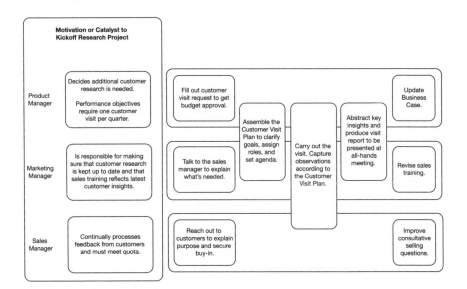

Step 4. Salespeople must reach out to the customers to make an appointment. That's the role of the salespeople, and it is their responsibility to get agreement from the customers for the visit.

Step 5. The product manager and the marketer need to decide how to structure the visit. To do so, they work on a Customer Visit Plan document. They may also have to refer to others within their departments for guidance. Their job is to negotiate with each other and with the salespeople on the protocol. The salespeople need to take the essence of the Customer Visit Plan to the customers and discuss the visits, the participants, and the tours and other activities that may take place—all of which ultimately help the salespeople secure the visiting customers' buy-in.

Step 6. Once the visit is agreed upon by all parties, the visit is carried out.

Step 7. Afterward, the product manager, marketer, and salespeople will meet to discuss what they saw and heard, and they will all collaborate on a visit report that contains the insights they uncovered. The product manager and marketer may reach out to their respective leadership teams to encourage their participation in a presentation of key findings.

This process explanation is just one small and simple depiction taken from the vast array of processes, subprocesses, and work flows that need to be synchronized across the Product Management organization. In the example just given, if the product manager cannot get a marketer to the table to have the initial discussion, a key outcome of the strategy will be unfulfilled, or at best only partially completed.

## A PRODUCT MANAGEMENT MATURITY MODEL

I will cover significant ground on this topic in Chapters 6 and 9; here, however, I want to explain some of the basic aspects of a Product Management Maturity Model. My intent is not to duplicate information but to kindle a spark that may inspire some ideas about your own organizations as you read the chapters that follow.

Most business leaders believe, and it is usually true, that consistent execution of key business processes will produce predictable business results. Setting some stakes in the ground doesn't guarantee success, but it usually does minimize risk and produce desired outcomes. The use of a Maturity Model allows leaders of product organizations to establish a framework for gauging the current usage of a given process so that decisions can be made on which processes to be fine-tuned.

To start, we need a definition for a Maturity Model:

A Product Management Maturity Model establishes a common foundation for the consistent, repeatable, persistent, and predictable execution of key practices, processes, methods, and documents for Product Management.

There are two dimensions of a Maturity Model: One relates to the maturity of the *product manager population*. The other relates to the maturity of the *Product Management organization and how it is governed*.

For clarity, I have assigned a unique term to each of these items so that you can distinguish the unique taxonomy behind them. When the Product Management Maturity Model (PMMM) is tagged with the designation "P," the resulting abbreviation PMMM-P stands for "Product Management Maturity Model, Product Manager Population." The PMMM-P is the model I'll be discussing in this chapter. In Chapter 9 where I discuss methods to govern and sustain Product Management, I will refer to the Product Management Maturity Model, Governance, using the designation "G," which stands for "governance," with the resulting abbreviation being PMMM-G.

This Maturity Model should not be confused with a product manager competency assessment. *Competency assessments* as described in this book relate to self-evaluations by individual product managers of their perceived level of experience. In contrast, *maturity evaluations* are carried out by managers or leaders to determine the degree to which product managers carry out work in a consistent fashion that (hopefully) produces positive outcomes.

I don't wish to confuse you. However, for the maturity evaluation to take place, we need something to evaluate. In this case, we use the meta-level competency clusters (again!). By using the same evaluative elements, we can uncover the product managers' experience level (as they report it on the competency assessment) and their maturity level (based on evaluation by their bosses). In Chapter 6, we will use both measurements on a *Product Manager Scorecard*.

To get going on the maturity evaluation, a rating scale is needed. The scale I suggest is as follows:

Choice 1. Very inconsistent and unpredictable (25 points)

Choice 2. Inconsistent and somewhat unpredictable (50 points)

Choice 3. Consistent and somewhat predictable (75 points)

Choice 4. Very consistent and predictable (100 points)

Next, we need to have some statements to elicit responses. I'll create a few for you, and then you can take over using the themes above:

1. "Product managers secure data to understand customer needs."
2. "Product managers understand competitor product positioning."

3.  "Product managers carry out competitor product analysis."
4.  "Product managers monitor industry trends."

Figure 2.8 is a table to show you how you might want to set up this evaluation.

After the maturity measurements have been taken for each product manager and the results have been rolled up to include segments or groupings of product managers in the organization, leaders will have a snapshot to help them decide which areas they want to improve upon. It is highly recommended that maturity measurements, like competency assessments, be done on an *annual basis*. This frequency allows leaders to ascertain progress and to fine-tune product manager performance objectives. It also provides snapshots that help determine Product Management process effectiveness. All of these reviews serve to set the stage for continuous improvement.

In short, greater levels of consistency in Product Management process execution should generally result in recognizable, sustainable results—and higher levels of overall efficiency in product manager work activities.

### Figure 2.8  Maturity Evaluation

| Maturity Statements for the Meta-Level Competency *"Derive Market Insights"* | Very Inconsistent and Unpredictable 25 | Inconsistent and Somewhat Unpredictable 50 | Consistent and Somewhat Predictable 75 | Very Consistent and Predictable 100 | Overall Maturity Score |
|---|---|---|---|---|---|
| Product managers secure data to understand customer needs. | | | | | |
| Product managers understand competitor product positioning. | | | | | |
| Product managers carry out competitor product analysis. | | | | | |
| Product managers monitor industry trends. | | | | | |
| *Total score* | | | | | |

## SUMMARY

There is no silver bullet that will keep products on top of their markets; and the process to achieve this kind of success is not some arcane, mysterious activity dependent on a few expert contributors distributed throughout the organization. The purpose of this book is to prove to leaders that Product Management can fulfill that function through its reliance on structured, repeatable, and measurable systems. However, in order to do so, Product Management must become an active, staffed, horizontal structure that serves as the backbone of the organization. A good Product Management organization should be composed of able and dedicated product managers who will translate strategy into viable, effective tactics in a dynamic way.

Getting the most out of Product Management means formalizing, measuring, and developing the organization. A Product Management Organization Master Plan helps to do this by chartering the Product Management organization and capturing all associated actions and precedents. Summing up, the most important parts of this plan are these:

- A Competency Model for assessing the knowledge, skills, and experience of your Product Management staff, based on a reliable Reference Model for effective Product Management.
- A method to assess and evaluate gaps between competency measurements and desired performance levels.
- An optimized, strategically aligned organizational design that encourages the various functions to work collectively on behalf of the product. You may have to make structural adjustments to roles and responsibilities in order to achieve this.
- A method to periodically evaluate the maturity of the Product Management organization so that it will evolve and progress over time.

Product Management should represent a stable, consistent method of managing products. It can and should be structured to remain relatively constant through any organizational or strategic changes. If Product Management is designed as the horizontal back brace, it can tie together the work produced by people in different functions on behalf of the product's business. With this in place, your organization will be more flexible and agile so that it can pivot more easily as market conditions change. With a properly chartered, structured, and measured Product Management team, you can track markets with much greater speed and precision and thus remain more profitable and competitive.

*Case Study I*

# THOMAS & BETTS

*By Bob Caporale, Vice President of Product Management and Engineering*

Thomas & Betts Corporation is a global leader in the design, manufacture, and marketing of electrical components used in industrial, construction, and utility markets. We have an extensive portfolio of over 200,000 products, marketed under more than 45 different brand names. Thomas & Betts traces its heritage back to 1898 when incandescent lighting was in the early stages of commercialization and the need for a related infrastructure was just being defined. Many of our products and brands are the result of a long history of acquisitions, beginning in 1917 and continuing right up to the present day. With so many different companies, products, brands, and even strategies coming together over the years, the glue that has held it all together has always been, and continues to be, our Product Management function.

## THE ROLE OF PRODUCT MANAGEMENT

Product managers have always held a critical and central role to the success of Thomas & Betts. We always say that Product Management is the "center of our universe." This is both metaphoric and literal. Metaphorically, we consider Product Management the core function that holds our strategies together. Like the central hub on a wheel, this team is responsible for working with nearly every other function in the corporation—Operations, Sales, Marketing, Engineering, Finance, Legal, and even Human Resources—to develop core business strategies and to see that those strategies are executed at every level. Our product managers do not have any of these functions reporting directly to them, but they are totally responsible and accountable for the output of all these teams. They are tasked to provide vision, direction, and motivation around their strategic plans, then to actively "sell" the organization on the merits and benefits of achieving the goals they set. This requires meticulous attention to establishing ownership among all functional leaders and, if applicable, addressing conflict in a collaborative way.

In a more literal sense, product managers are directly responsible for our product line strategies, and the product line strategies are the central focus of the overall business strategy, sandwiched between market strategy and operational strategy. Some companies begin with an operational plan and let it dictate their market and product strategies, but we believe that all things begin and end with our customers and, thus, with our market and product line strategies.

Notice I listed Marketing as a separate function from Product Management. We see Marketing and Product Management serving two very different, yet closely connected purposes. The Marketing team identifies our market opportunities, analyzes market trends, and defines our identity with our customers. In short, the Marketing team defines market strategy. From these inputs, our product managers develop product-specific strategies, set business and financial goals, and help develop operational and channel strategies that will satisfy market needs. The P&L responsibility lies here, along with all related communication, accountability, and leadership. The product line strategies are the basis for our overall business strategy, but they are not created in a vacuum. Instead, they are an integral part of a much larger plan that is developed collaboratively among all of the business functions.

Our products range from electrical boxes to specialty lighting products to high-voltage switches and switchgear. An equally diverse portfolio of brands goes with those products. Trying to adopt a one-size-fits-all approach to Product Management would be ineffective, to say the least. With every unique company, product, or brand we have acquired or developed over the years, we have also acquired an equally unique set of strategies, market approaches, and Product Management talent. Maintaining a balance between these different approaches while integrating them into the greater strategic direction of our company has been one of the keys to our success.

The strategy to sell a heavily distributed product like a steel box will look much different from the strategy required to sell a highly engineered product like a high-voltage switch. If these products were both treated the same in our marketing, selling, and operational approaches, one or both would almost certainly suffer. To achieve a balanced approach, Thomas & Betts maintains regional Product Management teams in each key global market, with local Product Management leadership to help customize each product line strategy based on the needs of the individual market being served. Additionally, local leaders can match the right talent and skill sets within their teams to the corresponding strategies where those strengths can best be utilized.

To ensure global coordination and support, the regional Product Management leaders come together as a team to ensure that local strategies are connected to an overall global product line strategy as well as to the larger corporate strategy. It is also the job of these leadership teams to ensure the implementation of common and consistent Product Management roles, responsibilities, and processes, while still allowing their respective teams enough flexibility to develop different strategic approaches for each different market and for each different product type within that market. To achieve this balanced Product Management culture, we focus on four main areas: strategy, structure, training, and tools.

## STRATEGY

Everything starts with the development of a good strategy. However, in terms of Product Management, it is so much more. The product manager's role is to bring the entire organization together to achieve each strategic goal. Having a well-developed, properly communicated strategy serves to rally leaders across different functions to work together to achieve that goal. But it's certainly not easy.

The first step to developing a strategy everyone can stand behind is to get buy-in from the executive team. To do this, our product managers are required to think at a different strategic level. There might be a natural inclination to create a strategic story from the details, but our approach is exactly the opposite. We encourage our product managers to develop the plot first, then fit the details into the story. Thus, they can sell the concept behind the strategies before writing the words of every chapter. Upon high-level approval of the overall direction, product managers relay the details to the leaders of every function. They allow the leaders to have authoring credit and ownership in the overall strategy. If everyone agrees on the 30,000-foot view, it's much easier to collaborate at 10,000 feet and below.

## STRUCTURE

We have a saying that "structure should always follow strategy." It may sound obvious, but it's often hard to practice. Companies are a collection of people, and some organizational leaders might want to take an inventory of their people and develop a structure around it. But this may not be the structure required to successfully implement their strategies. At Thomas & Betts, we always develop our strategies first; then we put the right structure in place to execute that strategy. This is vital when dealing with acquisitions. It is rare that any two companies will define their structures in exactly the same way. As a result, what is expected of product managers, as well as their required expertise and skill sets, may differ slightly from company to company. Because of this, it has been of pivotal importance for us to first develop the overarching strategy for acquired product lines and then to integrate their structures according to that overall strategy, rather than the reverse.

There must also be a careful balance between making drastic changes to existing structures and trying to develop skills not previously required of those structures. We have had much success, particularly with acquired businesses, in developing talent instead of summarily dismissing it. Rather than an inventory of structure, we take an inventory of skills, identify strengths and weaknesses in relation to our strategy, then fill in any gaps through focused organizational development. This could involve sharing of knowledge across Product Management teams, reallocating resources from one area to another, or providing training in specific developmental areas that are directly in line with our overall strategic goals.

## TRAINING

Some people are born with good instincts in certain areas, but few people are born with all of the skills needed to succeed in a function as demanding and diverse as Product Management. The role of product managers arguably spans more skill sets than any other job in the company. Product managers are responsible for developing and then selling the strategy, managing the product line P&L, forecasting, pricing, providing product support, managing product development and roll-out, guiding product marketing, developing their product brands, understanding the channel, helping to develop and drive operational plans, and, perhaps most importantly, having the right collaborative people skills to make all of this happen all at once.

It is virtually impossible to find a product manager who naturally possesses all of these skills at the levels needed to ensure ultimate success. We recognize that even the most able people require formal training or development, and so we invest in providing both internal and external training for all our product managers. In time, they develop the full set of skills necessary to perform their respective functions. In addition, training is targeted at the specific skill sets each of them needs—based not only on their own personal developmental needs but also on the needs of their product line strategies. For example, a product manager responsible for switchgear will need a high level of technical skill and competency, and he or she must understand how to serve the needs of utilities and engineers through training, product development, and marketing the concepts of safety and reliability. On the other hand, a product manager for electrical boxes must be more in tune with the distribution channel and may have to focus more on product placement, brand marketing, and developing a labor-savings value proposition to contractors and end users. These different skill sets can be fostered only through a combination of experience, training, and ultimately, identifying the right people for the right jobs.

## TOOLS

To set up a strong, successful Product Management team means giving people the right tools to do their jobs. For Product Management, this is more than providing the right technological tools; it is also about providing the right support functions to free up product managers so they can focus on planning and leading, instead of performing every task themselves. With so many responsibilities and accountabilities, product managers can fall into the trap of thinking that not only must they have a high-level understanding of many different functions but they must also perform all of those functions on a day-to-day basis. This could not be further from the truth. To prevent this kind of thinking, we have created separate teams in our Product Management organization to perform pricing duties, business analysis functions, product marketing tasks, and even project management functions. Having such teams ensures that our product managers have ample time to focus on their coordination and strategic leadership roles. We have also implemented many financial tools that enable product managers to track and analyze their product line P&Ls at the click of a button, so that they always work with consistent, accurate, and current data. In turn, this provides our company with a real-time knowledge of how we are tracking against our strategies, enabling us to make quick shifts when and if necessary.

## LIGHTING THE WAY

When we say Product Management is the "center of our universe," it is a high compliment, and it may appear hard to live up to. With a consistent and universally agreed-upon understanding of the product manager's role and a strong strategic story being told and being supported by all levels of the corporation, Thomas & Betts has been very successful in making this saying a reality. Still, with a portfolio of products and brands as large and diverse as ours, it is important to balance that consistent role definition with enough flexibility to allow product managers to customize their own responsibilities and skill sets according to the requirements of the products and markets they serve. Our focus on the four main elements of strategy, structure, training, and tools allows us to achieve the necessary balance and have our Product Management function lead us successfully into the future. Wherever electricity goes, so does Thomas & Betts, and we look to our Product Management teams to continue to light the way.

# MODULE II

# CLARIFY

Strategies cannot be created or implemented if there is no clarity of purpose or envisioned end state. However, even when a clear purpose has been delineated, it is often a challenge for leaders to get everyone on the same page. Many organizations are so dynamic, and their markets so fast-moving, that keeping everyone focused requires a Herculean effort. It becomes even more complex when you think about the many diverse roles and hidden agendas at work in the company's numerous functions.

For Product Management, the challenge may be even more difficult because there seem to be many varied interpretations of the function of Product Management and ambiguities about the roles people play in Product Management.

Product Management is the organic, interrelated ecosystem that touches, connects, and affects *all functions* within a company. A company exists because its products provide value to its customers in selected markets; consequently careful management of its products and portfolios is paramount. It is, then, axiomatic that the improvement of the function and performance of Product Management is essential to the success of the entire company.

In order to firmly establish the function of Product Management, *leaders must build a collective clarity of purpose for Product Management* that is viewed by, and bought into, across the entire organization. When the purpose of Product Management is understood by all, it will enable people to operate, cooperate, and interoperate more effectively. This is what clarity accomplishes for Product Management, and why these two chapters are so important.

The two chapters in this module convey several important perspectives that provide clarity. Chapter 3 establishes a clear definition of Product Management and its overall purpose in the company. Chapter 4 clearly shows how everyone in the organization is involved in Product Management. These two chapters are summarized as follows:

*Chapter 3. Everyone Is in the Product Management Sandbox:* This chapter has two primary elements. First, it brings to light many of the challenges that can emerge in any organization when functional agendas serve as a substitute for an integrated approach to "running the business" of products and portfolios. Then, it shifts to an explanation of what Product Management entails so that Product Management can be better understood by all. It concludes with six solid suggestions to get everyone into the Product Management sandbox.

*Chapter 4. Solving the Puzzle of the Product Management Organization:* This chapter is built on the premise that no matter what organizational structure a company chooses (geographic, functional, or a hybrid), Product Management must be able to thrive through its integration as a horizontal function. It provides an explanation of what should be expected of product managers and product *leaders* so that they can think systemically and holistically and respond accordingly. It then provides a model for organizational alignment so that everyone can get onto the same page and fit together the puzzle pieces of the organization with Product Management at the core.

CHAPTER 3

# EVERYONE IS IN THE PRODUCT MANAGEMENT SANDBOX

## EXECUTIVE SUMMARY

- In any organization, people who work in various business functions need to be unified in a way that helps the firm fulfill its strategic intent. That unifying force is Product Management.
- Product Management is business management at the product, product line, or product portfolio level.
- In the final analysis, *everyone* works in Product Management.

*People who work together will win, whether it be against complex football defenses or the problems of modern society.*

—VINCE LOMBARDI,
NATIONAL FOOTBALL LEAGUE COACH

Charles Darwin theorized that evolution was the result of *natural selection*. He coined the term "survival of the fittest" to describe the process by which species evolve, so that only the strongest and the best-adapted individuals survive in the ecosystem.

While survival is paramount in nature, it is important to understand that *Corporate Darwinism is not helpful or profitable* within a business. In fact, the opposite is true: teamwork and collaboration are more advantageous than individual or functional interests.

In this chapter, I propose some ways for businesses to overcome unproductive work situations created by functions that at times don't work collectively. I visualize a metaphoric "corporate sandbox" where everyone must cooperate with those they work with. My goal for this chapter is to describe why it's so important to get *everyone* into the Product Management sandbox and the important role that your leadership can play.

Here are some examples that show just how Corporate Darwinism can derail a company.

## ORGANIZATIONAL ISSUES AND DISCONNECTS

Several years ago, my firm worked with a midsize software and services company. Our project involved an organizational diagnostic, composed of competency assessments and interviews with 48 product managers and 9 managers of the product managers. We also interviewed the CEO and 12 of the leaders in other functions. Our findings revealed some challenges.

Although the majority of the population of product managers had "product manager" in their job title, most were generally referred to as "project managers." In fact, more than three-quarters of those interviewed used "product manager" and "project manager" interchangeably. Ultimately, we found 32 different job titles among 48 staff members.

In one area, there was a huge gap between how product managers actually monitored a product's financial performance and what their senior leaders expected. Although senior leaders mandated that the product managers were responsible, the product managers did not feel that examination of a product's finances was part of their job. It seemed as if no one felt accountable for product financials or for the product's overall performance. Our assessment showed that the scores related to financial acumen were the lowest of all of the categories. There was a reason for all of this. All of the people in these Product Management positions were former engineers and thus had little knowledge, training, or interest in financial matters.

There were many other significant findings. Aside from the financials issue, there were serious misalignments across the different business functions and a serious amount of role confusion. Product ownership was in chaos. Sales claimed ownership because they made the deals and monitored revenue. Marketing thought they owned the products because many of the product managers reported to them. Product Development had the loudest voice because they owned something called "the product life cycle process."

After we had completed all the assessments and prepared our diagnostic report, we briefed the CEO, and he asked us to present our findings and recommendations at a senior leadership meeting. At the meeting, we presented data and reviewed our insights. My team was then ready to facilitate a discussion that was supposed to (a) lead to better alignment of functions, (b) clarify roles and responsibilities, and (c) fortify Product Management—the reasons for the program in the first place. But from there on, the agenda was forgotten, and the discussions never took place. Instead, executives from some of the business functions grumbled that no one understood the value of what they brought to the table. Other complaints were also voiced. But worse, in an astonishing turnaround, the CEO backed off his intended objective and tried to placate everyone and "make peace" *without committing to any needed changes*. The rest of the "meeting" descended into a Darwinian fight for survival.

Although senior leaders in the company had commissioned the study, the business wasn't hurting enough to cause alarm, and there was little motivation to change anything. (Their survival did not feel threatened.) The leaders defended their territories (read: "silos") and left the conference room with a business-as-usual strategy. Even though this was a rare occurrence, is it possible that you recognize some of these behaviors in your own firm?

## THE IMPACT OF A GEOGRAPHICAL REORGANIZATION ON PRODUCT MANAGEMENT

There are many companies that have actually *had* vibrant, productive product managers—and then the company reorganized! As I learned from my research, such reorganizations can often cause some unintended consequences.

In Chapter 1, I related a story about a company that reorganized along geographic boundaries that shifted accountability for the P&L to local geographies. In fact, there were two companies I worked with in two different industries that chose this structure.

Both firms chose this path because it seemed logical to be closer to customers and to be more responsive to the needs of those customers. However, in addition to the problematic issues I raised in Chapter 1, there were some other challenges, involving Corporate Darwinism, and those also had a detrimental impact on the organization.

Prior to the reorganizations, product managers in both companies had worked directly with customers, salespeople, and others to secure inputs and prioritize solutions. However, the geographical reorganizations eroded the advantages of these procedures.

There's an old adage that says, "For want of a nail, a shoe was lost; for want of a shoe, a horse was lost; . . . for want of a horse, the battle was lost." In a parallel to the adage: Due to the structural changes, the companies lost the capacity to accurately characterize the operating profiles of the local customers and the distinct "need profiles" of various influencers. This meant they lost the capacity to recognize important facets of their customers' businesses. As a result, their capacity to uncover problems and find optimal solutions was inhibited.

When you have large accounts in a business-to-business environment, it may be logical to move some staff closer to primary customers. However, for more optimal results, it is important that *product managers be included in the plans,* instead of being left behind. They should (as often as practical) be part of the discovery and relationship building process, both with customers and with the local teams. If sales doesn't involve them or they aren't permitted to travel, vital signals will be missed. Also, if different product managers support different product lines but they don't regularly confer with one another, efforts can be inadvertently duplicated.

Our remedial advice was that each company set up a *centralized* product and portfolio rationalization group to reconcile all requests across geographies. This group would be tasked to oversee the many inputs and market insights that should influence overall decisions. Further, we suggested that product managers should be directly involved with customers and with the regional employees. In this way they would share and cultivate their diverse domain knowledge with the geographies, while ensuring greater customer satisfaction.

## WHEN ENGINEERING, OPERATIONS, TECHNOLOGY, OR OTHER ORGANIZATIONS DRIVE

Here are two more short examples that illustrate how other organizational paradigms keep the main players out of the Product Management sandbox.

In one firm, the Engineering function held sway over product strategies due to their avowed expertise. They claimed superior product knowledge because they received all the escalations and complaints. However, their focus on technical details impacted their overall objectivity. In an ironic twist, they didn't even realize that many of the complaints resulted from poorly conceived features or inadequate designs.

Product Management was *not* well established in this firm. In our estimation, they didn't have an adequate number of product managers; and those on their staff didn't have enough product or market expertise to credibly influence the strategic direction of the products. The senior leaders *claimed* they wanted to change the status quo and that they wanted to organize for more effective Product Management, but somehow, they never seemed to find the money to do so. End of story: Nothing changed. The engineers maintained their status, and the product managers wrote requirements, tested products, and dealt with customer or product problems on an ad hoc basis. Some companies seek advice, but they can't find the impetus to move out of their Darwinian comfort zone.

In the business-to-business division of a large bank, the Operations function held the reins. Since they were on the front lines, they believed they were the best able to evaluate and manage customer complaints. Due to their vaunted experience, they were brought into customer implementations and integration projects. However, they were ill equipped to act in the capacity of product managers, despite their frontline experience. Further, there was a conflict of interest and a lot of friction between the Operations group and the Information Technology group because IT felt they understood the product better than any other group.

Actually, it was the product managers who had the best functional and domain expertise, but they were relegated to roles akin to business analysts or project managers. The forward-looking senior leader of the division wanted the product managers to deepen their business acumen and try to come up with more innovative solutions, but he lacked the opportunities to implement this idea. Further, most of the managers of the product managers did not have the time, inclination, or expertise to support the growth and development of the individual product managers.

When different functions try to steer the products in different directions, for their own agendas, the effects of this disarray will result in undesirable consequences:

- When senior leaders are from Sales, deals dictate everything and other groups must follow along.
- When Development leads, technology tends to be pushed into the market.
- When Finance leads, then the value proposition is lost and prices are structured to meet cost targets or margin requirements.
- When product managers function in a disconnected way, it becomes a problem of "herding cats" even if there is a Product Management leader.

These may not be hard-and-fast, cause-and-effect organizational models, but I have observed enough such examples to be concerned. The first step to getting everyone into the sandbox is to inculcate a collective understanding of the role of Product Management in the overall organization and how it can maximize efficiency and teamwork.

## WHAT'S INVOLVED IN PRODUCT MANAGEMENT?

I believe that everyone in a company is involved in Product Management in some way.

If what I posit is true, then what is actually involved in Product Management, and what are the expectations? In this section, I explain it in two different ways:

- First, I'll give you the essence of the definition set forth in *The Product Manager's Desk Reference*.
- Second, I will explain the generic work activities—and *processes*—

contained in the Product Management Life Cycle Model (PMLCM) mentioned in Chapter 2.

## PRODUCT MANAGEMENT DEFINED

Simply stated, Product Management is the *business management of the product, product line, or product portfolio*. Products are the reason a business is in business. The Product Management function is the best way for a company to manage its products and services and to make them as profitable as possible. Product Management works to manage each product as if it were a mini-business within the structure of the whole business. In the big picture of the organizational structure, Product Management is a microcosm *of* and a model *for* a business organization.

When properly structured and utilized, Product Management acts as the "genetic material" that influences all supporting structures and business functions, just as DNA works in the human body. The word *organization* comes from the word *organ*, and DNA allows the organs of the body to function together, as they are supposed to. Ideally, all functions of the body—or the business—will work together, holistically, toward a single goal: the success and survival of the entity.

Just as Product Management is in all the "genes" of the organization, everyone in that organization has a role in Product Management, in some way, whether directly or indirectly. Thus, everyone in the organization needs to understand the roles, responsibilities, and interdependencies that make the business (body) work properly.

## THE INTERCONNECTED SYSTEMS OF PRODUCT MANAGEMENT

In Chapter 2, I discussed the Product Management Life Cycle Model as a Reference Model for Product Management. In that model there are three Areas of Work that bring products from idea to final sale. These were identified as New Product Planning (NPP), New Product Introduction (NPI), and Post-Launch Product Management (PLPM).

Separate but interconnected structures support these Areas of Work: processes, systems, methods, work flows, and documents. Although these structures seem to belong in one part of the life cycle, they are usually active, to varying degrees, across the entire life span of the product. Documents such as the Product Strategy, Business Case, or the Launch Plan that are created at a particular time have elements that reach out and touch everything from beginning to end. Events are constantly in motion, and responses must be sensitive to the situations that arise as the product moves through the market. As you can see, Product Management is a living structure composed of dynamic processes: it evolves; it changes; it creates, it responds; things wax and wane in importance. No matter what, Product Management is always an interconnected, living system.

While the Product Management Life Cycle Model does help establish a clear line of sight to the market, the creation and development of extraordinary products is not a linear or predictable process. Real business and market environments are vigorous, vibrant, and constantly changing. The same holds true for the *organizational design* of Product Management, in which many important activities are carried out at the same time. Decisions taken now affect future aspects of the product's performance. A small degree of difference at any given moment can make a world of difference later. Similarly, if you make decisions in the present to achieve a longer-term vision for the Product Management organization, you may require a stick-to-itiveness that is counterintuitive to many leaders.

Although the life cycle itself doesn't change very much structurally, what you learn along the way, as it moves forward, changes the *implementation* of the Product Management Life Cycle Model. Experiencing the product in the market can change the strategy or influence decisions about next steps. Actions taken by leaders or responses to competitors may suddenly change your firm's immediate goals or operating environment.

There are times when certain actions or pieces become more important; times when other parts are more fluid; and even times when one or more elements of the product environment must absolutely be static and stable. The Product Management Governance Board (see Chapter 9) should enable the management of each of these pieces separately, collectively, *and* holistically. Ultimately, that's how Product Management should be situated in the organization.

## PRODUCT MANAGEMENT PROCESS IMPROVEMENT REQUIRES EXPERT OVERSIGHT

In the several decades I have spent evaluating Product Management, I have seen many different depictions of Product Management processes and models. The people who create these models hail from a variety of different disciplines:

- In a U.S.-based money center bank, the Quality and Productivity group ran the Product Management process in partnership with their massive credit card operation.
- In a large industrial firm, the Organizational Development group came up with their Product Management model.
- In a major communications company a special task force was assembled to work alongside an outside consultancy to create a new model.

Here's the point: Product Management process improvement isn't a once-and-done project to be delegated to any organization. It requires comprehensive oversight by experienced, dedicated Product Management process specialists and ongoing oversight, as I will describe further in Chapter 9.

## NEW PRODUCT DEVELOPMENT PROCESS CONTINUITY

Not only do we have the problem of different process models, many companies don't stick with the program. Why? Those involved become apprehensive about the implications of additional work and perceived rigidity, and they worry that there may be an excessive need for constant governance. As a result, they either remake the model or reorganize. It is certainly easier to remake presentation slides than it is to monitor and respond to situational changes that enable continuous improvement.

In other analyses I've carried out, I've learned that executives become impatient because they don't see material returns such as cycle time reduction or improved decision making. In one situation, after a root-cause analysis, it was learned that the process model was *not* at issue. People and their politics provided the motivation. The "need" for process change was actually a way for newer senior leaders to leave their mark on the organization. In other instances, the New Product Development (NPD) process is avoided or important steps are skipped over because the people who are supposed to do the work do not have the requisite knowledge, skill, or experience.

The purpose of a phase gate NPD process is to serve as a business decision-making model so that the *best* opportunities can be selected—out of all that are available. In my firm's benchmarking, I have found that most companies do use some type of phase gate NPD process. However, some use it incorrectly—as a mere checklist of things to do to expedite work. Some companies are more interested in pressing everyone to use the process, and so "new" NPD models often miss the mark.

No model should overly govern or constrain business activity, though many companies take things in that direction. However, when dealing with phase gate NPD models, the process often becomes the focal point of too much activity. Take the amount of time people spend in task-based NPD activities, and compare it to the efforts being made to optimize the business and market performance of existing products. You may be surprised to learn that the time and energies expended on NPD activities are far greater than the time and energies spent on optimizing a product's market performance.

Another thing to keep in mind is that sometimes the NPD process is confused with Product Management. This is an easy mistake to make because it's the most pronounced linear representation of product-related activities. Process designs will usually be incomplete in key areas without some real perspective and expertise related to Product Management effectiveness.

## MAKING A LONG-TERM COMMITMENT TO PRODUCT MANAGEMENT

In some companies, Product Management task forces have been assembled to address shortcomings in one or two processes or subprocesses of Product Management.

Here's an example that shows several of the obstacles to even the best of intentions.

A Design for Six Sigma (DFSS) project in a large bank indicated some gaps in Product Management effectiveness. A task force was assigned to improve Product Management. However, the problem was that *no one on the team had ever held the job of a product manager!*

Before we started our program with them, we tried to set the objectives and agree on the desired outcomes. Some were understood clearly, but some were not. Our diagnostics showed that what they really needed was a measurement system to assess people prior to training and to evaluate results and behaviors after the training. We dealt with those issues in our workshops, which took place over a nine-month period. However, the team was disbanded shortly after the workshop deliveries ended, and the actual outcomes never had the chance to be realized. Later, it was learned that HR had stopped the project before completion because they hadn't been consulted or included in initial analysis and solution meetings. Talk about Corporate Darwinism! It isn't surprising that many Product Management improvement endeavors aren't "completed."

There are a few other important perspectives I would like you to consider in terms of Product Management process management. One of these should be the allotment of enough time for change to take place:

1. Task groups that are assigned to Product Management process improvement should be chartered for the *long term*, not just for a few months. This is important because the effects of any implemented changes need to be monitored. Without this connection, continuity may be lost.
2. Since there are impacts on people, processes, and cross-functional teams, buy-in from other leaders needs to be secured and followed—again, to ensure the long-term success of the initiative.
3. The executive leadership team or a designated Product Management Governance Board should drive the Product Management programs (a topic explored in detail in Chapter 9). Senior leaders can make or break significant initiatives. Most Product Management process improvement efforts involve active change management. A mere communication plan isn't enough to catalyze or complete the desired changes.

Many task forces recommend changes to processes and methods, and there is an expectation that behaviors will be adjusted. But change can't take place when people don't know how to move from one state of behavior or performance to another—whether due to skill gaps or lack of knowledge. Further, it must be understood by leaders and product managers that change isn't instantaneous. Otherwise, they are less likely to want to accept and implement the idea.

When their current work activities have not been realigned and product managers are asked to change their behavior and work activity to focus on other items, they become overwhelmed, and role confusion abounds. It is important to note that change *cannot* take place unless there is an overriding effort to nurture the actual transformation and provide a viable game plan for all.

As we all know, the ownership of a company can change with a signature. If you have participated in a merger or in the transition post-merger, you may have found that product managers and others associated with them are indeed confused. Another thing you may have learned is that you cannot change the people of the acquired company to adopt the culture of the new organization (or the new model that senior leaders envision) unless there is a plan. A *merger transition plan* can include "transformational" aspects that take into consideration the psychological and emotional dimensions of people who have to work in the combined organization. In order to effectively transform a company's Product Management organization into a vital function, senior leaders need to ensure that adequate planning, time, and thresholds are initiated to keep the program on track and to maintain employee engagement as roles are adjusted.

Even though there are many challenges, I am optimistic about the future for this field. More and more, Product Management is being regarded as a necessary structure. It is jelling far more solidly than in the past. I am encouraged by the many positive indicators that long-term Product Management governance is also beginning to take form.

## HOW TO GET EVERYONE INTO THE PRODUCT MANAGEMENT SANDBOX

There are some simple things that executive leadership teams can do to convince people in various functions to get into the Product Management sandbox:

1.  Everyone needs to understand the purpose and function of Product Management. The definition provided in this chapter should serve as a good reference point.

2. Product managers represent the Product Management "army." They must be capable, credible, and influential enough to get work done in complex organizations. Later chapters will describe how to hire and cultivate those vital resources. Product managers cannot inspire anyone to action unless they are equipped with a unique set of skills and abilities that places them in the roles of orchestrators and catalysts. This is particularly difficult if your company lacks adequate staffing levels of product managers.

3. Product Management thrives when every concerned person in every functional group understands the processes, methods, tools, and documents used to plan, develop, launch, and manage products. When people in the business functions know the roles they play, the responsibilities they fulfill, and the outcomes they provide, everyone can more easily "play" in the Product Management sandbox.

4. Product Management requires cross-functional participation and collaboration. Functional agendas must be subdued so that Product Management can take root. At the heart is the P&L. Product managers, as leaders, should *own* the P&L for their products, and Product Management should own the P&L for the product portfolios. It is amazing how behaviors change when this happens. This is not just my opinion. Many senior leaders maintain this as an operating model.

5. A realistic long-term view of Product Management is needed, especially if the company is just embarking on the Product Management journey. Small victories in the beginning will help leaders to communicate progress to the organization. These wins may allay the apprehension of leaders in the business functions so that they will contribute more heavily to the success of Product Management.

6. Product Management is *not* product development. Many Product Management models are represented as a New Product Development process. If this is the case, there will be a tendency to treat this as the overriding process for Product Management, which will result in a checklist or task list–driven enterprise.

Instead, think of Product Management as an interconnected set of processes and activities that support the product's business and the firm's strategy.

## SUMMARY

I see an organization as a big sandbox. The sandbox is a popular playground structure. But space is limited, and lots of children want to play there, so the competition can be a challenge. Because they come and go, the denizens of the sandbox change from time to time. And all of them have different ideas about what they want to do. Some want to build castles; some just want to move the sand around. Sometimes they start "battles" over territory, and other times they contest one another's creative efforts. Sometimes they need parental intervention. The possibilities for how to play and how to be open to rewarding experiences are up to the would-be players.

When I opened this chapter, I referred to the theory of evolution and the survival of the fittest and ended with the metaphor of a sandbox. Organizations, like sandboxes, may be finite in their physical space, but they have dynamic organisms working within those structures. We accept the premise that people need to grow and evolve, but in the organization, people in business functions need to be unified in a way that helps the firm fulfill its strategic intent. That unifying force *is* Product Management.

# CHAPTER 4

# SOLVING THE PUZZLE OF THE PRODUCT MANAGEMENT ORGANIZATION

## EXECUTIVE SUMMARY

- There are fundamental "puzzle pieces" that must be set in place to support Product Management; these foundational elements are essential to the long-term survival of Product Management.
- A stable Product Management Reference Model, covering planning, execution, and management of products and services, can greatly help to ensure that members of an organization are on the same page.
- Senior leaders can, and should, make Product Management work regardless of the firm's actual organizational structure.

*Every company has two organizational structures. The formal one is written on the charts; the other one is the everyday relationships of the men and women in the organization.*

—HAROLD S. GENEEN,
FORMER CHIEF EXECUTIVE OFFICER OF ITT

At times, I feel like an anthropologist, psychologist, and diagnostician, all in one—digging to discover the origins of problems corporations want to change. Being exposed to the inner workings of corporations has allowed me a remarkable perspective. Every client's business is a learning laboratory that teaches me more about company structures and how people carry out work. As they evolve, I learn more.

Through my work, I've seen corporations swing back and forth between new and recycled ideas, as they endeavor to find organizational models to meet the challenges and dynamics of the twenty-first century. The Bible tells us, "There's nothing new under the sun." I believe it. Sometimes it seems as if I'm watching reruns on television or remakes of old movies. Have business authors, university professors, and corporate leaders forgotten the lessons of the past? Or is it, simply, that new generations of leaders are replacing those who came before, and these new leaders are ignoring the lessons of the past? Can it be that all the collective learning has been forgotten or overlooked and, therefore, the errors of the past are being repeated?

Much that we know in life today is based on what was learned from history because past cultures have left us detailed records of their events and discoveries. So it should be with companies.

In this book I've used the simple metaphors of a jigsaw puzzle and a sandbox to exemplify the complex elements of an organization's culture and design. These analogies are intended to help companies understand that there are peripheral issues and challenges for product managers that exist alongside the exigencies of daily work. They require as much focus as the work itself.

When things are not working well, it's natural that corporate leaders, seeking better answers, may decide to restructure, rearrange, or reorganize. However, the results are not always stellar. It's not that change or reorganization is unnecessary—frequently it is. What I want to discuss is the need for rethinking what to change by adding greater weight and depth to the role of Product Management in the organizational formula. Therefore, in this chapter, I will talk about some of the structural elements that contribute to a more robust Product Management structure inside the organization.

## THE PRODUCT MANAGEMENT ORGANIZATION AS A LIVING SYSTEM

In Chapter 3, I compared the organization to the human body, and Product Management to the DNA that is in all the cells and organs. These overlapping, interlocking systems and functions influence each other in very complex ways in order for the entity to perform well. Changing circumstances (whether in the body or corporation) engender a fluid array of decisions driven by finely tuned protocols and methods. As we monitor our "bodies," we are supposed to recognize when something is wrong and take care of harmful situations.

In Peter Senge's book *The Fifth Discipline*, he refers to "systemic awareness" as a necessary characteristic of people working in corporations. *Systemic awareness* is defined as *"resources and activities that make us aware of the social, technological, and natural systems we are part of and that alter our beliefs and behaviors as part of evolving those systems."*

From my vantage point, Senge's proposition indicates that people who are the best leaders (and best product managers) in an organization "get it"; they're onto what systemic awareness means. They perceive how all the pieces fit together; they notice how the impact of one action affects other parts of the organization. People who truly "see" these interrelationships are usually more attuned to, and acutely aware of, organizational interactivity (cross-organizationally and cross-functionally). And as they process new signals, they are able to inspire others to be systemically aware.

Senge refers to this phenomenon as the "learning organization." By association, there are other effective terms like *institutional learning* or *tribal knowledge* used to describe the *communal* (or *collective*) *cognizance* that builds as an organization properly matures and grows.

Many senior leaders I talk to discuss systemic awareness as an always-desirable organizational characteristic. When they refer to the work of the business functions, they want the people in their product organizations to be more mindful of how the company actually works—regardless of individual structural composition.

## PUTTING ORGANIZATIONAL LEARNING TO WORK

If organizational learning is made up of the ongoing accrual of wisdom and awareness, then it makes sense to institute mechanisms and routines that will continually capture, share, and institutionalize data and synthesized information across the functions of the organization. Ideally, product managers should facilitate this work; it is an integral part of their jobs. They should be able to gather data, pull it all together, and effectively share the information with those they work with, even tangentially.

Through my benchmark work with so many companies, I found concrete proof of these assertions. Those companies whose employees gathered and shared data, particularly about industry trends, customer preferences, and competitor activities, tended to have greater levels of communal awareness. The proactive, effective product managers who capitalized on that capability earned greater levels of credibility with people up and down and across the organization chart.

The Product Management Organization Master Plan, discussed in the previous chapter, would be the ideal repository for this compilation of learning accumulated by the Product Management organization; the Product Master Plan, in Chapter 2 of *The Product Manager's Desk Reference*, would serve as the best repository at the product or product line level.

## ON THE ROAD TO CHARTERING PRODUCT MANAGEMENT

To further enhance the Product Management organization's abilities to achieve overall success, senior leaders must *formally* charter the function of Product Management, then sustain and support it over the long term. This goal becomes more attainable when leaders help their product managers (or a solid subset of Product Management leaders) cultivate and enhance behaviors and methods to bring about systemic awareness and holistic thinking.

> **Definitions**
> **Systemic:** Relating to or affecting the entire body (organization) or organism.
>
> **Holistic:** Relating to or affecting the whole and the interdependence of its parts.

Reorganizations have often failed because the leaders who catalyzed the organizational change did not fully realize the systemic and holistic implications of the change. They did not foresee all of the downstream interconnected impacts—what had to take place, with whom, and when. If, as asserted in other chapters, products or product lines are like mini-businesses inside the larger enterprise, then, logically, Product Management would be a microcosm of the corporate structure macrocosm. Therefore, Product Management should be systemically integrated into the firm. And since we expect product managers to think systemically and holistically, it logically follows that product *leaders* must think systemically and holistically and respond accordingly.

**A Success Story**

Although Product Management isn't as visible as I would like it to be, it must be said that many firms do have well-oiled leadership teams that effectively guide and focus the firm's resources. In one well-run company, a senior leader expressed great satisfaction with the company's Product Management function. However, that function had taken a number of years to cultivate. When I asked him for the "secret" of this success, the leader explained that what makes the firm's Product Management organization extraordinary is its *longevity*. It has been (and is) a work-in-progress for more than 10 years. He also noted that *its leaders have all previously held Product Management jobs* and that the Product Management leaders *cultivate product managers* as a matter of course. Like all good talent or sports scouts, these leaders also communicate informally with their peers in other functions, always on the lookout for product manager talent! Some characteristics the leaders continually seek are *the ability to see the bigger picture of how work gets done and the ability to influence people who work in other areas to get work done.*

## MORE PUZZLE PIECES

To assemble a holistic, sustainable backdrop for Product Management in an organization, we need to ensure that (in our figurative jigsaw puzzle) the following foundational elements are in place:

1. Processes should be documented and institutionalized so they become the referenceable knowledge base for finely tuned operations.

2. Systems and tools should be available to provide metrics, measurements, and indicators that can guide decision making, portfolio, and product investments.

3. A viable, flexible structure is needed, one that reflects the strategic intent and the value delivery methodology of the firm.

4. A staffing model should be established that allows for product managers and cross-functional product teams to be nurtured and sustained.

(Items 1, 2, and 3 are covered in this chapter. Item 4, the staffing model, is taken up in Chapter 5.)

## THE PRODUCT MANAGEMENT REFERENCE MODEL FOR ORGANIZATIONAL ALIGNMENT

Here's why all that preceded this is so important when establishing the Product Management organizational structure:

- No two companies manage products the same way.
- Product managers report to different functions in different companies.
- Organizations and policies in some companies don't always line up in ways that support strong Product Management.
- Executives split the roles that support important processes among too many departments, creating inefficient methods carried out inconsistently.
- A high percentage of typical product "practices" are nonexistent, deemed unnecessary, or made unnecessarily difficult because they are not based on a proven Reference Model.

In Chapter 2, I discussed the Product Management Life Cycle Model, telling you that it is the primary reference for the work involved in Product Management. To reinforce this tenet more graphically, I've inserted two diagrams in this chapter: Figure 4.1, "Product Management Process Mind Map," and Figure 4.2, "Product Management Life Cycle Model." They are intended to illustrate that Product Management is both holistic and recursive.

**Figure 4.1 Product Management Process Mind Map**

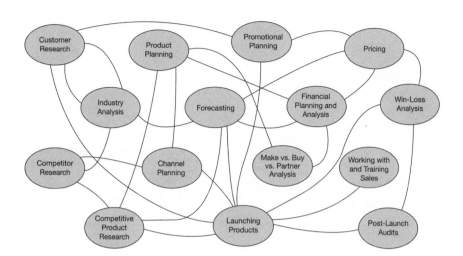

Looking at the Product Management Mind Map, you will recognize many of the processes and activities that are carried out within the purview of Product Management. The diagram shows the relationships between many interconnected and (at times) disconnected processes. It visually depicts the reasons that people in your organization may sometimes feel confused about who is responsible for participating in, driving, or producing outputs for each process. The diagram also indicates the areas in which cross-organizational or cross-functional interdependencies may be confused because of functional misalignments (see Chapter 3).

Looking at the Product Management Life Cycle Model in Figure 4.2, you can see the major Areas of Work first mentioned in Chapter 2. This certainly looks like a *much more organized* model! It's important because it presents very graphically how a well-structured business works. Think of each Area of Work as a "meta-theme" part of the product life cycle during which the phases of the life cycle proceed in orderly fashion. It also reinforces, once more, the idea that every product or product line is a business *within* a business—which, again, is why I maintain that Product Management is the business management of products! Therefore, all business models should account for each of the three Areas of Work and, in parentheses, its relationship to the Product Management Life Cycle Model:

**Figure 4.2  Product Management Life Cycle Model**

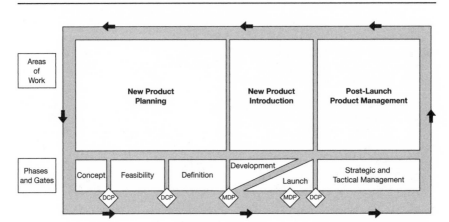

DCP : Decision Check Point
MDP : Major Decision Point

Source: Copyright Sequent Learning Networks.

1. Planning (New Product Planning)
2. Executing (New Product Introduction)
3. Managing (Post-Launch Product Management)

Now, I'll explain why the three main Areas of Work are so important to consider when evaluating the composition of Product Management in your organizational structure. The following sections show the description of the work and the work flows (and comments), which explain the interconnectedness of the processes and work activities.

### NEW PRODUCT PLANNING (NPP)

New Product Planning relies on the core competencies of people in the organization who are adept at securing, processing, and synthesizing market insights and other signals. This area serves as a backdrop for the exploration, the discovery, and the creative processes. New Product Planning is *intentionally* shown larger than the other two Areas of Work because the contrast in proportion represents the larger amount of time and effort that should be devoted to planning. Therefore, it is of the utmost importance that you utilize this part of the model as your guide for decision making.

As a side note, my hobby is woodworking. Woodworkers know that if you measure twice and cut only once (that is, if you plan better), you avoid time-consuming, frustrating, and expensive rework later on in the process. It also contributes to a better-quality product (and outcome).

The use of the adjective "new" for this important Area of Work is a matter of semantics. Whether the product being planned is actually new or it is an existing product that is being enhanced, there is usually something new or different being considered. Shown under the Area of Work, there are three phases and three decision gates within this Area of Work:

- *The Concept Phase*, where new ideas and opportunities are evaluated and screened
- *The Feasibility Phase*, where screened ideas are qualified and analyzed in greater detail and then further screened
- *The Definition Phase*, where the product's design and definition are finalized and can move on to be developed

The process also sets the stage for the *consistent* and *persistent* utilization of important documents such as Business Cases, Launch Plans, and Product Requirements Documents (PRDs).

Most companies utilize some type of phase gate New Product Development (NPD) process. In my firm's research, we learned that this process is used as a checklist tool for work activities and project planning because of its linear representation. In a recent survey I carried out, more than two-thirds of respondents indicated that the NPD process was used as a task management tool to expedite work.

However, the primary purpose of the NPD process should actually be *to serve as a business decision-making tool*. It is vital to keep this fact in mind. What it means is that a host of data elements are required in the process. Some of these pieces of data come from other process areas:

- Customer research
- Competitor research
- Competitor product research
- Strategic planning
- Forecasting
- Financial planning
- Promotional planning
- Pricing strategy
- Product definition
- Product performance management
- Launch planning

Now you can see how the Mind Map in Figure 4.1 more accurately represents the reality in an organization and why keeping track of all of the activities and deliverables can be so complex. This is also why Product Management needs an efficient staffing model for product managers and the staff associated with them. If you're going to fine-tune the function of Product Management, you will want to clarify the usage of the NPD process to ensure that it is effectively used to "funnel" ideas and make decisions on what to invest in and what not to invest in, instead of relegating it to a checklist function.

Another thing to keep in mind: When decisions have to made, the New Product Development process can often be misused because the necessary data elements are missing. *These data elements form the basis for effective decision-making criteria.* You can recognize these data elements when you ask the following questions:

- Is the market sizing accurate?
- Can we obtain the desired market share?
- Is the investment strategically important?
- Can we make money?
- What will the current and future cash flows entail?
- Can we integrate into the portfolio of products we already sell?
- Do we have the right technical resources to produce or develop the products?
- How does this investment impact other investments that have been approved and are in various states of development?
- Do we have adequate technologies in place to support the development?
- Will we have adequate resources to operate the organization?
- Will we have adequate resources to sell and service the products?

By exploring these questions (among others that can also be asked), product managers can demonstrate that they understand all the interconnected elements that must come together in order to bring a product or major enhancement to market and to have the product "digested" by the company. There is an implied outcome of the work activities carried out during New Product Planning; it is the *collective cognizance* mentioned earlier.

As an added and welcome benefit, each time a given team of (hopefully, the same) people, led by a capable product manager, evaluates product opportunities, they will find that they work together more easily and even tend to hold each other more accountable.

However, collective cognizance can be destroyed when Product Management is not taken seriously enough. Also, collective cognizance cannot be realized when the learning of a variety of people from diverse functions hasn't had the time or the opportunity to coalesce. Instances in which this happens are these:

1. When different individuals are delegated to work on projects that support the project
2. When team members do not feel any collective accountability for the product's business results
3. When leaders do not fully acknowledge the value of Product Management, especially before or after a major reorganization

In such cases, when organizational changes are made, Product Management gets remade, and it takes a long time to rebuild confidence in product managers. Further, because all this takes a long time, whatever happens may not survive the next reorganization.

## NEW PRODUCT INTRODUCTION (NPI)

The Area of Work called New Product Introduction (again, "new" may be optional) focuses on taking the agreed-upon plans, translating them into action, and getting the work done—in other words, execution. In most New Product Development models, the two subphases, *Development* and *Launch*, are often portrayed sequentially. However, this is *not* how work should be carried out during New Product Introduction. Optimally, while the product is being developed—under the watchful eye of a product manager or product leader—a cross-functional launch team *simultaneously* carries out the work needed to prepare the product for the market, and they prepare the market for the product.

The phases of NPI are important because they depict how teams work together to develop and deliver products, which, in turn, requires a thorough understanding of how the work actually does get done. The NPI work is also important because it serves as a validation point for plans that were assembled during the planning phases. While work is being carried out by various constituencies, their outputs are "sent" to a receiving party in another function while the product manager or product leader "assembles" the pieces into what will become the product's business when it is launched into the market.

During NPI, it is always important to verify that planning documentation and information is correct and that other assumptions remain valid. This is especially true for data produced from market insights, forecasts, and other documentation from the New Product Planning activities.

Product managers *must* oversee the process-related work flows between each function. If the plans have been properly established, roles should be clear, responsibilities spelled out, performance effectively monitored, and risks well managed.

### Product Development and Product Management Are Different

In terms of NPI, I'd like to quickly review the difference between oversight of development, which is the purview of the product manager, and product development itself, which is composed of actions performed by developers who design, build, and validate. *These two are always separate, like oil and water.*

Lately, I have seen product managers get drawn into what I call the "vortex of product development." In many of today's companies, a number of product managers have engineering and other similar backgrounds. Therefore, they comingle business and technical intellectual assets. This situation has become more noticeable in some of the rapid development techniques used by developers that call for intense product manager involvement. Leaders need to recognize this trend and respond to it by *staffing appropriately, with clearly defined roles and responsibilities*. If you expect product managers to be business managers of products, then you have to ensure that the right hand-offs and interdependencies are established from a process perspective. The alternative is to staff more rigorously with "hybrid" managers who can see *both* the business and technical aspects of the product's business.

### Launch Planning

Further, when discussing NPI, I've found that Launch Plans are often overlooked until someone realizes that a launch team needs to be put into place.

Recently, I carried out a post-launch audit at a major medical laboratory equipment company. The CEO was unhappy with the outcome for several reasons: The product was late to market; it was delivered below the desired quality standards; and customers were very unhappy. Here is what I observed from this post-launch analysis:

1.  The Launch Plan was not formally assembled because no one "owned" the launch except an overworked product manager.
2.  Since an actual "need by" market window had not been established, the launch activities were carried out with a hastily cobbled together spreadsheet as the project plan.
3.  The importance of the launch was overlooked by senior leaders because they assumed it was being attended to.
4.  The product manager did not fully comprehend that all of the other operational functions needed to be throttled to ensure that the product could be ordered and delivered.
5.  A sales training plan was not assembled on time.
6.  The salespeople didn't have any quota in their plans, nor was their compensation structure changed to encourage the sale of the product.

It all sounds simple enough. Everyone involved ought to have gotten this right.

It's possible that senior leaders may not have paid close enough attention to these necessary steps. In the final analysis, experienced product managers and other delegated stakeholders must be knitted together by their leaders, the functions must be staffed accordingly, and the leaders must be committed to the collective efforts of all. And there should be clearly defined roles and responsibilities for everyone involved.

## POST-LAUNCH PRODUCT MANAGEMENT (PLPM)

Post-Launch Product Management takes place after a new product (or a significant upgrade to an existing product) is launched into the market. This requires the product manager and other delegated team members to focus on optimizing the business and market performance of the products. It should be accomplished within the context of the strategies of the firm, division, product line, and, of course, the financials. Such work may include the following:

- Adjustments to the marketing mix (product, price, promotion, and channel)
- Changes to the product's business with respect to Operations, Service, and Support

In many companies, those who carry out this work seem to be doing "just-in-time" Product Management. During interviews, product managers have indicated that dealing with products in the market demands a lot of "blocking and tackling." Their day-to-day work is often highly reactive and seemingly disconnected from the overarching strategy of the firm or the business division. Another problem during post-launch Product Management is that leaders may not know whether work flows and processes are fully understood by all concerned. Roles are often unclear as to who does what, where, and when—and responsibilities are similarly vague. Therefore, product managers have to fill in and take care of seemingly urgent tasks—tasks that should be the assigned responsibilities of people in other departments.

## MONITORING KEY PERFORMANCE INDICATORS

Product managers will always encounter cross-organizational or cross-functional challenges. Beyond the role clarity issue, I find that many of those who work with product managers do not understand or appreciate many of the key performance metrics that are, or should be, used to monitor the product's progress. This is where many firms' process-related shortfalls become apparent. Notable among these deficiencies are:

- Limited market insight due to a lack of ongoing market research
- Inattention to vital key performance indicators and measurements
- Neglecting to examine operational control systems that should support products and portfolios

There is no linear phase gate process with existing products and portfolios. When such is the case, the function of Product Management would be to set the organization's posture, enabling product managers to create order out of what can be an often-chaotic, unpredictable set of circumstances.

Here is the true test of good product managers: that as they orchestrate the multiple activities to optimize the performance of current products or portfolios, they also demonstrate their ability to get through myriad inputs (customer requests, sales demands, quality issues, logistics, operations, service issues, financial tracking, and so on) and still maintain close connections and relationships with various people in all of the business functions.

In fact, *this is really where the function of Product Management "shows its stripes,"* by "taking care of business" as it should be done. When it is run properly, Product Management utilizes employees (product managers, business analysts, and others) to view all the pieces of the product's business holistically and systemically. Product managers need to have the ability to adapt—or pre-empt—as necessary. In other words, those in Product Management should be able to understand a variety of key performance indicators, apply their intelligence, and create an effective "feed" into the "front end" of the model. Those who see the entire picture of the product's business from a holistic perspective usually perform more effectively. This big-picture perspective is also why the role of the product manager can be considered equivalent to the role of the general manager. It's also why leaders seek this quality when recruiting new talent.

## DIFFERENCES THAT DETER PROGRESS

At the core, Product Management is the most effective organizational structure to enusre that products are effectively managed, from beginning to end, in a holistic manner. As I've shown thus far, the Product Management Life Cycle Model represents that position, with the purpose and context for each Area of Work described earlier.

Unfortunately, in some environments, this beginning-to-end approach to Product Management is not applied as I believe it should be. The diagram shown in Figure 4.3 will show you what I mean. Notice that the New Product Planning box is smaller, the New Product Introduction box is larger, and the Post-Launch Product Management box has dashed lines around it

**Figure 4.3 Development-Centric Approach to Product Management**

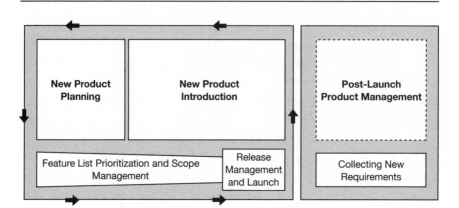

and is disconnected from the other boxes. The best way I can describe this situation is that it is a *development-centric approach to Product Management*.

There are several reasons this happens. In some organizations, people responsible for products do not devote sufficient time to holistic planning. Instead, the activities involved in planning are geared toward feature planning, or attribute planning, or prioritization. Product road maps and feature backlogs are evaluated based on incomplete or ineffective decision criteria in these environments.

Some executives have explicitly stated to me that there isn't enough time for them to make the necessary detailed plans. Or there isn't enough data, or they are short on resources. Or they must simply get the work done and get the "release" out the door.

Companies that operate Product Management in this way do not utilize a structured approach to decision making, nor do they pay attention to the other processes and interconnected work elements that are vital to the ongoing health of the product. In fact, the decisions are more often related to "what's next" in the development work queue (rather than eyes on the big picture), thus limiting decision-making criteria to work complexity, resource availability, or perceived customer requirements. When people in an organization operate within this model, they don't usually pay close enough attention to the ongoing market analysis and the tracking of key business performance indicators.

When we perform our interviews and surveys, we learn that in the majority of cases, product managers do not examine the financial impact (incremental contribution) of prior product development efforts that added more functionality. That's what they should be doing when crafting strategies for their product lines. Possibly, they are not geared to seeing the big picture, or they are not being held sufficiently accountable for the product's financial contribution. There may not be an opportune climate for people operating in this manner to develop the collective cognizance that would build a shared accountability for the product's success.

As complex and daunting as it might seem, one of the ways to make improvements in Product Management, and to put the "release train" approach into some perspective, is to view the product's business from a more holistic perspective. To move in this direction, you may wish to adjust your Product Management operations to include the following:

1. Ongoing examination of current product business and market performance indicators
2. More frequent evaluation of market information
3. Strategic profiling of the product line, conducted often enough to ensure that strategic and market objectives are being articulated and fulfilled

On the other hand, you may find that your company is well staffed and your product managers *are* able enough to carry out full-stream Product Management activities that allow them to balance the inputs at the front end (NPP), effective oversight of development and launch (NPI), and Post-Launch Product Management (PLPM).

In my benchmarking, I have learned that some companies have varied their structure so that they have some product managers who focus on the New Product Planning and New Product Introduction work areas and other product managers who pay attention to Post-Launch Product Management, or the optimization of current products and portfolios.

If you opt for this approach, make sure that the product managers from both areas are communicating and linking their work. Roles and work activities for explicit processes must be spelled out clearly and agreed to by leaders of concerned functions. For instance, post-launch product managers may

**Figure 4.4  Post-Launch Product Managers May Have a Broad Strategic Role While NPP and NPI Managers Have Tactical and Planning Roles**

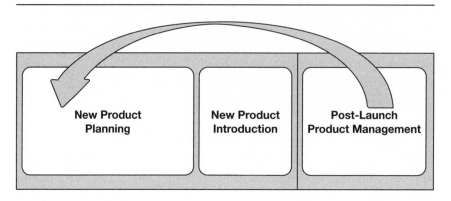

work more closely with the market research function to improve customer and competitor insights.

Those insights garnered by PLPM product managers will create valuable inputs to the product managers who are working on planning and introduction activities. To be clear, and at risk of repeating myself, the separation of these key product manager roles *requires constant communication and interaction* because the PLPM managers may be taking on a broad strategic role, while the NPP and NPI product managers may have to focus more on tactical planning and execution. Figure 4.4 shows that emphasis. Mind you, strategy and tactics may make up elements of both areas.

If you perceive a disparity in alignment of the roles of product managers where the focus is supposed to result in full-stream Product Management, your own focus will be required in terms of the hierarchy you set forth. For example, you may find that in the present alignment, a product line manager has full-stream product line accountability, while other product manager associates have tactical types of responsibilities. You can align roles effectively when you understand the vital processes and work flows used to carry out Product Management work. Then you can plan or adjust the work of the product managers and their teams in the systemic fashion that promotes more efficient product operations.

## KEY POINTS TO KEEP IN MIND

Based on what I have discussed thus far, there are some key points that leaders can consider to more effectively guide and evolve the Product Management organization. These include the following:

1.  Be sure that calendars are used to keep track of routine events, activities, and processes. These notes might include the agendas of product team meetings, reminders to conduct market checkups, and even budget or product performance check-ins with senior leaders. Calendars can be set to give a "first reminder" in advance of upcoming events, which could help leaders with prioritizing and scheduling.

2.  Provide a steady stream of reliable, accurate data for product managers and their teams such that they can spend more time analyzing and less time acquiring data. Many firms now use business intelligence tools to extract data from disparate systems. They use key performance indicators that allow for timely tracking, analysis, and action. They also use dashboards and other unified visual tools to explain, at any time, the current state of a product's business.

3.  Put key Product Management processes under the microscope to look for areas to improve efficiency, work flow, and decision making.

4.  To improve cross-organizational or cross-functional communication, have some of your product managers contribute or participate in process evaluations, role negotiations, and other activities. This will enhance decision making and fortify the ability of product mangers to earn the empowerment they need to be effective.

## IS THERE A CORRECT STRUCTURE FOR PRODUCT MANAGEMENT?

I firmly believe that using the Product Management Life Cycle Model as a stable reference point can greatly contribute to getting members of an organization on the same page in terms of planning, execution, and management. But there can be times, as mentioned in Chapter 1, when an appraisal of prior transformative efforts may be needed, especially for the Product Management organization. I believe that some of what I cover below may be helpful for you because it is based on what I learned from observations, diagnostics, and interviews carried out for this book.

In many of my interactions with senior leaders, I am often asked about organizational design and the optimization of those designs—especially with respect to Product Management. As you might guess, there are no hard-and-fast answers. However, there are two main areas that are important to think about:

1. What is the current structure, and why is it in place? How does this structure help or hinder Product Management?
2. Where do you want to link your strategic intent: to the roles that people carry out, to the work they are responsible for doing, to the interdependencies between those people, to the overarching decisions for which they are responsible, or to the measurements that are necessary?

To address these questions, here's a quick reference summary about organizational design. You may already be familiar with these principles, but even if you are, I suggest a quick skim.

## THOUGHTS ABOUT ORGANIZATIONAL STRUCTURE AND DESIGN

All companies are organized to fulfill the strategy and objectives of the firm. Everyone I spoke to and surveyed for this book validated this point. My research also indicated that some structures have a strong bias toward products or technologies; some seem motivated by corporate policies and politics. Some structures are put in place because they help the company save money, achieve efficiencies, or improve revenue—typical drivers you'd see in any text or consultant report. Some change from functional structures to geographical structures; some move from product focus to customer focus; and some make other types of transformations. No matter the reasons or motivations, the impetus to view change as a panacea will continue.

One thing I've learned is this: The more that people in the organization relate to the rationale and purpose, the higher the probability that the reorganization's goals will be realized. For example, an airline executive told me that all employees, product people included, understand that their focus must always be on the traveler and the traveler's experience.

As I stated earlier in this chapter: As organizations evolve, the function of Product Management should be "front of mind." The community of people who work in all the functions that are carrying out the organization's strategy (which includes those who lead product managers), should be the primary orchestrators of this work. When Product Management is not considered an intrinsic and comprehensive element of the firm's design, then those who work in or around Product Management just "go with the flow."

During any organizational adjustments, if the role of product managers (the primary orchestrators) is deemed unimportant, their sense of their purpose and fit will be diminished. If the reorganization does not consider how work flows should be adjusted and whose roles will change, overburdened product managers may end up with even more work, and in the extreme, they may have to shoulder the increased workload with *fewer* resources.

One senior leader admitted his concern about this. After a major reorganization, his company had significantly reduced the number of product managers. This kept the firm from having an effective "force" of product managers, while their main competitor maintained twice the number of product managers for a similar amount of work.

In a sample survey of hundreds of product managers in our workshops, I asked about their view of these same issues to counterbalance what I had learned from senior leaders. One of the conclusions was that many senior leaders do not fully comprehend how an organization's redesign impacts Product Management. As a consequence, leaders may be in for some unfulfilled expectations.

My research for this book included surveys and interviews with senior leaders, as well as those with product managers. I wanted to formulate an appraisal of what motivated shifts in focus and how they impacted the results achieved, or not achieved. One of the most obvious things learned was that in reorganizations involving Product Management, there were wide variations in organizational goals, about who was involved, and what the desired intent was. In most instances, members of leadership teams collaborated on setting those goals.

Reasons cited for the changes included these:

- To locate the business closer to customers (in geographic settings)
- To excel at product and technology excellence
- To improve operational performance
- To build greater levels of intimacy with customers

In a quote from Andrew Grove, former CEO at Intel, he said, "A corporation is a living organism; it has to continue to shed its skin. Methods have to change. Focus has to change. Values have to change. The sum total of those changes is transformation."

## DIFFERENT TYPES OF COMPANY STRUCTURES

I want to recap some of the types of structures that companies utilize. Some companies have organized into business functions (Marketing, Sales, and so on). Some have organized according to their product lines (including brands or categories). Some have established geographic boundaries, and some have aligned to focus on specific customers or segments. Others have organized using some type of hybrid (function/product) model. In my research for this book, the following statistics emerged:

- 29 percent of firms reported that they organized functionally.
- 27 percent by product lines.
- 13 percent by geography and customers.
- 24 percent as a hybrid of product and function.
- 7 percent indicated that they organized to focus on industries and "other" types.

What I'll try to do here is tell you a little about each type. If you're well versed in these structures, you may wish to skim this section.

## FUNCTION-ORIENTED STRUCTURE

A *functional structure* can be helpful when you find value in having vertical groupings such as Marketing, Finance, Operations, R&D, or Customer Service. Each function has a specialty. This type of structure can be effective if the organization's product lines are fairly narrow or if they serve defined market areas.

Software companies, financial firms, and the like may find happiness as a functionally aligned shop. A variation is to have a functional organization operate in a "matrixed" mode built on the idea of cross-functional collaboration.

When you have a smaller or moderately sized firm with an effective leader like a general manager (GM), this type of structure can be highly effective. I worked with a company that had 100 people, one CEO/GM, and one Product Management leader. The company had a fairly narrow line of specialty products, and it was functionally organized, which worked well for them. If, in a functionally organized company, the product managers report to the GM, the head of Marketing, or a defined, respected Product Management leader and these leaders are able to exert their sphere of influence over the functions to get work done, then this can be a favorable modality.

## PRODUCT-ORIENTED STRUCTURE

A *product-oriented structure* is used by midsize to larger companies who divide their firms into product groups or product lines with business or specialty functions that support each product line's business. Product groupings in these structures are profit centers. Product companies are equipped with the capability to improve product cycle times or to create product enhancements or variations for given market segments. Presumably (best-case scenario), these firms employ people with deep industry or domain expertise.

Firms that organize this way include automobile companies, insurance companies, food companies, industrial equipment firms, and others with the same type of product lines. Consumer goods and food companies may organize into brand groups or category groups that have similar supporting structures.

Product organizations can (or should) effectively manage their individual product line portfolios in a holistic manner and be able to utilize resources based on the strategy for the product group. Product organizations may also be more inclined to try to improve product quality, invest in specific technologies, and gain other efficiencies that will impact the product line's contribution to the organization.

Companies that operate as a conglomerate or complex multidivisional firm should be able to effectively support a product-focused structure. During my corporate career, I worked in product companies, and I believe that this is the best structure for Product Management. One of the challenges in that type of organization was that quite often executives in the product divisions did not share their strategies and plans. Therefore, it was not unusual to find similar products from the same company in the market at the same time, which served to confuse customers. *Some companies have harnessed this challenge by forming platform committees and cross-product councils that seek to rationalize product investments from a portfolio perspective.* While adding a layer of complexity, this level of oversight serves a unifying purpose.

The other aspect that requires attention in this structure is to ensure that there is a unified channel strategy—and specifically, a good account management structure, so that there aren't any channel conflicts (multiple salespeople, overlapping products, and so on).

Lastly, in many product companies, there is no dedicated functional structure for each product line. Instead, the functions such as IT, Development, Marketing, and Finance are shared. This could cause a lot of conflict. In a product company, the product line owner, who should be a Product Management executive, owns the P&L for the product line and serves as an executive-level cross-functional product team leader. *The more product areas that exist in a company or in a business unit, the greater the need for process definition and role clarity.*

## GEOGRAPHY-ORIENTED STRUCTURE

A *geographically based structure* is used by a company that decides to focus on a given region. This type of company sees a need to be closer to its desired market segments or customers. The company may find that doing business locally can reduce the costs of all the factors of production, such as materials, labor, and overhead, that characterize tangible products in capital-intensive industries.

In companies that provide infrastructure products such as communications equipment, oil and gas, industrial chemicals, large-scale computing platforms, and electric power, the geographic structure can work well. Service providers like large information technology firms, systems integrators, or professional services firms can draw on local talent and capabilities to meet local market needs quickly and efficiently.

Geographic positioning may also be required to support cultural adaption and market acceptance by localized firms. For example, although GM is a U.S.-based company, it has a significant local presence in China. Baker Hughes, an oilfield services firm, has a presence in areas where oil companies are drilling for oil. In these types of firms, you may have regional general managers who own the P&L, and they may call upon a centralized product organization to produce the products for their local markets, or they may call upon local suppliers to fulfill local needs.

Geographic firms may suffer from some of the same problems as product organizations that must share resources that are in remote locations. For example, if product managers and product developers are in a region different from that of the localized organization (based in the United States versus Asia), there could be problems in terms of product manager overload (too many requests from too many regions) or resource limitations that may hinder product development.

In order to minimize duplication of efforts, capitalize on cross-geographic learning, and help in balancing product manager workloads, I advise firms to utilize a cross-functional product portfolio council, as I will discuss in Chapter 9.

## HYBRID STRUCTURE

An *amalgamated* or *hybrid structure* that encompasses what might be called "front office" and "back office" arrangements could be used to enable the product-oriented structures to function on one side and the supporting structures of the product organization to function on the other. This amalgam of structures is an effective solution for complex organizations with diverse product lines in diverse markets. It means that the functions on the organization chart get separated by the degree to which they are catalyzed by internal or external forces.

To get a sense of what this means, please refer to a modified representation of the Product Management Life Cycle Model as visualized in Figure

4.5. Notice that it contains the essence of what I portrayed in Figure 4.4. However, this diagram shows *both* New Product Planning and Post-Launch Product Management on the same plane. The implication to be derived is that the current product and portfolio market and the business performance "stimulate" back-office work because there is greater latitude for greater creativity and resourcefulness.

The model offers executives an interesting way to think about organizing for Product Management, one that reinforces the position that being "market oriented" can stimulate ideas and innovations. In this situation, the back office (where New Product Introduction resides) serves as the supplier of products to the front office. Therefore, the front office (think "storefront") is "front of mind" for people in the organization, but that's not true for the back-office people who supply the technologies and the infrastructure to support the operation of the organization. Also, I strongly recommend that a product portfolio council be effectively deployed when a hybrid structure is utilized.

**Figure 4.5  Modified Product Management Life Cycle Model**

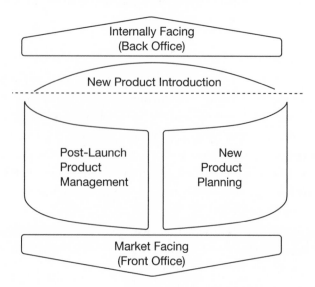

## NONNEGOTIABLES FOR PRODUCT MANAGEMENT ORGANIZATION

Product Management as a function earns its reputation as the orchestrator of work across functions and geographies to help the company fulfill its strategic intent. I definitely prefer product-oriented structures, but it doesn't really matter what structure is used. No matter the structure, *Product Management should be able to thrive in any type of organization.* Therefore, *Product Management as a primary organizational element should be nonnegotiable.* Companies need Product Management to build the products and portfolios that provide for the financial well-being of the firm. Product Management is the function that harnesses the cross-organization and cross-functional resources required to strategize, plan, develop, launch, and manage products and portfolios. To achieve this stature, Product Management must work in the following ways:

1. Utilize a model for the holistic, systemic scheme to manage products and portfolios, represented by the Product Management Life Cycle Model. This model should allow for effective planning, developing, launching, and managing of products and portfolios.
2. Establish a clear recognition of each and every process that allows for the following:
   a. Gathering and sharing of market insights
   b. Comprehensive data that enable strategies to be formulated up and down the organization
   c. Agreement between key stakeholders that ensures clarity around roles and responsibilities, as well as clear methods to promote rapid, data-driven decision making
   d. Methods to ensure that executive support will be available as needed
3. Bear in mind that strong, influential people (product managers) will (and should) be supported by senior executives as they harness, synchronize, and orchestrate the contributions of people who work in specialty functions that will ensure that high-quality, market-driven products are produced and successfully marketed in the targeted market segments.

4.  Ensure that systems, data, tools, and other resources are available to support and guide the work of product managers and their teams at every phase of the product life cycle.

## SUMMARY: AVOIDING ORGANIZATIONAL INDIGESTION

Perhaps this heading seems a little odd for a summary and concluding comments. However, it describes the manner in which Product Management can contribute to the organization's success—and some stumbling blocks to that success.

I talk about "organizational indigestion" when a great product idea doesn't get to see the light of day, either because there aren't enough resources or an executive thinks he or she has a monopoly on creativity. Or the executives put up some organizational obstacles. Organizational indigestion happens when systemic obstacles stand in the way of success. This can be particularly problematic (especially if there really is a market for the product!) if a product's success is thwarted because of an inability to gain alignment across functions.

It takes a lot of corporate energy and effort to get a product from the initial concepts into the hands of customers. I learned this from extensive personal experience and from my research. Best-in-class companies and best-of-breed product managers have an uncanny knack of getting everyone onboard early and keeping them onboard as concepts are mulled over, as prototypes are developed (yes, this applies to both tangibles and intangibles!), and as customers adopt products. Keep in mind, too, that there are many points of potential failure that effective Product Management can help to *circumvent*. Product Management is the function that has the people who see the big picture and how the puzzle pieces fit. When you have an "army" of people who see how all of the corporate gears work and are so well able to get those gears synchronized, the only thing that will cause product failure is a bad product.

*Case Study II*

# TD CANADA TRUST

*By Thomas Dyck, Senior Vice President, TD Bank Financial Group*

TD Canada Trust is Canada's largest retail bank. It is respected throughout the world for its ability to deliver a *consistently superior client experience* and industry-leading earnings growth.

About 30 years ago, forward-looking senior management decided that the ability to deliver a unique client experience was vital to the company's future success. To achieve this goal, a group of very competent and knowledgeable people would be needed to provide beginning-to-end oversight for its products and services. For the answer to those needs, they turned their attention to the Product Management function. The growth and success of TD Canada Trust 30 years later have fully justified this decision.

I will discuss two important areas of this case. The first depicts the role of the product manager; the second describes our Product Management organization.

## THE ROLE OF THE PRODUCT MANAGER

One of the more noteworthy aspects of TD Canada Trust's approach to Product Management lies in how we utilize our product managers. First and foremost, we are a distribution-centric company. We bring our brand to life through several channels. These include bank branches (face-to-face), the phone, automated teller machines (known as "automated banking machines" in Canada), and of course, online. The challenge for product managers, then, is to develop and support the sale and service of complex financial products in a way that strengthens the client experience in each of these channels.

In our bank, product managers are accountable for the profitability of their product lines through each channel—and *every* product must be profitable. Product managers cannot employ a "bundling strategy," which other companies often use to achieve product line balance.

To live up to these high standards and fulfill their objectives, our product managers possess a robust set of skills and capabilities. They must harness a vast field of data, understand the dynamics of a complex organization, and produce positive outcomes.

Product managers understand the drivers of earnings. Therefore, they must recognize the unique needs of customers in each channel and build durable pricing strategies. They also know the costs and expenses associated with the production, delivery, and sustenance of their products.

To carry out their work, they lead a cross-functional team. As an example, to ensure that they have the right data to track customer behavior and analyze key trends, they are given enough latitude to influence the work of our market research department. Product managers also work closely with our Finance function to develop Business Cases, analyze financial reports, set prices, and perform other analyses.

## WHY OUR PRODUCT MANAGERS PERFORM WELL

Our product managers are well-educated and trained; they possess highly sophisticated capabilities that help them evaluate many different indicators and leverage key processes. There is also a high degree of technical expertise required because transactions are processed through national and international payment and financial systems. In order to help the bank manage risk, there are many aspects to keep in front of, such as the myriad complex regulatory and compliance guidelines to which transactions must conform. These finely tuned business and analytical skills are vital for planning strategies and making optimal business decisions.

Another dimension of the role of product manager is how they influence behaviors within the channels. As many may know, in a bank, "shelf space" is limited, so there is little room for slow-moving products. At TD Canada Trust, we subscribe to the "easy principle." In other words, "simple" sells. Product managers have the responsibility to make sure their products are easy to understand, easy to sell, and easy to use. To enable this level of simplicity, product managers are expected to be the bank's experts about customers who use their products. They accomplish this through their analysis of research and branch visits. They also work with people in the back office and call centers, and they frequently engage Sales and Marketing people.

In addition, thousands of employees, both on the front line and in the back office, must be trained in how to sell and fulfill their products. It is not enough to communicate the "how"; employees must understand the product strategies because they need to handle unscripted client questions and exceptions in a consistent manner. Ultimately it is the quality of *all* these efforts that enables the superior client experience, and our product managers are on the front line of these efforts.

Ultimately, it is the role of the product manager to utilize and optimize key business processes by cutting through all the complexities. They must always be on the lookout for ways to streamline processes, reduce paperwork, and simplify the approach to meeting the bank's legal requirements. It is their extensive knowledge of the IT systems and regulatory requirements that contribute to this capability.

## THE PRODUCT MANAGEMENT LEADERSHIP ORGANIZATION AT TD CANADA TRUST

Recognizing the importance of the Product Management function, a significant commitment has been made through the development of people and a structure that communicates to the broader organization.

An executive vice president (EVP) of retail banking products and services reports directly to the CEO, TD Canada Trust, and has direct oversight of all Product Management teams. The EVP ensures that broad product strategies are aligned with the TD brand and the promise of an extraordinary client experience. He or she assists the team by identifying *cross-product strategies* and the insistence on a *holistic view* of the client's relationship with the bank. Ultimately, the EVP is responsible for ensuring that the many products and services offered meet the expectations of shareholders.

He or she is also a member of the Senior Executive Operating Committee for TD Canada Trust, which serves to underscore the importance of Product Management to the bank. In that capacity, he or she is often called upon to provide leadership and support for broader bank initiatives.

Senior executives, reporting to the EVP, are responsible for major lines of business—secured lending, credit cards and unsecured lending, and retail banking products. To ensure a solid understanding of the bank and a breadth of perspective, these senior leaders must be *generalists*, with significant experience not only in Product Management but also in a variety of other fields. Their teams are staffed with people who also have a broad range of capabilities, along with a number of specialists who deal with the areas of project management, risk, pricing, and analytics. The teams also include junior product managers who are responsible for individual lines of business including oversight of profitability, day-to-day monitoring, and ultimately product strategy development and execution. Depending on the line of business, some senior leaders have dedicated sales teams of several hundred; others have large call center operations supporting their lines. What's most important is that they can all count on *direct support* from a number of corporate functions such as Finance, Human Resources, and Technology.

Although hundreds of people work in the Product Management department, implementation requires broad support from a variety of other functions in the bank's organization. However, product managers have no direct authority over these areas. Instead, product managers must leverage a collaborative approach, utilizing their ability to influence others to solicit their input, and achieve buy-in to product strategies. Key support partners from Finance, Human Resources, and Technology are usually permanent members of the management team and decision-making process. Well-defined project management procedures ensure that all appropriate stakeholders are also included. At conferences, team meetings, and one-to-one discussions with senior leaders, product managers always look for opportunities to communicate their strategies and plans to the entire organization.

## TALENT DEVELOPMENT

As a sign of its importance to TD, Product Management is widely viewed as an excellent place to develop management talent for the broader TD organization. When other functions in our organization have high-potential managers and executives who need to increase their perspective, business acumen, or financial capabilities, they encourage placement of these people on our Product Management teams. On the other hand, when we source our future product managers directly from universities across the country, they do not immediately join the ranks of our product managers. Instead, they are often placed in positions elsewhere in the bank, in order for them to grow their capabilities, share their experiences, and expand their breadth of view.

Leveraging the Product Management function this way not only increases management capability for the bank but also serves to prove the critical role of that function.

This approach has been successful for TD Canada Trust because we have ensured that the Product Management function has been diligent in aligning products and services to strengthen its value proposition. This also ensures that the earning potential of the organization is optimized, fueling future investments in the line of business. Further, this fully integrated function is respected and supported as a distinct capability within the organization. *In short, Product Management is critical to the bank's ability to maintain its winning ways.*

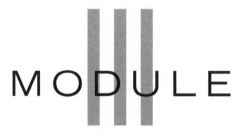

# MODULE III

# CULTIVATE

The two chapters that compose this module serve as important elements of transformation for the Product Management organization. The reason is simple. It's about people: the product managers and their leaders.

Leaders responsible for staffing face myriad challenges in the search for the best product manager candidates. These problems surface because most hiring managers have conflicting standards about the requirements for the job of the product manager. I've personally encountered so many different job descriptions and job titles, their infinite variety as never ceased to amaze me.

The prevalence of such challenges can throw an organization out of balance through a cause-and-effect, domino type of misalignment. It starts when people in other functions have specific expectations for product managers that may be beyond the capabilities of their product managers. Next, these unmet expectations cause functional leaders to default to their own paradigms, and they are forced into carrying out the work that remains undone. Another deleterious effect is that managers in other functions discount the contributions of product managers, based on the disarray they have observed. They have no way of recognizing the value of contributions that *properly equipped product managers should bring to the table.*

But it's not one-sided. There are challenges for product managers too. Functional weaknesses can cause the work of product managers to shift to meet the exigencies of the moment, which casts a shadow on their performance. Whatever the case, these situational inconsistencies cause role confusion and organizational imbalance, and they are counterproductive.

When senior leaders and managers of product managers understand these issues, and when they are provided with the proper context, they can surely make better hiring decisions. Furthermore, if they have proper guidelines for the cultivation of product managers as vital human assets, the organization will operate with greater precision.

Therefore, the content of these two chapters is designed to help leaders bring order to the organization and situate Product Management, and product managers, for greater levels of success. The two chapters are summarized as follows:

*Chapter 5. Clarifying the Role of the Product Manager to Improve Staffing Strategies:* High-performance product managers can be powerful allies to unify a company's efforts and achieve business excellence. This chapter helps leaders understand how to clarify the role of the product manager based on the most effective set of core competencies required for the job. The methods set forth in this chapter serve to guide leaders to optimally select, hire, and deploy product managers.

*Chapter 6. Cultivating and Shaping Product Managers:* This chapter offers leaders and managers some logical, actionable guidelines to continually improve the contribution of product managers. It includes several good ideas that suggest how leaders can establish job levels and progression plans using a unique *Product Manager Scorecard*. It also provides six critical steps that leaders can put into place to better cultivate product managers. The overarching goal is to create a more stable portfolio of product managers who contribute to the firm's performance objectives.

# CHAPTER 5

# CLARIFYING THE ROLE OF THE PRODUCT MANAGER TO IMPROVE STAFFING STRATEGIES

**EXECUTIVE SUMMARY**

- How a company hires and places product managers and how it enables them to excel as strategy-minded business managers can have a major impact on whether that company merely survives or flourishes.
- Exceptional product managers catalyze action across the organization in a manner similar to those of CEOs or general managers.
- An effectual staff of product managers can equip the firm with greater potential to achieve competitive advantage.

*Every prince needs allies, and the bigger the responsibility, the more allies he needs.*

—MACHIAVELLI

Good product managers don't mystically materialize when needed, nor are they found through sheer serendipity. Earlier in my career, I learned the value of good—and consistent—hiring practices. While at AT&T, I was a member of a task force that supported a global leadership development program for high-potential managers. This gave me insight into corporate leadership development and how to best recruit, select, and cultivate leaders. As part of that leadership development group, I served as a member of the Ivy League campus recruiting team, and I was able to influence the feeder population from the top business schools. From this corporate experience, I learned the importance and the benefits of a finely tuned, consistently used process for recruitment and selection of businesspeople. Furthermore, I learned how exceptional candidates can, and do, positively impact the business.

With this context, I have several aims for this chapter:

1. To show leaders that it is necessary to have the right staff with the right knowledge, skills, and experience to deliver the potential of strong Product Management.
2. To offer leaders guidance and support so that they may improve their recruitment procedures and minimize the inconsistencies in the recruitment and selection strategies used to *hire* and *place* product managers. Even when you have product managers who bring a lot to the table because of their technical or domain expertise, uneven staffing patterns can prevent Product Management from properly maturing in the organization.
3. To help you fortify your staffing methods and procedures and improve the population of product managers in your company.
4. To clarify the role of the product manager and how this role is situated within the firm. This clarification is necessary because there are so many variations in the job descriptions and scope of responsibilities.

## YOU KNOW IT WHEN YOU SEE IT

While on AT&T's Product Management task force, we had the opportunity to carry out benchmark interviews with a major imaging products company. One of the senior leaders we spoke with was responsible for approximately 50 product managers in his division. The conversation turned to a discussion of the characteristics that separated excellent, high-performance product managers from the others under his aegis. His face lit up when he referred to a small subset of his product managers. He felt they had an instinctual, almost "magical," sense of "knowing everything" about their product's business. "They just know how to *work the system* and *get things done*," he said. When asked how many there were, he said he could count, on one hand, those on his staff who fit that description—that was only 10 percent! Further, those top-performing product managers had such a good reputation that senior executives in other divisions of this company knew about them.

Through research for this book, I found that about two-thirds of companies do not have any sort of formal method to benchmark or analyze their population of product managers. In my interviews with leaders, half of them told me they use informal, undocumented methods to discover the high-performance product managers.

Analyzing and segmenting the product manager population offers great opportunity for organizational planning. However, in most cases, the segmentation is done only during periodic rating and ranking routines; and varied criteria are used for rating and ranking, across companies. What's more, very few companies have a designated individual or body of individuals to track this data over the long term. Without a well-ordered formal process, it will always be a challenge for any company to harness the potential energy that a population of good product managers can bring to the firm. What's needed is a reliable method that will purposefully and proactively identify these top-tier product managers and cultivate their skills in order to achieve top-tier performance that benefits the entire company.

Before going any further, it will be helpful to provide additional context on the role of the product manager. Here is the role definition for product managers provided in *The Product Manager's Desk Reference:*

- The product manager is a person appointed to be a proactive product or product line "mini-CEO" or general manager.
- The product manager leads a cross-functional product team.
- The product team's responsibility is to optimize the product's market position and financial returns, consistent with corporate, business unit, or division strategies.

(*Note:* At the beginning of the book, I indicated that I would use the term *product manager* as a generalized role to avoid repeating all possible levels ascribed to the job. The description above seems to portray someone in a leadership capacity—a senior product manager, product director, or equivalent title. Regardless of that connotation, I will continue to use the term *product manager* as an umbrella term.)

One of the issues that surfaced from work with my clients and research for this book was this: In some (though not all) companies, the product manager job seems to be a "stop-off" job, a rung on the ladder upward, as opposed to a "destination" job that has a highly desirable professional status. This creates a problem: It tends to limit the talent pool of those who are capable of making Product Management their career. I believe that the product manager job category deserves more attention and recognition than it has received up to this point. You would never settle for substandard engineers or computer programmers, so why settle for substandard product managers? Good, *experienced* product managers enable the company to be more efficient and productive, and they make notable and visible contributions to the company's performance and bottom line.

The time has come to change the stop-off job perception about the position and recognize it as a *professional job category* (akin to engineers and other similar experts) that is deeply embedded in the company fabric. It is vital to target the subset of the population who are motivated (or rewarded) product managers to convince them to remain in the role so that they can be cultivated as impactful individual contributors in the present and possibly as corporate leaders in the future.

High-performance product managers can be powerful allies in unifying a company's efforts to achieve business excellence. That's why I also recommend formalizing a population of highly performing *product leaders* who are equally necessary for the leadership of a professional staff.

Peter Drucker, the well-known father of modern management, once said, "Executives owe it to the organization and to their fellow workers not to tolerate nonperforming individuals in important jobs." I suggest leaders consider this advice since one of the most important high-performance jobs in the company is that of the product manager.

## IT TAKES A STRATEGY AND A TEAM

Just as we need a strategy for the Product Management organization (to avoid having to reinvent the wheel), we also need a product manager staffing strategy. Similarly, just as any generic strategy would be methodically formulated, so should a strategy be formulated to construct and sustain the product manager population. This methodology is extremely important because it should be used consistently as the organization matures, and it should be utilized as leaders periodically take the pulse of Product Management.

In order for the strategy to be structurally sound and durable, it should accomplish the following:

1. Define a sequence of events and activities—and arrange them in order so they can be viewed collectively as a complete beginning-to-end process. To uncover areas for improvement as the organization matures, it is important to view the contents of this staffing process as a whole, but also to study each of its individual components.

2. Define an agreed-upon set of goals—to ensure better staffing procedures, improvement in hiring decisions, and, ultimately, better-performing product managers.

3. Designate and set in place clear roles for the *staffing strategy team*. I use the word *team* because this strategy cannot be carried out by one individual. A team of cross-functional experts is needed. The team would include a partner from Human Resources and/ or the Organizational Development functions, plus leaders from other relevant functions (such as Sales, Marketing, Finance, and/ or Engineering), and of course, Product Management leaders.

4. Acknowledge that there are good reasons for this team to be cross-functional. For one thing, product managers are expected to extend their reach and influence to people across the organization. For another (equally important) reason, the staffing strategy team members must agree on the expertise they should contribute and on the work they are expected to produce (e.g., competency assessments, job descriptions, and salary reports). This team may, in fact, be the Product Management Governance Board that I will discuss in Chapter 9.

5. Create a feasible set of rules for decisions that will be made by this staffing strategy team. This means that once a practice or policy is formulated, the team has agreed on it. The people on the

team will decide on the issues and policies collectively, or it will be up to the leader to make the decisions. Another option would be for a policy council or governing body to make the ultimate decisions.

6.  Set up communication policies that govern the dissemination of information to concerned individuals. Information would be given to hiring managers and others who would need to be trained or developed to carry out the policies as defined by this team.

## THE STRATEGIC REFERENCE POINT

Consistent with one of the themes in this book, the staffing strategy for product managers will be made relevant by having a reference point. As discussed in Chapter 2, the Product Management Life Cycle Model provides this reference point. The model also serves as the basis for a Product Manager Competency Model as discussed earlier in this book. The Competency Model consists of seven broad competency groups, or "meta-themes":

- Developing market insights
- Crafting effective strategies
- Planning and carrying out effective, timely product launches
- Managing and monitoring the financial and market progress of products and portfolios
- Translating information from many sources into cohesive decisions
- Driving action throughout the organization and building shared accountability across all contributing functions
- Using basic work management skills

There is a significant level of activity encompassed within these seven key competency groupings.

As discussed earlier, many senior leaders agree that only a small percentage of their product manager population can fulfill these requirements—*at present*. Yet there are many capable product managers at varying stages of their professional development. Some may fulfill the ideal definition; some may be at varying levels of development; some have leadership potential; a number will not move beyond their present capabilities.

In order to implement and execute an effective staffing strategy, it is important to understand the key elements and core competencies of this job category. The diagram shown in Figure 5.1 illustrates some additional context. In this diagram, which really looks like a Venn diagram, you can see that the product manager job is composed of five general elements that overlap one another. Of the five elements shown, the set of requisite core competencies is a central, dominant figure due to its overarching importance. Though shown slightly smaller, the other four elements are critical characteristics or attributes that better enable the success of product managers. In Chapter 6, these qualities, and others, will be referred to as "product manager attributes and behaviors" which will be used in a unique tool referred to as a the Product Manager Scorecard. In the diagram, there is an intersection between the core competencies and the other characteristics. For example, competency for driving action across the organization requires the ability to lead and influence. Some other required competencies are critical thinking and decision-making skills. In the definitions that follow, many of these intersections will become apparent. Consider these intersections as complementary to each other.

## CORE COMPETENCIES FOR PRODUCT MANAGERS

As I indicated before, there is no shortage of product manager job descriptions. They all describe the position from unique angles, based on how the role is perceived or utilized or who is defining it. When job definitions and descriptions are being outlined, *this variation can be minimized through the consistent application of a common set of core competencies and complementary enablers,* as shown in Figure 5.1. You can also minimize variation by specifying the degree to which any supporting work activity is carried out or specifying the frequency of usage.

However, and without equivocation, the basic principle remains: Core competencies should be the *nonnegotiable sets of knowledge, skills, and experience that every product manager should have.* These nonnegotiables serve as the constant backdrop used to describe and situate the role of the product

**Figure 5.1  Five General Elements That Make Up the Product Manager Job**

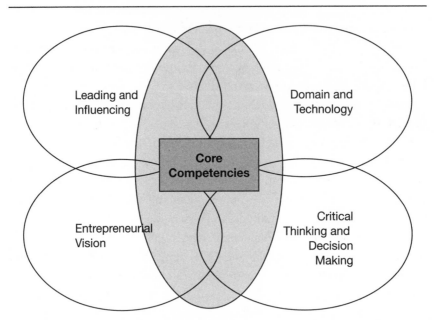

manager in any company. They must be applicable in all situations, no matter whether the product managers are new or experienced or whether they are assigned to new or mature products. They also apply regardless of level and regardless of whether a product manager is an individual contributor or a product line leader. Whatever the category, each of these core competencies must be cultivated and mastered to the greatest extent possible.

Refer to Chapter 2, where I set the context for the maturity model, to review the descriptions of the competencies listed there. I've modified those details in this chapter to provide you with some additional context and to reinforce them as vital anchors of the core competencies, in preparation for the staffing process to follow.

## DEVELOPING MARKET INSIGHTS

It is important to understand that market insights require adequate ongoing research. Insights come into better focus when product managers have access to timely, relevant market data. Without the proper market perspective, it is a challenge to surface ideas and opportunities and to influence others to build consensus across the organization. There are many skills and techniques needed to gain these valuable perspectives. Therefore, leaders should ensure that all product managers know the following:

1. The market segments or areas in which their products are sold
2. Every customer type based on their stature as a buyer, user, influencer, or decision maker
3. The motivations and changing preferences of each customer type
4. The industry environment in which the products are sold, including the sectors in which companies compete and the external influences that characterize those sectors
5. Each and every competitor in the sector and how each product is positioned against each competitor's product

## CRAFTING EFFECTIVE STRATEGIES

Without a doubt, every product manager should understand the strategy formulation process. This means they should be able to accomplish the following:

1. Put the past and present performance of the product or product line into an explainable baseline view.
2. Set the end-state vision and objectives.
3. Establish the plans to achieve those objectives.
4. Create the future metrics and key performance indicators to track progress.

They should also understand that every product in a company or division is part of a broader investment portfolio, chosen by the company's leaders to help it achieve its desired competitive advantage. Therefore, product managers should know how product strategies should be set within the context of the portfolio. With this perspective, product managers will be able to understand the concept of strategic alignment when evaluating future opportunities.

Product managers must be able *to think collectively about many inter-connected elements.* At a high level, these comprise the "marketing mix" of pricing, promotion, and channel. Any product strategy can be derailed if it does not consider the other marketing mix elements. You can see how marketing mix elements are connected to many other items in the Product Management Mind Map diagram shown in Figure 4.1 in Chapter 4.

There are a couple of other key points I would like to leave you with, as you consider this specific core competency for product managers:

1.  Many documents used by product managers involve some alignment with the overarching strategy—for example, Business Cases justify product investments that should be aligned with the strategy. Leaders should be sure to consider this within the evaluative context for assessing competencies.
2.  Product managers cannot overlook the strategic planning process for product lines, even if they're busy with tactical day-to-day tasks. Therefore, product or product line strategic reviews and resets should be carried out as often as needed—at the speed of the market. The Product Management Governance Board (Chapter 9) should ensure that this framework is in place.
3.  Strategic planning means product managers can and should see the "big picture" of the product's fit within the market. This demands powerful insight, which involves critical thinking skills, complemented by relevant domain context.

## PLANNING AND CARRYING OUT EFFECTIVE, TIMELY PRODUCT LAUNCHES

When companies introduce new products, enhancements, and upgrades, product managers should either lead or work with those who are responsible to execute the launch. However, launches are very often delayed due to a lack of proper planning and coordination. It is up to product leaders to make sure that product managers play a significant role in the process that shapes launch plans and launch execution. To ensure that product managers can fulfill this charter, leaders must guide product managers to ensure the following:

1.  An appropriate market window is selected.
2.  Cross-functional team members are engaged at the right time.
3.  Adequate time is allowed to construct launch plans and to execute on those launch plans.

## MANAGING AND MONITORING THE FINANCIAL AND
## MARKET PROGRESS OF PRODUCTS AND PORTFOLIOS

Product Management is business management of products; therefore, business and financial acumen are important to proper job performance. Product managers should understand basic practices for accounting, finance, budgeting, and forecasting, which are the essential "tools of the trade." They need to be able to use the array of tools, metrics, and key performance indicators to track vital signals about the product's performance. Coupled with market insights, these evaluative skills and tools serve to validate or revise the strategic and tactical plans.

## TRANSLATING INFORMATION FROM MANY SOURCES
## INTO COHESIVE DECISIONS

Agility of thought and comprehension are of infinite value for product managers. *There are always decisions to make because there are always problems to solve.* Product managers at any job level must recognize and deal with many situations that arise. Experienced product managers should be able to think on their feet and decide their way forward, always strategizing, restrategizing, and motivating action across the organization.

Product managers may encounter challenges in making decisions; the process usually involves other people who need or want to be included. *Leaders should recognize that there is an important intersection between decision making and personality types.*

Some product managers require an endless barrage of data, which can *delay* vital decisions. They are the ones who often engender "analysis paralysis." At the other end of the spectrum, there are those gifted product managers who are comfortable with "just enough" data and are able to formulate more salient situational profiles to manage the decision-making process in timely fashion. They often have a "third eye" into the more nebulous areas of the business environment, and they always see the big picture. Leaders should be sensitive to temperaments because extended analysis can cause a delayed decision and expose the company to a competitor's action. Therefore, effective product managers must be able to balance the need for speed against the need for data.

## DRIVING ACTION THROUGHOUT THE ORGANIZATION AND BUILDING SHARED ACCOUNTABILITY ACROSS ALL CONTRIBUTING FUNCTIONS

Product managers have an overarching charge. They have to get work done, and they have to make sure everyone else gets their work done. Not only do product managers "manage" by crafting strategy and setting direction, they catalyze others across the organization. Leaders can pave the way by making sure that roles and responsibilities across functions are clearly spelled out.

Product managers must influence others in order to effectively drive action across the organization. Influence requires leadership. However, leadership, like the role of product manager, may come in a variety of "shapes." Some have an innate gift; others have only bits and pieces. Some can learn to lead with proper guidance. To others, learning to lead may feel natural only after they understand how the interconnected pieces of the product's business come together. Even though senior leaders want all product managers to lead, not all product managers can fill the bill. This is not necessarily a bad thing: you can't have an army with only generals. Who will do the work? Who will follow the leaders?

## USING BASIC WORK MANAGEMENT SKILLS

Not only must product managers ensure that work across the organization is carried out, they must understand how to effectively complete their own tasks. In a nutshell, product managers must also know *project management*. (Remember, to minimize role confusion, product managers should *not* be referred to as "project managers" even if they do have to oversee or coordinate the work of others.)

Another important aspect of Product Management work is that the processes and methods by which work is carried out are, or should be, subject to constant improvement. Therefore, product managers should be mindful of the need to always look for areas of efficiency through routine analyses of operational processes. This will help uncover efficiencies, which can save time and money. The Deming work activity cycle model, referred to as the Plan-Do-Check-Act (PDCA) Cycle, is a great reference for this required mindset.

# THE META-PROCESS FOR THE PRODUCT MANAGER STAFFING STRATEGY

The product manager staffing strategy is a "meta-process," and it involves several steps. Here, in sequence, are the nine steps that describe an effective model for product manager staff planning:

Step 1. Assess the current population of product managers.

Step 2. Segment the population into logical groups.

Step 3. Determine the need for domain or technical expertise.

Step 4. Calculate the market pay scales.

Step 5. Identify the required interrelationships.

Step 6. Validate or rewrite job descriptions.

Step 7. Improve interviewing procedures and protocols.

Step 8. Introduce competency assessments into the recruitment plan.

Step 9. Decide to decide: improve hiring decisions.

## STEP 1. ASSESS THE CURRENT POPULATION OF PRODUCT MANAGERS

In order to determine strategic staffing options for product managers, it is necessary to carry out an appropriate assessment. Most human resource or organizational development professionals agree with this. I've seen the varying range of diagnostic tools used by differing groups who work in these companies (e.g., Human Resources, Organizational Development, and others). Although they are not Product Management subject-matter experts, they all try to create some type of assessment. They base these assessments on an internal discovery process in which they interview product managers and Product Management leaders.

During the interviews they will ask those leaders, "What should product managers be doing?" Of course, the answers vary widely based on the paradigms of those interviewed. This effort may produce some sort of outcome, but it may not necessarily be on the right track.

After studying dozens of the Competency Models for product managers put together by my clients, I must say that the sheer inconsistency in how companies carry them out, along with the absence of a consistently applied foundational Reference Model, is *cause for concern*. Another issue is that these assessments are usually carried out at a single point in time and usually, in response to a one-time corporate initiative, aimed at improving the capabilities of product managers. I have evaluated many of these initiatives to determine their effectiveness, and I have learned that they're really not designed for longevity because they are only singular events. Add to this the fact that reorganizations and staff turnover do not typically allow for continuous measurements and related evaluations of other performance improvement efforts.

Chapter 2 focused on the use of a Competency Model to assess the overall population of product managers to improve the *function* of Product Management in the organization. Earlier in the book, I showed you how to (a) set up the assessment, (b) establish the rating scale, and (c) apply a method to evaluate gaps. I also focused on using the Competency Model as a means to clarify the role of the product manager. Remember, the assessment uses the Product Management Life Cycle Model as a reference. Before you continue, here are a few other points to take into consideration in a product manager competency assessment:

- Presume that every person who has a product manager (or related) job title has some competency level. Although there is the nonnegotiable set of competencies, leaders must always take into account the general background and experience of each person being evaluated.
- You may also want to factor in your specific industry or domain areas. However, these should be added as an overlay afterward, not as part of considering the generalized core competencies.

In my company's diagnostic programs, we use 11 competency clusters and approximately 80 activity statements. We also utilize a five-element experiential rating scale. The key to this instrument's success is the consistent use of a common set of clusters and themes that reflect the core competencies of product managers. The main point is that these themes do not speak to an explicit industry, technology, or domain. *They focus on the skills and experience that are the essential enablers for effective Product Management.*

Here is another important point: Assessments should be carried out annually, regardless of shifts or changes in the product manager population. Such regularity is critical in order to track performance over time—as well as to equate investments in organizational and professional development with desired outcomes.

## STEP 2. SEGMENT THE POPULATION INTO LOGICAL GROUPS

It is a given that product managers need a significant amount of business acumen. However, they are by no means equals. This inequality is due to their varied levels of innate talent, experience, and functional paradigms, as well as the corporate culture of their company and even their ability to lead and influence others.

Product complexity and maturity also matter. In several services-based firms we worked with, senior leaders expressed frustration about the lack of creativity and innovation exhibited by their product managers. After our diagnostics, we were able to explain to them that the product portfolios were filled with mostly mature products. These portfolios did generate a significant contribution to the business; therefore, the main duty of their product managers was to be reactive to customer requests. With such limitations in scope, their product managers were ill equipped to envision a wider field of opportunity.

Firms like these miss potential opportunities in adjacent market areas if their staff doesn't include some entrepreneurial-minded product managers—people with the vision to look beyond the current boundaries of the organization. When funding for product manager resources is limited, it may be a challenge to carry out these two separate, but integrated work streams in any company. However, it may become possible to work out a more productive staffing strategy when you have a better understanding of the composition of your product portfolio and organizational structure.

You use a variety of research methods to segment markets in order to identify desirable areas and target customers. In similar manner, you can segment the product manager population using a variety of factors, including the following guidelines.

## Whether They Manage an Entire Product or Only an Aspect of a Product

Consider whether the product managers work with or shape (a) a grouping of attributes, (b) a component or subsystem, or (c) an element of the product's design. It is important to identify the people who have the ability to see a larger picture of the product's business versus the people who work within a narrower context. Some product managers can manage multiple products or an entire portfolio; others have lesser capabilities. People need to be classified in groupings that weigh various factors such as (a) product complexity, (b) product or market maturity, and (c) degree of sales activity or volumes. Depending on the type of company and its products, there may be other aspects that could serve to classify areas where product managers are assigned.

## The Life Cycle State of Products within the Organization

Product manager work plans and activities are often aligned with the product's market maturity. Some mature products remain on the market for many years, providing predictable cash flow to the business. In this instance, product managers will tend to process and prioritize customer requests or be reactive to competitor actions. Other companies have rapid product-refresh cycles that require a more actively engaged group of product managers who are attuned to the market's pulse.

## The Degree to Which Customer Exposure Is Required

In a B2B setting, some product managers are effective in dealing with customers who work at any level, including key influencers and decision makers. Others are adept at being "in the field." Some are uncomfortable or are not equipped with the basic skills to carry out these important interactions. Understanding these classifications can provide important clues leading to professional development efforts.

## Product Complexity or Technology

Some product managers are well suited to working in advanced technology or domains because of their ability to understand complex systems (not all "systems" mean computer systems). In Step 3, I will speak to this point in more detail.

### Primary Interfaces and Interactions

As noted often, product managers reach across many organizations and work with many people. This attribute can be an important determinant of a product manager's potential for success. Many companies utilize personality profile tools such as the Myers-Briggs Type Indicator, Keirsey Temperament Sorter, and the FIRO-B personality test. These provide a context for clarifying work preferences, and they can help to identify programs that improve interpersonal effectiveness.

### The Preferred Working Styles of the Product Managers

Some people like to be assigned "tasks" that they can complete. These are linear thinkers who like a degree of control and predictability in their work. On the other end of the spectrum, some see a different picture (or different pictures) and can deal with abstractions. They are not fazed by the amorphous nature of a fast-moving, dynamic job or the unpredictable nature of markets. These are the desirable self-starters. The latter are better suited to becoming product leaders.

### The Prior Background and Experience of the Product Managers

Education and experience generally matter, to a certain extent. However, pure passion, vision, and natural abilities serve to motivate successful entrepreneurs and businesspeople—and this includes product managers. I strongly recommend a deep exploration of employees' prior on-the-job experiences and their own understanding and rationale behind the roles they assumed and what they learned. It is also imperative to understand the prior successes and failures of prospective product managers, or those who are vying for promotion. Product managers and leaders who assimilate these aspects of their prior work use these valuable experiences to shape their own success. Understanding an employee's academic *and* career journey will help in identifying placement opportunities in any organization.

### The Current Scores and Findings of the Competency Assessments

Organizations that routinely administer an assessment to evaluate core competencies of product managers can do an effective job of assessing and cultivating the product manager population. As suggested, carrying out these evaluations on an annual basis can provide invaluable insight into performance planning possibilities.

### Years of Product Manager Experience

It may make sense to evaluate the population if a company is seeking to rationalize its *portfolio* of product manager staff. When you have some people who have been in a role for many years and perform predictably for a stable, mature product, it is important not to penalize them. In fact, there are some companies who have product managers who excel in a narrow set of performance characteristics and add valuable product, domain, or cultural context. Leaders would do well to align the product's strategy with the person assigned, regardless of years of experience.

### The Interpersonal Skills of the Product Managers

The so-called soft skills are often overlooked attributes for product manager effectiveness. Since the success of the product manager is so vastly dependent on the person's ability to relate to others, it is imperative that product managers are competent in this area. Interpersonal skills include verbal, written, and presentation categories.

1. Verbal skills can communicate knowledge and expertise and can be used to persuade others.
2. Written skills are important for creating appropriate documentation and artifacts, or communicating with customers and other stakeholders.
3. Presentation skills focus on face-to-face human interactions, body language, and other visual cues used as tools to lead and influence others. Presentation skills have little to do with how a person stands up and runs through the PowerPoint slides.

### The Leadership Abilities of the Product Managers

Leadership is an important aspect of the segmentation model. It's an indispensable asset for high-performance product managers. There are many dimensions of leadership. In some cases, it covers the demonstrated acts used to influence and inspire others. In others, it can be related to the degree to which authority is assumed or direction provided for others. As I said before, not everyone can be a leader. There are people who do not possess the temperament or nature to be leaders. However, it is possible to improve such skills in the population of prospective leaders. One way would be to tap into the leadership development resources in your company; another would be to seek support from external sources.

## STEP 3. DETERMINE THE NEED FOR DOMAIN OR TECHNICAL EXPERTISE

In today's companies and economy, leaders need their staff members to perform in their jobs almost immediately, often without an effective start-up plan. Therefore, people are often named to product manager jobs based on their perceived product or domain familiarity. These can include the following:

- Operations people who know products based on how they support them
- Salespeople who are familiar with the product's functionality and have good customer relationships
- Engineers or developers who know the inner-workings of any product

Most "new" product managers are dropped into their roles. (More about this subject later in this chapter under "Onboarding and Socialization.") They don't know what they don't know; and they don't know what to ask or whom to go to with questions. Often there is no supporting or historical documentation. They simply begin by answering e-mails and attending meetings. As they continue in the job, they can do only what has to be done at the moment because they do not have the necessary information to perform properly.

Technology companies with dominant Engineering or Development functions tend to be motivated by tools and techniques. As more products are developed rapidly, product managers are being asked to spend more time in the lab. Because of this, they may not be able to spend the time focusing on other important aspects of the business. You get undesirable outcomes when products are ready before the rest of the organization can catch up and "digest" them. Keep in mind that staffing models may require adjustments to ensure that there are enough product managers to support the development team as well as to manage the product's business.

There is nothing wrong with taking domain or technical experts and placing them in a product manager job. Before this takes place, however, executives must determine *how much of the core competencies the incumbent is presently able to bring to the product manager job*. Then a development plan can be put into place such that the employee can be purposefully guided to become proficient at being a product manager.

## STEP 4. CALCULATE THE MARKET PAY SCALES

Admittedly, salary administration is a complex area. Companies need expertise and data that can help guide human resources and other leaders to determine market-based scales. Human resources leaders should keep an eye on the most relevant market indicators such that competitive salaries and compensation packages are aligned with the roles assigned as well as to consider the financial contribution for which product managers are accountable.

## STEP 5. IDENTIFY THE REQUIRED INTERRELATIONSHIPS

There are complex and interconnected webs of working relationships that must be navigated by product managers. The questions that need to be answered are these: Whom does the product manager work with, when, and for what purpose? The answers to the questions require an understanding of several interrelated organizational elements. Of primary importance is the organization's design. Please refer to the section of Chapter 2 entitled "Organizational Design Considerations." The intent of that section is to help clarify the roles and responsibilities that lead to a specific outcome in relation to a given process.

To develop effective staffing strategies for product managers, all possible Product Management processes need to be identified, categorized, and visualized. I strongly recommend the creation of a "process library" because it offers an organization the ability to maintain role clarity and improve interrelationships between cross-functional constituencies. Process libraries could be organized by meta-level competency groups. For example, a "market insight" library of processes might include a "customer visit process" or a "competitive product analysis process." When all processes and subprocesses are documented and understood, it is easier to align the role of the product manager and the role of others. It is also easier to depict the interdependencies between people in different functions. In the final analysis, when the role of the product manager is clear, other roles become clear as well. When role confusion is minimized, work flows more easily and efficiently through the organization.

## STEP 6. VALIDATE OR REWRITE JOB DESCRIPTIONS

At various times, clients ask me to evaluate their job descriptions. When I first started doing this, I was surprised at the high level of variation. I feel it is a cause for greater attention. In some companies, there may be a universal job description for a product manager. In other companies, there are sometimes dozens of descriptions. Having so many descriptions can be confusing and can also lead to incorrect hiring decisions. Creating or improving job descriptions can begin with what was described in Steps 1 through 5 in this section.

What I provide here is a general outline for the product manager job description. Your HR department should have the necessary templates that can be used to capture the inputs based on what has been discussed thus far. The objective for you is to align this description (or these descriptions) with the degree to which any competency or other attribute is needed and with the way you have come to agree on the role in your own firm. In the next chapter, I will talk about job hierarchies and employee planning. However, there's no doubt that you will need to have a few job descriptions that contain common elements and are suitable for the level within the hierarchy of the product managers in the company.

If your HR department does not have a standard template for a job description, here are the primary elements. If you are already familiar with these, I suggest you skip to the next section. Aside from the basics of the description identifiers, job codes, and business nomenclature, the product manager job descriptions should contain the following:

1. A reference for where the job rests in the organization chart.
2. The reporting relationships (manager, manager's manager, and so on), both superiors and subordinates.
3. The major purpose or principal focus of the job, including what the product managers are responsible for achieving, and why.
4. The major work processes, work activities, and general frequency with which those work activities are expected to be carried out. *This is where it is important to make sure that the core competency*

*areas are spelled out* so that the employees know what the foundational work is and so that the candidates can be tested for that knowledge by their hiring managers. These major activities can be listed in order of importance as well.

5. The minimum sets of knowledge, skills, and experiences required. This would include formal education and various experiences that are desirable. These can also be ranked in order of importance to the role.

6. An indication of the minimum performance requirements or time commitment required to progress to a subsequent level. Many product managers are ambitious and want to know what's next in line if they deliver on the job description.

7. The required working interrelationships. As discussed in Step 5 earlier, the working interrelationships need to be called out. These can include a listing of organizations and/or people and the frequency and purpose of the interactions.

8. The critical systems, tools, and resources that the product managers will have to work with or that they might actually have to create. This information can be especially important in relation to activities undertaken to plan and monitor the product's performance.

9. Decisions for which the product managers are accountable.

10. Budgetary or financial authority.

11. Supervisory responsibilities, if any.

12. Performance planning (how objectives are set and evaluated). This might include revenue or profit targets, customer measurements, or even peer evaluations.

13. An optional section might address key cultural or organizational issues and obstacles that the product managers may expect to encounter.

## STEP 7. IMPROVE INTERVIEWING PROCEDURES AND PROTOCOLS

As I mentioned earlier in the chapter, when I participated on the global leadership development team at AT&T, I was also trained as a campus recruiter—with the focus on the top MBA schools. It may sound really *easy* to be a campus recruiter. However, the training alone was a grueling week-long event. The most important benefit for me was that I learned to use a standard set of questions and a standard set of questioning techniques. In modern business parlance, it was analogous to learning how to sell in a consultative manner.

Individual managers have unique interviewing styles and a particular line of questions they like to ask. If an organization wishes to standardize some of its practices related to Product Management, then the interviewing process is a good place to start. Since I often serve as a point of validation in clients' staffing processes (interviewing prospective product managers), here is a description of the technique I use when I help them with their product manager hiring.

My strongest emphasis is focused on creating the kinds of questions that relate to the core competencies. As I explained earlier in the chapter (where I listed them in great detail), they are the nonnegotiable competencies that product managers must master and for which they must earn top grades in their responses. For example, in the category related to strategy, one could ask the following sequence of questions, starting with one main question:

1. Have you ever created a strategy for a product or product line?
2. Describe the process you followed.
3. What data did you use?
4. Where did you get the data from?
5. What were the key themes you uncovered?
6. Whom did you work with on the strategy?
7. How did you communicate it?
8. How did you get others to buy-in?

There are a host of questions that can be asked that seek to uncover how candidates think, how they secure data and insights, how they gain the support of others, and how they secure buy-in.

Not only is it a good idea to create the interview questions related to the core competencies, it can also be highly efficient to train all the supervising managers in the techniques used to carry out this type of questioning.

It is important to maintain consistency when asking questions and recording responses. That's because the technique establishes a format and structure that can be used by all managers who interview and hire product managers. There will be less ambiguity when everyone is asking the basic, foundational questions related to the core competencies. I have another proposal: Think of how great it would be if the interview forms and interviewer notes were kept in a single repository. This is an example of the advantage this would bring: Suppose that after you interviewed your first-choice applicant, you found that your second-choice applicant also had potential. Two weeks later, another hiring manager had an opening. The records of the interviews would be available, and they could be scanned to consider the recent candidates who were interviewed. That second-choice person could be brought back in for another look—because the interview data was available.

Another benefit of using a standard interview protocol is that it builds up another dimension of the organization's maturity model. If, for example, metrics are kept on hiring statistics, as well as other success factors such as the turnover rates or the number of employees who are delivering better results, these can be tracked over time. If you demonstrate a higher level of predictability in hiring results, then it suggests that the organization is operating in a more mature manner.

I also recommend that leaders establish a series of questions that speak to a variety of situations that a product manager might encounter. These can relate to any number of areas, including how candidates deal with prioritization or negotiation. I particularly like to ask, "How do you get others to work with you when they don't work for you?" Another question I may ask is, "Have you led a cross-functional team on a complex project?" And as a follow-up question, "How have you had to resolve a conflict between people who work on a team?" Asking open-ended situational questions may help you derive a greater level of insight into the candidate's qualifications.

Additionally, managers who hire product managers can set up a peer review council. This can work in a number of ways. For one thing, managers can co-interview candidates and then critique one another to build more consistency into the process. For another thing, once the process is clearly understood, it can pave the way for various improvements and greater efficiencies. More focused questions could be created, or a different variety of interviewing steps could be considered, based on the candidate's profile.

My last comment in this area concerns the space outside of the core competencies. Some interviewers, especially those with strong domain or technical experience, tend to hire people who are aligned with their own experience or paradigms. Moreover, they may not be familiar with the nuances of the job because some of them have never been in a job as an individual contributor product manager. In such cases, it's easy to see why poor hiring decisions might be made. This is an important reason the standard questions that focus on the core competencies should remain the steadfast benchmark for all hiring decisions.

## STEP 8. INTRODUCE COMPETENCY ASSESSMENTS INTO THE RECRUITMENT SCHEME

In some instances, I strongly recommend the use of testing in the hiring routine. This provides hiring managers with a comprehensive data set that helps to evaluate prospective candidates. It also sets up a common array of criteria on which to make hiring decisions. In my practice, the competency assessment is often utilized as a precursor to the interviewing process. It stands to reason that if you are going to use ongoing competency assessments to track employees' progress over time, it's also a good idea to use the same protocol for new hires or transfers.

## STEP 9. DECIDE TO DECIDE: IMPROVE HIRING DECISIONS

The part of the hiring process that is most challenging is the decision-making process. It is too easy to "like" one candidate over another. You can be captivated by one element of a person's experience, even if you know that the person is weak in other areas. Don't forget that candidates are often coached to sell themselves to you. The implication is that the hiring manager is the "buyer" and therefore, must take precautions and have a goodly amount of "sales resistance."

The entire interviewing and testing process is not the only precaution available. Using a structured decision tool, each like a decision matrix, can be a great help! If a decision matrix can be used to screen product ideas, why not use one to screen employee candidates?

To construct the decision matrix, you need to consider what criteria you want to use in order to objectively rate each candidate's credentials against each criterion. The criteria would start with items that are contained in the

**Figure 5.2  Decision Matrix for a Hiring Decision**

| Candidate Name | Secure Market Insight | Strategic Mindset | Product Planning | Product Launch | Business and Financial Acumen | Leading and Influencing | Decision Making |
|---|---|---|---|---|---|---|---|
| Candidate A | | | | | | | |
| Candidate B | | | | | | | |
| Candidate C | | | | | | | |
| Candidate D | | | | | | | |

core competencies and other enabling areas. The matrix could look like the one shown in Figure 5.2.

In the table, each criterion should be assigned a score that is as objective as possible. For example, use a scale of 1 through 10 with 10 being the best score. You will have to come up with the definition for the score—that is, *the degree you have determined represents the value for each number from 1 to 10.* For this, we can borrow from our organizational maturity rating scale. For example, a 10 might mean that, beyond a reasonable doubt, the candidate's experience has been validated by evidence (documents, tests, and so on) so that this is a very strong attribute. A score of 5 might mean that the candidate's experience is somewhat predictable and that he or she might require more supervision. A 5 does not necessarily preclude accepting the candidate. You need to look at the overall picture and evaluate the strengths and weaknesses, and then you need to decide which of those is sufficient or not sufficient for your needs. There are important trade-offs that can be considered as you and your peers work through this process. The more often this process is practiced and shared, the easier it becomes to institutionalize. The more efficient this process becomes, the more predictable your hiring decisions will be.

Once the decision is made, follow your company's policies that focus on the standard methods and protocols they use to extend the offer and process the acceptance.

## ONBOARDING AND SOCIALIZATION

In many instances, product managers are brought into an organization, either as transfers from other departments or from outside the company. Often, they do not know where to begin their work. Often, there is no Product Master Plan for them to refer to (see Chapter 2 of *The Product Manager's Desk Reference*)—and they might not know whether there even is such a plan. Consequently, there has to be some formality that helps you to get them started, comfortably. Even for those product managers who are good self-starters, there should be a framework for them that might resemble a checklist of things to do. This checklist should be put into a calendarlike format.

A variety of general routines take place on the day of arrival. Then in the subsequent days the formalities are usually handled by the general onboarding program that exists for all employees. However, I want to go beyond these formalities to talk about some of the key methods that get product managers started in the actual work. These would be aside from the myriad meetings and other obligations that materialize on Day 1. Rather than provide detailed explanations, here are the basic facts that the new product managers should be given so that they are aware of them from the start. It's important to do this because it saves time and improves the necessary ramp-up. This information should include the following:

1. The company's business model, organization chart, and key players.
2. The physical locations and contacts for all those in each function associated with the product.
3. Any product-related documentation including strategy documents, Business Cases, Product Requirements Documents (PRDs), Launch Plans, financials, and product performance information. Also, all marketing materials should be made available. As I've pointed out before, time can be saved if there is one repository or central location for the necessary information and documentation.

In addition, new product managers should be introduced to their peers and the company's senior leaders in an informal, relaxed manner such as over a lunch.

## SUMMARY

Many companies use sophisticated techniques to determine where to invest in their product portfolios. Better product investment decisions tend to yield improved business results. Furthermore, most executives know that productivity and efficiency can be improved by placing the right people in the right jobs.

If we accept that product managers comprise an important dimension of the company's portfolio of assets, it makes sense to do the best we can to improve how we attract and hire this vital corporate asset. While this seems intuitively obvious, there is, in reality, a vast disconnect between staffing strategies and product portfolio strategies.

Why does this happen? One reason is that the role of the product manager is subject to many interpretations—because a common definition of the role of a product manager is not fully understood. Therefore, I addressed this issue in the first half of this chapter in order to provide a common definition for the role.

The second issue is related to the actual product manager staffing strategy. One of the reasons the portfolio of product managers is suboptimal in many firms is that the practices and techniques to recruit, select, and hire product managers are vastly inconsistent. Therefore, in the second half of the chapter, you were provided with some ideas about what you can do to fortify your staffing practices. Some of these include ongoing assessments, segmenting the population, understanding working relationships, interviewing effectiveness, and improving decision making.

All executives are concerned with business success. This success can be enhanced when the best product managers are brought in and correctly positioned within the organization. When positioned correctly, these product managers will meaningfully impact both the *top line* and the *bottom line*.

# CHAPTER 6

# CULTIVATING AND SHAPING PRODUCT MANAGERS

**EXECUTIVE SUMMARY**

■ When companies consistently classify and evaluate product managers, they ensure that the right product managers are in the right jobs at the right time.

■ Leaders who cultivate product managers and enable them to think holistically and systemically about their products will ultimately preside over robust product portfolios.

■ Targeted product manager development programs can improve overall product manager effectiveness and organizational efficiency.

*Correction does much, but encouragement does more.*

—JOHANN WOLFGANG VON GOETHE

Marketers, advertisers, corporate leaders—and writers—recognize the importance of titles. Naming things is part of basic communication from the primal level, to the complex terms used in the sciences and the arts, to the brand names created for business purposes. Titles should convey the essence of the idea—whether for product, brand, book (or even chapter)—and they should attract the audience they want to contact. The writer Flaubert was adamant about finding the right word (*le mot juste*).

As I pondered the title of this chapter, I went over many different words and their nuances. I thought of the word *nurture*, but it reminded me of nourishment and eating and implied spoon-feeding, which is counterproductive. The word *develop* seemed apt but was too similar to *product development*. Then the word *cultivate* came to mind, and it resonated strongly with me. *Cultivation* connotes careful planning and preparation and mindful tending, which, like taking care of crops, relates to productivity and yield. It works as well with people as it does with plants. *Shaping*, the other word in the title, is also important because adept senior managers can be instrumental in deftly shaping each individual's capability and ensuring that he or she is well integrated with the culture of the organization. Cultivating and shaping product managers can contribute powerfully and tangibly to the value of product managers as corporate assets. This, in turn, can help the firm achieve its desired competitive advantage.

In his book *Good to Great*, noted contemporary author Jim Collins suggests that a company cannot ascend to greatness without the right people in the right jobs at the right time. His advice is: "Get the right people in the right seats." I cannot agree more!

To paraphrase an old adage, good product managers are made, not born. First, in order to have the right people, they have to be properly recruited, selected, and segmented (see Chapter 5). The next step: "Get them into the right seats." This involves giving product managers the tools to learn and earn their "seats." You achieve this through the skillful cultivating and shaping of their capabilities.

This chapter is devoted to providing you with the content and context to help you accomplish this. I've outlined six areas to be addressed:

1. Establishing the optimal job levels and progression plans for product managers
2. Guiding product managers to think and act holistically and systemically about their product's business
3. Motivating product managers to be conscientious about the performance of their products
4. Inspiring product managers to make informed, fact-based decisions
5. Making sure that product managers can effectively influence and lead others
6. Creating targeted development programs for product managers

## ESTABLISHING THE OPTIMAL JOB LEVELS AND PROGRESSION PLANS FOR PRODUCT MANAGERS

In many companies, product managers are categorized based on whatever fits present needs or seems convenient. These elements include salary band, perceived level of experience, or a title they may have held in another job. Sometimes the title is given away as part of the deal to sweeten the offer.

### PROGRESSION PATHS

In the years I've spent interviewing leaders and employees, I've learned that very few companies use *consistent methods* to *classify* product managers and to *progress* them through their organizations. In surveys made prior to writing this book, I asked the question: "Does your company have a formal hierarchy or progression path for product managers?" In responses from executives in 144 companies, collectively employing more than 6,700 product managers, 73.9 percent of leaders indicated that they did not have a formal hierarchy or progression path for product managers.

In cases where criteria for progression planning *were* established, the top three criteria for product managers (shown below) that were selected as "extremely important" or "important" included these, in order of precedence:

- Has the ability to influence others
- Is a self-starter
- Knows how to get things done in the organization

At the next lower level, the criteria included the following:

- Market knowledge
- Reputation with customers
- Product knowledge
- Domain and technical knowledge
- Ability to achieve financial and business objectives

A third level listed a host of other criteria, including these:

- Is recommended by other leaders
- Helps others
- Is at the top of the salary band
- Has an "easy-to-get-along-with" personality
- Makes task force contributions
- Demonstrates company values

## HIRING PROCEDURES

It's a well-known fact of corporate life that executives and Product Management leaders talk among themselves about product managers or other people they know who have potential. It's thought of as a "whisper system" or an unofficial talent hunt. In fact, companies often place a premium on the informal opinions of leaders and managers when it comes to assignments and promotions. Although this (talent scout) practice is common, it is difficult to harness it as a documented procedure because it cannot be quantified or measured. However, these discussions should not be discounted because they are an important aspect of the hiring process. In other words, "water cooler" conversations have merit. What would help would be a set of notes that were provided by referrers and kept in a human resource talent management system.

One interesting point about filling Product Management positions: *poor decisions are seldom corrected by employers.* In some cases, an external hire is made, and the product manager is placed in a salary band based on leaders' beliefs that the incumbent can perform at a given level. Later on, they may find it was an error in judgment. Since employers don't rescind salary packages after the fact, these employees become a part of the general population, although they may not pull their weight. In fact, they may even undermine the desired efficacy of the product manager population. Thus, companies are not getting enough return on investment from such employees.

In another example, a current employee from a different function (for instance, Engineering) makes a lateral move into a product manager position at an equivalent salary band level. This employee has no demonstrated experience as a product manager and so may require extra help to fulfill job requirements. Such assignments are made with the expectations that employees will perform at the expected level. These intracompany transfers are complex and can be problematic; often, the anticipated results are less than satisfactory.

To modify these situations in the future, I suggest that leaders establish a trial period of about three to six months for transferees at a lower level of performance and no reduction in salary. This way, the performance expectation can be managed, the employee's morale can be maintained, and allowance can be made in advance for the cost issues. During this period, particular attention would be directed toward cultivating the person's skills and competencies. The payoff might be that you have created an unexpected asset. If not, then the person (with an explicit understanding that it really is a trial) is returned to his or her prior role. In sum, it is easy enough to situate product managers on the organization chart, but it is a much greater challenge to position product managers so that they fulfill the company's strategic intent.

## PRODUCT MANAGERS AND THE TRADECRAFT TRADITION

It may be a stretch, but try to think about product managers as if they were tradespeople: plumbers, electricians, brick masons, or others. I'm not implying that product managers are mechanical contractors; rather, I'm only making an analogous comparison to the trades. Now, think about the following: A newly hired electrician would not be assigned to wire a building his first day on the job; nor would a newly hired mason be assigned to construct a new brick façade on a building without supervision. Before being given added responsibilities, these workers would need to prove themselves and show what level of work they were capable of. If they were beginners, they would need further experiential development; if they were experienced, they would need to be exposed to more complex situations; and if they were top tier, they would be accepted as full contributors to the trade. The same applies to newly hired product managers. They need to be assessed to see what level of performance they are capable of and, therefore, the contributions they can be expected to make.

Since they began long ago, the tradecrafts have used three phases of initiation. The terminology used to designate these three phases—apprentice, journeyman, and master—is familiar to us. This terminology may not be considered politically correct in today's diverse world. Accordingly, I'll adjust the terms and refer to levels of product managers and relate them to the trade roles: *associate product manager (apprentice), product manager (journeyman), and senior product manager (master)*. In your own company, you may use similar titles, or others that essentially connote the same levels. These simplified classifications are being used to illustrate three basic levels for the classification or segmentation of product managers.

(*An important note*: For the intended purposes of this section, I will temporarily depart from my stated position at the beginning of this book, which was that the term *product manager* would be used to refer to product managers at all levels. At the conclusion of this discussion, I'll drop this temporary departure and return to my original position. Furthermore, higher levels such as director or above will be excluded from the discussion of the three levels because I would like to focus on my key points about progression management.)

In the following three subsections of the chapter, I'll provide:

1. A general overview of the primary job levels so we can define what can or should be expected of a person in that level
2. A Product Manager Scorecard, which will prove to be a *very helpful tool* to help you classify a product manager's current situation
3. Some guidance to help you establish a purposeful direction for each employee

## JOB LEVELS FOR PRODUCT MANAGERS

*Associate product managers* are equivalent to apprentices. Placement in this category is dependent on the employees' level of experience. Those who are at this level have had little or no experience as product managers. They may have some familiarity with the role, based on having worked with or having closely observed product managers in action. Like apprentices, the associate product managers may have studied for the work (through their academic education) and might therefore be familiar with the basic terminology, tools, and methods. Also, some of them may understand the basic functionality and technology underpinning of a product, perhaps because they worked in Engineering, Operations, Marketing, or Sales before their lateral move. Here is the challenge: It doesn't matter what their education was or what they seem to know about various business areas; it also doesn't matter if they have had some general exposure to the product through work experience. *None of these are substitutes for firsthand performance of Product Management work activities and tasks.*

This means that associate product managers require structure, close management, and purposeful coaching. As with apprentices, masters (senior product managers) should be doing the coaching. Within this structured environment, the associate product managers would be put to work on a variety of activities and tasks, some planned, and some ad hoc. Aside from some natural competence, the associate product managers should also begin to demonstrate increasing product manager skills within a reasonable time. Associate product managers may stay at this level for a year, or even up to three years. Whatever the time period spent as associates, the candidates for promotion must meet a set of criteria, based on core competency measurements and the ancillary areas as discussed in Chapter 5, plus their ranking on the *scorecard*, shown later.

*Product managers* are analogous to journeymen. People who move up into the role of product managers have been coached, shaped, and cultivated under the watchful eyes of senior product managers or the senior product managers' managers. Therefore,they should be equipped with a collective portfolio of skills, core competencies, and experience gained from their role as associate product managers. As with the other levels, some of their work is planned, and some is ad hoc.

It is important that product managers keep on developing the right connective tissue—the thought processes that help them to think holistically and systemically. They should be able to discern patterns and trends and synthesize a variety of inputs into tangible outputs. They should also be optimizing their portfolio of competencies, enabling them to move easily in and across the organization. Competent product managers should continually strive to build credibility with peers and others and, ultimately, to produce tangible business results. At the start of their assignment, product managers should be able to take responsibility (generally) for one product. As they make progress and expand their span of control, they should be able to take responsibility for more than one product. Acquiring some portfolio perspective builds a broader business context that enables them to recognize products in various parts of their life cycles and adds a layer of complexity to their role. In order to move further up the ladder, product managers should have demonstrated that they can carry out a portion of their work with minimal coaching or supervision. To attain that level will take about two to four years in this role. They should be required to meet a set of criteria for promotion based on their ranking on a scorecard.

*Senior product managers* are the masters. I like to think of senior product managers as those who have developed a collective portfolio of knowledge and skills. They have also acquired a certain level of *wisdom* that can come only with several years of experience. In other words, senior product managers get things done, deliver results, and have earned credibility and a greater level of empowerment in the organization. Senior product managers are actually effective self-learners; they deal with unexpected situations with aplomb, and they guide associate product managers and product managers.

Some senior product managers may actually be assigned to supervise others (as masters). Some may remain as individual contributors for many years because they have found a niche in which they can be productive and satisfied. Others may be included in the pool of high-potential leaders.

By now you may be wondering, who are the masters of the masters? Be assured that senior product managers are not left to languish because they don't have a master. In fact, senior product managers have usually established *informal* mentor-protégé relationships with many other senior leaders as they encounter different situations. They may also have great bosses who are adept at cultivating and guiding them through difficult situations. However, at this level in their career, they will have learned enough about corporate navigation, politics, and influence, and they will have delivered sufficiently stellar results, that they are able to earn higher levels of empowerment and stature.

(*Note:* As indicated earlier, I will now return to the use of the term *product manager* to refer to all product managers, regardless of level.)

## PRODUCT MANAGER MATURITY AND PROGRESSION PATHS

In Product Management, you cannot make an appointment with experience. You have to "sign in" and be there. For product managers, there is no substitute for situational *and* predictable work experience, seasoning, and maturity. If product managers are not correctly categorized in terms of their experience and capabilities, situations may arise that they are too inexperienced to handle. Those with less experience tend to spend more time on reactive activities than on purposeful, planned activities. When there is a problem (a customer complaint, a product quality problem, or an unplanned proposal), the assigned product managers may lack the requisite experience to resolve it.

It's regrettable, but sometimes the product managers have no one to turn to, or their managers may not be available; on occasion, they may even be fearful about raising the issue with their managers because they feel their managers may react negatively. This point has been validated by a number of participants in my workshops and those whom I interviewed. They have complained, quite often, about many such situations. However, there is a light at the end of the tunnel. When product managers are correctly categorized, these situations can be minimized. Further, if nonthreatening channels of communication are open between product managers and their managers, experiential gaps can be quickly uncovered, and the main issues can be more adequately addressed.

The creation of simple hierarchy and progression paths requires some effort. But they can be easier to digest if we utilize two contextual areas discussed previously. The first is based on the Product Management Maturity Model for the product manager population (PMMM-P), mentioned in Chapter 2. The technique shown is intended to help evaluate the population of product managers in order to determine the level of maturity of the Product Management organization. The second is based on the hiring decision criteria discussed in Chapter 5, where a decision matrix was used to rate prospective product managers.

In order to set the stage for making structured evaluations, baseline data will need to be collected and organized for *each* product manager in the population. The HR department should be included so that talent management systems can be kept up to date. To create the baseline, the following steps need to be followed:

1.  Assemble a current profile of the product manager population, including the following information:
    a.  The number of people in various levels and their titles as uncovered in your competency assessment

b. Evaluative measures that can serve to classify product managers, which may include the following:
- Competency assessment scores
- Maturity scores that determine how consistent and predictable the product managers are when they carry out work activities

c. The number of locations where product managers currently work. This will be a factor if the product manager workforce is distributed, whether because of current organizational requirements or because they work in acquired companies.

d. Product and portfolio maturity levels. Classify product portfolios into categories: Products being developed, products in growth, products in maturity, and products in decline. (For context, if product managers have too much experience with mature products, it may mean that they are missing experience in new opportunity development.)

e. The business, market, financial, and other performance indicators for each product and product line across the portfolio. This may help in associating product managers with the degree to which their product impacts the portfolio and the company's market position.

2. Create a Product Manager Scorecard to capture evaluative elements as described above. This would also contain other information that current managers may have provided (or can provide) as a historical record of the employees' work.

Figures 6.1 and 6.2 show the two sides of the page of the Product Manager Scorecard. I believe that a more structured approach to evaluating product manager employees, based on the scorecard content, can contribute greatly to your efforts to fine-tune your performance planning and appraisal process.

One of the themes developed throughout this book focuses on documentation and evidence. When it comes to the evaluation of and career planning for product managers, data accumulated and used consistently and persistently is an effective method to help leaders align the product manager workforce with the organization's strategy to improve Product Management. The scorecard, in and of itself, can serve as a powerful contribution in this regard.

## PRODUCT MANAGER DEVELOPMENT

At the outset of the chapter, six areas were identified as essential to cultivate and shape product managers. Up to this point, I concentrated on the first area. For the balance of this chapter, I will focus on the other five areas.

## GUIDING PRODUCT MANAGERS TO THINK AND ACT HOLISTICALLY AND SYSTEMICALLY ABOUT THEIR PRODUCT'S BUSINESS

The Product Management Life Cycle Model represents the product's path across its life in the market. It is a dynamic model that is, of necessity, represented in a linear manner, almost like showing a map of the world on paper instead of on a globe. It's enough to drive any product manager to distraction.

People who think in linear terms or prefer task-oriented work may be frustrated with market, organizational, and other dynamics. People who are amorphous thinkers and can shape something from anything (think of a pottery maker, artisan, or others who can deal with abstractions) and can think in more than one dimension do not have as much trouble with seeing the whole picture. But it takes focus, and learned skills.

Good product managers must have the breadth of mind and scope to handle all these styles. It requires a kind of critical or inferential thinking that has been the subject of study by many academics and consultants—this one included. Aside from examining the outcome of studies, research projects, and books, *how do leaders of product managers teach product managers to think holistically and systemically?* I will share some of what I've learned from my own research and experience.

The idea behind teaching people to think is to help them build a suite of skills. Mastering these skills should help them comprehend their work world in greater depth and broader dimensions, which can lead to development of insights. Therefore, these skills will help them to appreciate that there is a constant and ongoing stream of situations or problems that need

## Figure 6.1 Product Manager Scorecard, Page 1

**Product Manager Scorecard**

| Employee Identifying Information | Date: _____ |
|---|---|
| Name and Contact Information: | |

| Employee number: | Date of hire: |
|---|---|
| Current job title and band: | Manager's name: |
| Time in current job: | |
| Prior job title and time in level: | Manager's name: |
| Education/degrees: | |
| Recent training: | |

| Work location: |
|---|
| Product assignment: |
| Date of initial assignment: |
| Life cycle state (Introduction-Growth-Mature-Decline-Discontinued): |
| *Product revenue/gross margin:* |

| | Prior Score—Date | Current Score—Date | Target Score |
|---|---|---|---|
| *Competencies* | | | |
| *Maturity* | | | |
| *Other attributes* | | | |

Competency and Maturity Scores

| Meta-Level Competency | Competency Assessment Score | MATURITY ASSESSMENT | | | | Overall Maturity Score |
|---|---|---|---|---|---|---|
| | | Very Inconsistent and Unpredictable 25 | Inconsistent and Somewhat Unpredictable 50 | Consistent and Somewhat Predictable 75 | Very Consistent and Predictable 100 | |
| Developing market insights | | | | | | |
| Crafting strategy | | | | | | |
| Launch planning and execution | | | | | | |
| Product performance management | | | | | | |
| Translating information and making decisions | | | | | | |
| Driving action across the organization | | | | | | |
| Using work management skills | | | | | | |
| *Total score* | | | | | | |

*Note:* Competency assessment scores are collected from another instrument.

Competency and Maturity Evaluation

| Meta-Level Competency | Competency Assessment Score | Maturity Assessment Score | Total Current Score for This Employee | Desired for This Performance Level | Gap between Current Total Score and Desired Level | Score Required for Promotion |
|---|---|---|---|---|---|---|
| Developing market insights | | | | | | |
| Crafting strategy | | | | | | |
| Launch planning and execution | | | | | | |
| Product performance management | | | | | | |
| Translating information and making decisions | | | | | | |
| Driving action across the organization | | | | | | |
| Using work management skills | | | | | | |
| *Total score* | | | | | | |

# Figure 6.1  Product Manager Scorecard, Page 2

Evaluation of Attributes and Behaviors

| Product Manager Attributes and Behaviors | Not Evident 1 | Minimally Evident 2 | Somewhat Evident 3 | Generally Evident 4 | Extremely and Persistently Evident 5 | Total Score |
|---|---|---|---|---|---|---|
| Domain knowledge and experience | | | | | | |
| Technical knowledge and experience | | | | | | |
| Demonstrated industry thought leadership | | | | | | |
| Entrepreneurial mindset | | | | | | |
| Self-starter, initiates projects | | | | | | |
| Persuasive presentation skills | | | | | | |
| Clear and concise writing | | | | | | |
| Listens carefully and courteously | | | | | | |
| Builds positive relationships in the organization | | | | | | |
| Excellent customer relationships | | | | | | |
| International experience | | | | | | |
| Efficiently manages time and work | | | | | | |
| Helps or coaches others | | | | | | |
| Effectively negotiates (internal and external) | | | | | | |
| Manages and balances risks | | | | | | |
| Considers diversity and cultural issues | | | | | | |
| Adaptable and flexible | | | | | | |
| Big-picture thinker | | | | | | |
| Works effectively with outside partners | | | | | | |
| Total score | | | | | | |

Documented evidence of work and location of evidence:

_____

_____

Recommended work plans for skill and experiential development:

_____

_____

Recommended education and training:

_____

_____

Required work and evidence for promotion:

_____

_____

_____

Other career path notes and comments:

_____

_____

to be addressed. Product managers should be able to come up with ideas and solutions to address those situations. If you can break down some of these situations to discern patterns or themes that are applicable for the product managers, you will contribute greatly to their development. As an example, showing how to tell time is one thing; looking inside the clock to see how it works is another. Product managers need to do both. Here are some ways that might help.

## CREATE SITUATIONAL PROFILES OR STORIES

Create situational profiles or stories to search for common themes. For example: Product managers who work in a business-to-business environment would visit a customer's office to observe people in action. After the visit, they would then write an actual "day in the life" story about each person encountered. If they have not done this before, it is their managers' job to guide them into the environment, work on the profiles together, and discuss the findings. In such a discussion, I have found it's better to ask open-ended questions (but don't "spoon feed" answers even if patience grows thin)—questions such as, "I wonder why that analyst was working on that report? What do you think was going on?" Or, "When you were observing repair technicians, what do you think they were doing, and what would you want to ask them?" Leaders should want to inspire product managers to look at situations with wider-open eyes and demonstrate the relationships between observations and problems. That is one of the first steps in building the skills that require *insight* (as in market insight)—the most important meta-level competency.

## FIND COMPARABLE SITUATIONS

Find comparable situations among other people to see how they uncover or solve problems. Such situations can serve to demonstrate how they were handled by others and if the results were favorable or not. These situations can then be evaluated in relation to issues the product managers have to cope with. However, product managers need to find the comparable situations themselves instead of waiting for applicable examples to occur to them. If product managers are not "natural" networkers, introduce them to senior level product managers in other business areas. Encourage the product managers to talk to those senior-level product managers and learn about situations the senior product managers have encountered with respect to similar products, customers, or competitors.

Help your product managers by offering a set of open-ended questions that they can use to learn about how other people might have carried out situational analyses and how those translated into strategies or tactics. Sit in with the product managers on initial interviews with others to help them improve their ability to elicit responses and probe more deeply (and learn to be good listeners). Conducting short debriefings will help them build some of the connections in their minds that relate to different situations; in turn, this will help improve confidence and move them toward more independent and associative thinking.

## BRING PRODUCT MANAGERS TOGETHER IN CROSS-FUNCTIONAL SETTINGS

Bring others together to discuss customer or market situations. A valuable skill for product managers to acquire is the ability to leverage the combined expertise of a cross-functional team. Newer product managers may be challenged in this area. You may wish to have the product managers reach out to a couple of people for an informal discussion, say, over lunch. The product managers can introduce situations they observed on a customer visit and share some of their discoveries. Have them ask for help from others to derive meaning from the observations. The answers provided (as another example) to customer questions may provide a helpful context. This approach serves to put the product managers in an advantageous position because it allows them to build a market-oriented dialogue, gets others to see that the product managers care about others' opinions, and helps inspire a shared approach to problem solving. It also helps the product managers build credibility, which ultimately leads to greater levels of influence.

## EXPOSE PRODUCT MANAGERS TO SITUATIONS THAT ARISE IN OTHER FUNCTIONAL AREAS

Expose product managers to situations that will inspire them to draw conclusions and derive meaning from various areas such as market research or internal operational studies. There is no shortage of information inside the company. Despite the complaints from product managers about the shortage of market research, there is nothing to stop them from making their own investigations. In another instance, perhaps the product managers can work with someone in the supply chain organization to learn how an order is processed, from time of receipt to time of delivery.

Product managers can ask those people to show them actual process diagrams—but they shouldn't stop at, "Show me how the order gets processed." They need to delve into the whole process, step-by-step. They should be asking, "Where does the order form go after it is received?" "How long does it take to get to the next person?" "Who is that next person?" "What do they do with it?" "What forms or documents are used in each step?" And so on. This is important because product managers should be collecting information all the time.

Further, they should strive to create a library of processes and methods for research. It will be of great help to them as they seek to uncover inefficiencies and to improve aspects of the product's business. If they do create a library of processes, they can bring others into conversations that might reveal opportunities to fine-tune or streamline a process or method.

As product managers gain more experience and understand how work gets done—key processes, work flows, timing, hand-offs, and logistics—they will substantially increase their value to the company. That can improve their efficacy. Also, there are many processes that can be improved upon, which could ultimately have an impact on product quality, customer perceptions, and organizational efficiency.

When product managers operate with single-threaded work flows (product requirements from development to launch and then back again), they don't get to see how the business operates as a collective whole. Product Management leaders should guide product managers as much as possible to help them build on their knowledge and learn about those connections, much as the master plumbers take the apprentices on all the plumbing jobs during the term of apprenticeship. That way, the apprentices learn how the system works, and from that, they learn how to diagnose where the trouble may be and how to fix it. Thus the apprentices can move up—and so it should be with product managers.

## ENSURE THAT PRODUCT MANAGERS CAN CARRY OUT ROOT-CAUSE ANALYSES

Problems always pop up. Root-cause analysis is a structured method that helps people understand the main reason a problem occurs. It is also a valuable tool to help improve processes and increase efficiency.

*Managers of product managers* should act as coaches for those who do not have the requisite experience in this area. As an example, if the customer service department reports that the number of incidents of late delivery of products is mounting, the product managers can work with the customer service department, and perhaps others who would also want to investigate the situation, by assembling the data and evidence. They may have to dig into data that spans a year or two; they may need to actually listen to call center tapes or examine physical products that have been sent back for repair or return; they may also have to go into the field and visit and interview customers; and they may need to observe the environments into which the products were received. From this data collection, people working cross-functionally can better understand the problems.

To take this example further, suppose the real problem is based on the fact that the procurement department employees, in conjunction with the shipping department employees, had to meet a corporate edict to lower the cost of shipping supplies. To do this, they purchased cartons and packing material that was not as sturdy but cost less. The product managers could point out the types of product damages, show the damaged cartons to leaders or to the purchasing unit, and conclude that the cost reduction effort was flawed.

However, the problem may not have stopped there. Suppose that the marketing department was carrying out customer satisfaction surveys and noticed a precipitous decline in satisfaction scores. The product managers will have had to bring those marketing people into the equation. Even if the shipping carton problem is fixed, other related challenges may emerge based on the primary root-cause study. In this case, perhaps a promotional program would be needed to win back the confidence of customers who may have defected to the competition. Further, those promotional programs might have to include a pricing adjustment to induce the customers to return.

In these situations (as in some others), the root-cause analyses and solutions can ultimately involve many people in many functions. The people who have to see and comprehend how all of these elements work together are the product managers. If the product managers are not doing this work in a thorough manner, it becomes the responsibility of the *managers of the product managers* to make sure the product managers can ultimately succeed. That means they must ensure that the systems and data to accomplish this

164 MODULE III CULTIVATE

work are available. This work cannot be completely delegated; it must be overseen until the product managers can capably and consistently carry it out independently.

## MOTIVATING PRODUCT MANAGERS TO BE CONSCIENTIOUS ABOUT THE PERFORMANCE OF THEIR PRODUCTS

In Chapter 6 of *The Product Manager's Desk Reference*, I stated that finance is the common language of business. Product managers should be accountable for the financial contribution their product makes to the business. They must be able to assess how a product's financial impact affects the business and the product portfolio. In addition, they need the financial acumen to wisely manage future investments in their product.

Other key performance indicators (KPIs) should be monitored as well. It is up to senior leaders to make sure that the most important KPIs are available and that they can be tracked at the right intervals. This will be discussed in Chapter 9 as a responsibility of a Product Management Governance Board. Further, the board should ensure that product managers have these analytics and tools at their fingertips so that they can respond or escalate as needed. Having a good product performance scorecard or dashboard that graphically depicts the product's financial state is a great tool. For this to become a reality, it is vital that financial reporting systems be tuned to report product-specific financial data, along with any other relevant business data and KPIs.

In many situations, product managers complain that they do not have product-level financial data or other KPIs. If they have failed to gather the data or they have it but do not use it or they don't know how to get it and apply it, the senior manager or the board must decide if the product managers are able to properly do their jobs. Here is where product managers might require a little extra coaching.

In a lot of interviews as well as discussions in my workshops, I have often found instances in which product managers just don't have the interest to monitor performance indicators. If you find that some product managers do not have a natural inclination or curiosity about the numbers or KPIs, they need to be motivated to do so. Their managers need to make the time to show them how to review the results and show how the numbers or

KPIs come together—and what they mean. A Product Management leader may also want to assign product managers to work with financial people or other experienced product managers to carry out a variance analysis of an actual indicator against its planned number. Using techniques such as root-cause analysis or related auditing principles may help the product managers develop a better set of analytical skills and improve their overall business acumen. Working with, or experiencing, the fiscal processes with someone coaching or guiding can sometimes be an eye-opener as things begin to make more sense and the bigger picture is revealed.

## INSPIRING PRODUCT MANAGERS TO MAKE INFORMED, FACT-BASED DECISIONS

The success or failure of a product can be linked to good or bad decisions. Therefore, one of the most powerful capabilities that should be cultivated in all product managers, regardless of level, is their ability to uncover data from many sources, analyze the data, and make decisions. To me, managing the product's performance is a *nonnegotiable competency* for product managers. However, going through the process of assembling and analyzing data leads to some big questions like "So what?" or "What should we do?"

When product managers make or contribute to informed, fact-based decisions, they earn empowerment and credibility. When product managers synthesize data from many sources to form conclusions or solve problems, they are seen as contributing positively to the product's business. However, conclusions drawn from data collection and analysis often result in revealing more ideas and opportunities than there are resources to execute. When a situation like this arises, product managers should be able to evaluate the situation and decide what to do. If they do not demonstrate this thought-driven capability, they need to be taught how to make decisions in a structured manner.

I won't say that decisions cannot be made rapidly with minimal data or even a gut feel—provided those who are experienced enough in a given area make the decisions. However, on the whole, those are usually in rare instances.

Managers in any discipline need to verify that their employees can do the work. In the case of product managers, their managers should coach them in the basic techniques of decision making. I'm listing a few of the techniques here with a very brief description of each. If you want to delve more deeply, decision making is discussed in greater detail in Chapter 5 of *The Product Manager's Desk Reference.*

Here are three methods designed to support decisions and provide a degree of perspective and insight into how the problem might be solved:

1. *Combining options:* This technique is easy to use. It considers the complementary characteristics of two alternatives. If product managers are analyzing customer complaints and they find a quality problem, there may be two different solutions. This decision technique allows them to consider the possibility of implementing either or both solutions through the evaluation of resources, marginal costs, and marginal value. After such an analysis, they may find the better solution, or they may find they don't have to choose one over the other and can do both.

2. *Putting options into a morphological box:* This is a simple technique that allows product managers to put an informal structure around a problem to frame possible solutions. It's a great tool to use for coaching product managers when they are challenged to quantify the impact of choices. The morphological box is also a great ideation tool. When you have to prioritize feature possibilities for a product enhancement, you can try to align them around some common themes, such as improving the customer experience or enhancing the product's quality and reliability. Using this technique allows the product managers to group similar features that contribute to the achievement of one or more of those criteria.

3. *Putting options into a decision matrix:* This method provides an added level of structure to the decision-making and problem-solving sequence. A basic decision matrix can be used to classify options according to a variety of criteria. For a new product, the criteria could include strategic value, financial impact, available technology, capable resources, and others. A more complex decision matrix might include weights for any criterion so that collectively, possible product attributes can be evaluated according to the criteria.

Helping product managers make better decisions also means that they need to be able to easily secure relevant and timely facts and data. The suite of data could include information from customer, industry, and competitive research. It could and should include financial data, operational performance metrics, and other KPIs too. The product managers need to be familiar with the data sources, have the ability to evaluate data quality, and be aware of the frequency of evaluation required. It is important for product managers to learn that data should be evaluated both on a fixed interval basis (e.g., when conducting monthly product performance reviews) and on an as-needed basis (e.g., when key performance indicators pass certain thresholds). Not only should data be evaluated but it should also be organized in such a way that the KPIs are prominent visually. Dashboards and scorecards make great tools for this.

The key points of this decision-making section all add up to the fact that Product Management leaders must recognize the need to cultivate this decision-making capability in product managers. When product managers have the facts, data, and ability to analyze that data and ultimately come up with logical, fact-based decisions, they will be more satisfied and more engaged—and Product Management leaders will then feel rewarded because better decisions often lead to better business performance.

## MAKING SURE THAT PRODUCT MANAGERS CAN EFFECTIVELY INFLUENCE AND LEAD OTHERS

In my conversations with executives, they speak as if there is a universally accepted theory that all product managers should be leaders. However, there is also a saying that an army can't have all officers and no soldiers. It is wrong to assume that every product manager can, or even should be, a leader. From your own experience, you have no doubt found that different people demonstrate different degrees of influence and leadership ability. Some are naturals, but that's rare. Any bell curve will show natural leaders are at one end of the curve. Anecdotally, we've found that perhaps 10 to 15 percent of a population of product managers in any one company can influence the right people at the right time to get things done. Roughly, another 33 to 50 percent of the population may possess varying degrees of the raw material and the potential to be better influencers and guides to people in other functions.

Your job (and the job of the Product Management Governance Board, see Chapter 9) is twofold. One is to continue the cultivation of people who demonstrate solid leadership abilities. The other is to identify the potential leaders (the raw talent, so to speak) and cultivate them so that they can be more impactful in the organization. In a broad sense, the managers of product managers (and the Governance Board) must help the potential leaders acquire and improve their leadership skills. Once they have attained these skills, they will be better able to improve their own credibility and effectiveness.

But how do you teach people these skills in order to help them to develop leadership abilities? First, you might refer to Chapter 3 in *The Product Manager's Desk Reference*, "Leadership: Creating Influence," to provide some helpful context. On another level, for the enrichment of high-potential employees, there are external resources that many firms use that serve to cultivate general leadership skills. Perhaps you can tap into those. However, there are some other techniques, explained below, that you can use to stimulate product managers to act in a way that inspires more confidence and earns greater respect from others.

## ENSURE THAT PRODUCT MANAGERS ARE MARKET EXPERTS

Product managers who are market experts actively monitor customer, industry, and competitor data, and they understand what all that information means. Not only do they need to be market experts but they also have to communicate what they know to their team members and managers. They must also get others involved in market-sensing activities. Some product managers lack the initiative to secure the data, and when they don't, they miss opportunities to share this data with those who would benefit. Your job is to *make sure that they know it's their job* to acquire needed data and keep others up to date and furthermore to be relied on as the go-to person, the constant beacon for market insights.

## HELP PRODUCT MANAGERS TO THINK AND ACT STRATEGICALLY

Product managers can earn greater levels of credibility if they are seen as strategic thinkers. Of course, this usually takes native talent, and it may be easier said than done; but its importance means it should not be overlooked. A person who can think strategically knows how to take many different inputs and indicators and weave them together into a story about what it all means for the product, the portfolio, and the company.

This synthesizing skill can be cultivated. One way to do so is to collaborate with the product managers in the creation and maintenance of *periodic strategic product reviews*. This type of review captures all inputs (market, financial, operational, and so on) and establishes a baseline profile that shows the path the product has traveled and where it is currently situated in the market. Leaders can "test" the product managers by asking questions about the product's current situation. These questions might include, "What do you think caused the product's sales to increase during this period?" Or, "Why do you think the gross margin improved during the year?" You might also send them on analytical journeys to speak with other people who work in other business functions. Or better yet, you could show them how to get a couple of people from other functions together for lunch to talk about one or several aspects of the product's business that may require investigation. In this way, you're inspiring them to draw cross-functional team members into conversations that create connections in their own minds.

Ultimately, the true test of leadership for product managers is their ability to set the direction for the product and to gain the confidence of people in other functions to follow. When the product managers get everyone to move in the same direction and the product achieves its envisioned success, then the product managers will have earned their leadership positions.

## CREATING TARGETED DEVELOPMENT PROGRAMS FOR PRODUCT MANAGERS

James Joyce once wrote, "I am tomorrow, or some future day, what I establish today. I am today what I established yesterday or some previous day." There are others who write of the benefit of experience. No doubt, you have your own favorite quotes and your best experiences. These make for great stories that extend your earned wisdom to others. *Many of my best experiences were, in fact, my worst mistakes.* To extend this to another Joyce quote: "A man's errors are his portals of discovery."

Ultimately, it will be the managers of product managers and leaders across organizations who will contribute to the efficacy of Product Management. You will accomplish these strides forward through the targeted development of product managers. In the same way that you wouldn't introduce a product if you didn't know your target market segments, it can be a great benefit to know where the developmental needs of the product managers in your company are and how to cultivate and shape them to allow for the growth that is beneficial to all.

## USING THE PROJECT MANAGER SCORECARD

For targeted developmental programs the best place to start is to use the Product Manager Scorecard. This data-driven approach allows you to identify the most important competencies or characteristics that reflect the needs of the business. You would then use these criteria to assess your product managers for the abilities you seek. It is always helpful to involve the product managers in the process since they will have to do the work. By using the scorecard as the starting point, you can create a targeted developmental strategy for one or for many product managers. Note that there is also a space for developmental projects on the second page of the scorecard.

## CREATING DEVELOPMENTAL PROJECTS

*Developmental projects* are those that consist of structured work activities that are designed to build up a given competency or fortify a behavior. In Chapter 22 of *The Product Manager's Desk Reference*, I supplied a structure for an "applied learning project." I recommend that product managers carry out one or more of these projects during any appraisal period. Further, the managers of the product managers need to agree to the scope, techniques, and practices that will be applied, as well as the anticipated outcomes, and the time frame within which to produce the outcomes.

This project plan will include an employee report that captures what was done, the process followed, the team members involved, the decisions made, and a description of the outcomes. A formal report, written by the product manager, would be required because it would serve as the documented evidence of the work. This report would be validated by having the product manager's managers and perhaps other managers sign off on the report.

Accomplishing the project does not prove that the acquired skill or experience is repeatable, but it's certainly a lot easier to repeat something if it's been done at least once. This evidence is also transportable, just as an artist's work can be transported. That means product managers can use this report to prove that they have actually carried out specific projects. As I have learned from many interviews, an employee's "folder" of work and experience can get lost in the organizational shuffling. Therefore, aside from what is revealed on the curriculum vitae, this evidence can help product managers demonstrate their work.

To undertake the coaching of product managers, one of the challenges that managers of product managers may face is the fact that they may not actually have the experience in a given area. So, yes, even managers should have a scorecard. If there is a development project that requires coaching and the immediate manager isn't equipped to advise the product manager, a *peer referral network* would be the way to go. Such a network should exist (or be created) inside the company to provide go-to managers whom the product managers can turn to for guidance and coaching on a project-by-project basis.

The most important aspect of developmental work programs is that they provide a focus that optimizes the product managers' time in the job. There will always be tactical day-to-day firefights. However, explicit work projects can add a particularly powerful dimension to the product managers' experience.

Different programs can be structured according to where product managers are in the segmentation model. If, for example, the product managers need to have their experience fortified in building customer insights, a learning program could have them plan and carry out a customer visit. Another program might have the product managers play the role of note-taker on a sales call. Or a program could pair the product managers with people in marketing to work on a customer satisfaction survey. There is a wide array of work activities that can be associated with each competency cluster. *A reminder:* It is extremely important (as indicated earlier) to make sure these work projects are accompanied by adequate documentation and evidence that will be kept in a talent management system as well as in the individual employee files.

There are some other types of developmental programs I will summarize as reminders. Before I do so, I want to share a recent experience with you. After carrying out a series of interviews and competency assessments in a company with about 80 product managers, one of the findings was that product managers did not have sufficient financial knowledge, let alone any experience in analyzing key financial indicators. It wasn't surprising because they were formerly operations and IT people whom the organization had shifted to a new structure. The leaders were anxious to address this issue and wanted to contract with me to deliver some basic financial training for the product managers.

What I recommended surprised them! My suggestion was that they identify about 25 percent of those they believed had high potential for leadership—and then have those people attend a local community college. In the first term they were to take a basic accounting class; in the second term, a basic financial management class. The senior manager was taken aback at such a suggestion. He felt that there was no time for the people to take time off from work and that the company could not wait nine months for results. I told him why I made the suggestion: You cannot "inject" accounting and finance in a day or two. To learn this material, you have to learn it from the basics on up—journal entries, balance sheets, ratios, and the like.

However, seeing that it was out of their paradigm to send people to college, I suggested an alternative: Perhaps they could contract with the college for the instructor to come on site for lunchtime or after-work classes, two or three times a week for an hour at a time. Academic programs do serve a purpose, and where there are shortfalls in knowledge, they should be utilized. In fact, they took the advice, and later they thanked me because they realized that the process did not interfere with their work and that the participants were able to digest and, ultimately, use what they learned.

Another time-tested developmental method can also be used, and that is *job rotation*. Think of it as an on-the-job, full- or part-time applied-learning project. Or you can think of it as an internal internship. If the product managers have never worked in a factory and are responsible for a manufactured product, an apprenticeship might include working on a loading dock (if they are physically able), working on a production line, or even counting inventory. If they cannot do this full time, have them spend some time—a day or even a week—in the factory watching and possibly lending a hand in the various processes.

Another experiential activity would be to have product managers sit with call center agents and listen as the agents take orders, resolve complaints, or any other aspect of the customer service process. At one point in my career when I was working in the communications industry and my product was a technician dispatching system, it was helpful for me to go on "truck rolls" where I went with the technicians to see how they did their jobs. Anything you can do that provides another perspective on an aspect of their job will contribute to their experiential perspective. One might think product managers would seek and find such developmental opportunities on their own. However, not every product manager is able to overcome some of the obstacles to initiating these activities. Some don't have an innate enterprising nature; some lack confidence; some don't want to challenge a company culture that discourages this (who can blame them?); and some won't do so because other work tasks may slip. However, I cannot emphasize enough that developmental work should be part of the portfolio of activities undertaken to fortify the pool of product managers.

## SOME GUIDELINES

A few guidelines may help you to ensure that these plans result in successful learning. The first is this: Don't try to do too much at once. Instead, consider working on one or two competencies in a given appraisal period. Think of learning activities as seeds that must take root over time. Another is this: Personal development plans should be linked to the needs of the business in order to reduce skill deficiencies and to meet the individual's personal and professional career goals. There should be *obvious relationships* between the developmental activities and the skill deficiencies. If possible, select developmental activities that improve multiple skills or multiple competencies, and ascertain that the completion of those developmental opportunities will actually improve the needed skills and knowledge. There is no need to limit the scope of these developmental activities to those within your own purview. Therefore, the plan should also include a *combination of developmental activities*. These might embrace a variety of technical skills (related to a product or domain); functional skills (related to a specific competency area); and soft skills (such as team building, negotiating, or facilitating).

# SUMMARY

The Roman philosopher Seneca once said, "As the soil, however rich it may be, cannot be productive without cultivation, so the mind without culture can never produce a good fruit." Wow! Companies that cultivate and shape product managers can expect better human performance and better business results—in other words, better "yields" from investment in human capital.

This endeavor may seem overwhelming, and it does take a lot of effort.

It may not happen in a day, or even a month or a year, but I urge you to think of this as an investment in time and energy that will fine-tune your portfolio of business managers and leaders. By using some of these techniques, you will find out how to improve your staff, remove poor performers, and fine-tune your cast of high-performance product managers. When you have a better "cast" on hand, and a few people as "alternates" (apprentices) who are watching in the "wings" and learning in a purposeful manner, you can't help but stimulate productivity and produce better results.

*Case Study III*

## SPOTLIGHT ON PRODUCT MANAGEMENT EXCELLENCE

# FEDEX SERVICES

*By David K. Payton, Director, U.S. Product Management*

Product managers have one of the most pivotal roles at FedEx. They work shoulder to shoulder with the top executives of FedEx, and they are accountable for the core service areas of FedEx. Product managers occupy a peerless yet critical role at FedEx. While they're accountable for a large part of the operations at the company, they don't have direct control of the separate operating units of FedEx or authority over the managers that run these units. Their role is similar to that of the chiefs of staff who advise the president of the United States—they are the nation's highest-ranking military officers but they have no chain of command that directly reports to them.

So how do product managers influence the operational decisions at FedEx that they see as necessary for success? By providing invaluable counsel about market analytics, product features, and business strategies—in short, by earning a seat at the table.

## FEDEX AT A GLANCE

FedEx provides businesses and consumers, all over the world, with a broad portfolio of transportation, e-commerce, and business services. Under the umbrella of the trusted and respected FedEx brand, the company offers a wide range of transportation services through operating companies that compete collectively and are managed collaboratively. FedEx is led by a unit called the FedEx Corporation, which oversees the operating companies that collectively compete under the FedEx name worldwide: FedEx Express, FedEx Ground, FedEx Freight, FedEx Office, and FedEx Services.

FedEx Services coordinates sales, marketing, information technology, customer service, and worldwide supply chain services support for the global FedEx brand. This includes the Product Management group, which is responsible for managing the transportation service "products" for the FedEx Express and FedEx Ground operating companies. Since they are employees of FedEx Services, the product managers do not wear the same "badge" as those in the operating companies they support.

For this reason, the question arises: How does an individual contributor in one unit of the company effectively influence product-related decisions made by executive management in the independent operating unit of the company that actually performs the service? The answer is that their influence is earned, repeatedly and consistently, by demonstrating market mastery and valuable product expertise and by providing organizational alignment and outstanding results that executive management cannot get anywhere else in the company. This places Product Management at the heart of the enterprise.

## THE PRODUCT MANAGER ROLE

The Product Management group earns credibility with executive management because product managers, first and foremost, expertly demonstrate a mastery of the market. Second, product managers serve as product experts, possessing detailed knowledge of product features. They are frequently called upon by sales executives to determine if existing products can meet unique market or customer requirements. Similarly, IT management seeks guidance from product managers to determine if planned data structure or logic changes related to FedEx transportation services will function properly.

Central to this product expertise, product managers understand the value proposition extended to each market and customer segment, which serves to drive demand for the product. They do this by putting all market dynamics to work to stimulate and maintain the company's competitive advantage, and they are adept at recognizing emergent customer requirements, either as explicitly requested or implicitly understood. For example, during a recent economic downturn, many customers reduced safety stock of their merchandise or critical parts in order to minimize investment in inventory holdings. The FedEx product managers reasoned that when replenishment was needed, it would be needed fast so they took steps to expand the availability of our fastest overnight service. This ran contrary to conventional thinking that during a recession customers would shift to lower-cost transportation services. The results confirmed the product managers' expectations as actual demand for the premium service outpaced the forecast demand multiple times over.

One way in which product managers can fall short is by too narrowly defining product requirements and developing plans to meet the needs of external customers only. Effective product managers at FedEx must also connect their market and customer mastery to that of critical internal stakeholders including the heads of Operations, Sales, Marketing, and IT. They must understand the strategy of the company, the processes and systems that drive the company, the financials, and the objectives of executive decision makers. They must understand how the organizational pieces fit together, which groups and stakeholders perform what roles, and the processes necessary to make things happen.

Because of their breadth of knowledge about customers and competitors, *and* internal capabilities, product managers can interweave the objectives of their product plans with those of the executive team. Done well, the result is truly win-win for all: the customers, the company, the product managers, and the internal stakeholders. The product managers clearly support the goals of the operating company, and the operating company executives become strong advocates for the product goals, as communicated by the product managers. As a result, at FedEx, product managers are sought out for their point of view on strategies, and they become involved with major decisions for the company. Ultimately, product and operating company goals are indistinguishable.

## DETERMINING THE BEST FEEDER AIRCRAFT ROUTES

FedEx Express is the world's largest express transportation company. It provides fast and reliable delivery to every U.S. address as well as to more than

220 countries and territories. To accomplish this, the company uses a global air-and-ground network to speed delivery of time-sensitive shipments—usually in one to two business days—with guaranteed delivery times. The company's fleet of 697 aircraft serves more than 375 airports around the world.

Recently, the FedEx Express officer team developed a list of potential markets for planned deployment of feeder aircraft—small planes used to transport packages to smaller regional markets and connect to larger hub markets. Feeder aircraft can greatly improve service through later pickup times and earlier deliveries to smaller markets, but cost can be a factor.

As the FedEx Express engineering teams worked through flight schedules, network design, and load balancing issues, the Product Management team was asked for an opinion on the viability of the markets being considered. The product managers performed a thorough assessment on the targeted markets, including these areas:

- Economic and business characteristics of the market opportunity
- Identification of potential target customers and industries
- Packaging tendering options, including pickup, drop box availability, and staffed retail locations
- Competitive assessments

The product managers presented their findings along with their recommendation for "go" or "no go" for each of the markets considered. Through the process, they clearly demonstrated mastery of the markets and the customer demand (or lack thereof) for FedEx Express services. Their analysis suggested the presence or absence of the market conditions needed to justify adding feeder aircraft routes to the markets in question. The product managers proved their understanding and support for the FedEx Express executive team's objectives by utilizing critical assets for the most productive return. They thereby reinforced their credibility and earned their seat at the table. The key was their market expertise along with their ability to relate that knowledge to the financial obligations of the operating company.

The FedEx Express Product Management team is now considered a charter member of the regularly scheduled strategy development and planning sessions with the FedEx Express executive team. The FedEx Services Product Management teams that represent the ground transportation and residential services have also followed suit. Executives from the various operating companies also look to Product Management to participate in and to lead strategy development and tactical deployment efforts.

## FOUNDATION FOR THE FUTURE

The detailed market knowledge and organization acumen of the FedEx product managers are also used by other stakeholder groups within FedEx, like Pricing and Forecasting. They discuss and agree on pricing strategies, and they also influence annual revenue business plans and assess long-range outlooks. Moreover, people in the FedEx Product Management group are consistently sought out for their insights by those in the Pricing group when they need guidance on price adjustments. Similarly, the Forecasting group works closely with Product Management to estimate volume projections for the next fiscal year.

This influence and involvement strengthens the internal alignment with senior management in the operating companies and has further solidified Product Management's seat at the table. Providing predictable performance, market mastery, and cross-organizational credibility have helped secure the function of Product Management and a foundation for the future of the product manager at FedEx.

# MODULE IV

# CONTINUITY

All organizations go through changes and transitions. You might think of these changes as parallel to product life cycles with their associated crests and troughs. As mentioned throughout this book, organizations will always seek to fine-tune operations, refine products, and expand into new markets. Since Product Management is not immune, adjustments are also made to resources, processes, and portfolios.

Earlier in the book, I compared Product Management to a jigsaw puzzle where different companies often reassemble the pieces of the Product Management puzzle without a "picture on the box" to follow. The picture of the puzzle is ultimately reconstituted based on leadership's understanding of Product Management itself and what improvements can be expected based on an analogous fine-tuning of this function.

Sometimes, making changes to Product Management can upset the balance that had been attained when prior organizational adjustments took place. At other times, a change might be welcome because it turns out to be for the better. However, in both cases, the ebb and flow of other areas in the organization can actually be counterproductive to the achievement of high-performing Product Management.

As I have explained (perhaps repeatedly!), a shared understanding of the role of Product Management across the organization is of vital necessity; it can go a long way toward ensuring that Product Management is well stabilized—so that it can thrive for the long term.

To this purpose, I've shown you a more ideal version of the picture of Product Management that could be placed on the figurative puzzle box to holistically restructure the organizational puzzle. This picture of Product Management is portrayed as a "framework" that lets you reconstruct your own company's picture. The picture gains greater meaning as you clarify the role and purpose of Product Management. The picture is then put into even better focus so that you can cultivate your portfolio of human assets— the product managers. Now we turn our attention to the last details of the picture to achieve Product Management *continuity*.

Why continuity? Because every time there is an organizational change, leaders choose their players (other executives) and pick their battles (themes and strategies), but often exclude Product Management from consideration. *Continuity*, as I define it, requires the creation of some structures that will ensure that Product Management is more deeply embedded or rooted within the firm so that it can withstand any organizational "tempest."

I will speak to three key *structures* in the three chapters that comprise this module. One relates to the establishment of a community of practice that provides a "shared environment" for product managers. The second serves to fortify an important work structure—the cross-functional product team. The third establishes the governance model for Product Management. These are summarized below:

*Chapter 7. Building a Knowledge-Based Community of Practice for Product Management:* Communities of practice have existed for eons, from times before the craft guilds of the past to the professional networks of the present. The main point is that professional communities contribute to the exchange of knowledge and experience. Many suggest that people who want to perfect their skills in a given profession need to engage with others who encounter similar challenges and situations. This chapter talks specifically to the community of practice that can serve to ensure that product managers, and others with whom they work, have a way to share knowledge, understanding, experience, and insights.

*Chapter 8. Designing and Sponsoring Cross-Functional Product Teams:* Most firms use cross-functional teams to get work done in complex organizations. Often, however, there is confusion between the cross-functional *project* team and the cross-functional *product* team. This chapter provides some insight into the differences between the two types of teams. From there, it goes on to explain, step by step, how senior executives can effectively create an empowered, accountable, highly performing, cross-functional product line (or product portfolio) team. This team serves to synchronize the efforts of all business functions, and it warrants that all business and financial objectives of the product line or portfolio are optimized.

*Chapter 9. Embedding a Governing Model for Sustaining Product Management:* This chapter represents the *apex* of this book. Initially, it provides the justification for a *Product Management Governance Board* to ensure that Product Management can survive for the long term. After explaining the importance of this board, the chapter provides an important tool to help leaders work out the company's current Product Management maturity level and to prioritize some improvements to attain greater maturity. It does this using a 10-point maturity assessment. As the chapter progresses, it lays down explicit instructions for setting up the board and for taking action, over time, to successfully embed this board into the fabric of the firm.

# CHAPTER 7

## BUILDING A KNOWLEDGE-BASED COMMUNITY OF PRACTICE FOR PRODUCT MANAGEMENT

### EXECUTIVE SUMMARY

- Because Product Management is a dynamic, interconnected living system, the firm will benefit greatly from a dynamic, interconnected knowledge-based community of product managers.
- Companies will profit from a vibrant community of product managers who easily transfer explicit *and* tacit knowledge and experience within and across the organization.
- A well-organized Product Management community can enhance creativity, deepen understanding, and sharpen collective problem solving.
- An energetic community of product managers requires tangible support and funding in order to take root and grow inside of the organization.

*Changing the ways professionals work, not installing new computers, is the best way to leverage intellectual capital.*

—ROBERT KELLEY AND JANET CAPLAN,
*harvard business review*

At the conclusion of each of my workshops, I distribute an evaluation form. Aside from the usual ratings, some open-ended questions are posed. One of those is, "What were the most valuable aspects of the workshop?" The most frequently written comments are about how much they valued, and benefited from, the networking and knowledge sharing that took place in the program. They indicated their appreciation of the spirit of *community and fellowship* engendered by the interactions with their peers as they exchanged information and discussed business practices with one another during the workshop. They felt stimulated and enthusiastic about their jobs, and they felt their horizons had broadened.

Here's the problem: What happens when they are back at work? As time dims the effects of the workshop and things go back to the status quo, people revert to their old, reliable routines. Soon they forget the enthusiasm they felt. The net result is that most people do not continue the relationship and network building, especially when they work in different locations.

A couple of years ago, I worked with a very large communications company. The senior vice president of Product Management decided to have a big off-site meeting for his team of 120 product managers. My staff and I facilitated the work of five product line managers so they could deliver showcase presentations to illustrate the positive contributions of their efforts. We also provided some content and facilitated the two-day program. A senior executive cabinet member flew in to give an inspirational talk to the product managers and the Product Management leadership. I was amazed at the enthusiasm, excitement, and passion exhibited by all who participated.

The program was a big success! After the workshop, everyone returned to their respective offices in different cities. People continued to talk about this event for weeks. But as memories faded, enthusiasm evaporated and things went back to normal. As a postscript: In the intervening months, a round of staff reductions was announced due to economic factors. The community that was envisioned was replaced by other work and the needs of the business.

Many companies recognize that some sort of community structure is needed to draw people together and keep everyone in the loop. Their answer is to utilize electronic repositories for posting templates, procedures, and documents. But document sharing and electronic collaboration does not allow for participants to impart the thought process and logic behind what is suggested; they don't capture tacit (instinctual but unstated) knowledge that often emerges when people discuss situational learning, especially when they meet in person. No matter how efficient modern methods of electronic information exchange, the vital *human* element cannot be discounted. We are all social beings, and despite the advantages of technology, there is no really good substitute for person-to-person interactions and communication.

Some companies start initiatives that go beyond electronic document repositories, in the hope of building a Product Management community. Unfortunately, their efforts are dependent on budgets and finances, which often overshadow the potential value of building a durable community.

I am a strong advocate for the establishment of a vibrant Product Management community. Such a community would bring together product managers and those they work with, through mutual collaboration, shared knowledge, and collective experience. These communal processes would go far to help everyone involved build on and improve their competencies and collective cognizance. The value derived from the formation of this type of community cannot be overestimated. However, deciding to build community is one thing. *Continuing and sustaining the community is another.*

As you read this chapter, I hope to give you food for thought about the benefits a knowledge-based Product Management community can bring to a company. Though many product leaders have considered the idea, and many have even made attempts to accomplish it, the bottom line is that it's not uppermost in their thoughts. But it should be. In my opinion, a knowledge-based Product Management community is one of the pieces of genetic material that needs to be spliced onto the organic tissue of every organization.

## WHAT EXACTLY IS A COMMUNITY OF PRACTICE?

Communities of practice are composed of groups of people who share a common set of interests or a common set of roles in an organization. You can compare such communities to market segments that are also composed of people with common needs, interests, or motivations.

Communities of practice are nothing new. They've been around since ancient times. Think back in history to the guilds in the Middle Ages. Each trade craft occupied its own sector or section of a city. This provided a "built-in" community of people with similar interests and strong connections to each other. In more recent times, the garment industry was centered in the "garment district" in New York City, and it was a trade-oriented community. Today, one can walk into a bar or café in the financial district in New York City, London, or Singapore and observe the social interaction among traders or investment bankers. Whether in Medieval times or today, people who work in the same profession like to gather to discuss happenings, pass on information, and catch up on the gossip related to their business. This reinforces the feeling of affiliation and community.

In our global business community, technology has made it possible for people to work anywhere. Unfortunately, this prevents people from working together in person and keeps people, especially those working in Product Management, from building a knowledge-based community.

Communities of practice actually do exist in many parts of an organization. You might have, among others, a community on diversity management, a community on environmental policy, a community of scientists, or a community of innovators. Some communities are formed on a short-term basis to solve a problem. Some groups stay connected over the long term because of common interests, such as R&D, engineering, or marketing. For the most part, communities are voluntary efforts; some can sustain themselves, and others are unable to.

Peter Drucker, the esteemed author and management consultant, has suggested that people who want to perfect their skills in a given profession need to engage with others who encounter similar challenges and situations. Communities fill a need because they help interested individuals accomplish personal and professional goals through the sharing of experiences and the exchange of ideas, and such communities can serve as effective means of improving the function of Product Management.

## THE KNOWLEDGE-BASED PRODUCT MANAGEMENT COMMUNITY OF PRACTICE

The community of practice I suggest for Product Management would utilize some of the tools and techniques described in previous chapters. This Product Management community of practice should serve to ensure that product managers, and others with whom they work, have a way to share knowledge, understanding, experience, and insights.

The value of this community cannot be overestimated because product managers handle all sorts of situations all the time—just as surgeons encounter unexpected situations in the conduct of similar procedures from appendectomies to complex heart surgery. When product managers get together or are brought together, either informally or formally, they take advantage of the opportunities to explain to each other how they handle different situations and problems—and the logic and rationale for what they did. The explanations about what they encountered provide for the *tacit knowledge* exchange that adds tremendous value to what a community can accomplish. In my opinion, a community can and should help capture the vitality of a dynamic base of intellectual assets that can help a company mature in unimagined ways.

*Note:* For reference, the expression *tacit knowledge* refers to the uniquely individual inner-understanding that one develops over time through varied situations and experiences. It may include the generalized knowledge one possesses, but usually is not consciously expressed.

In many topics mentioned throughout this book, I have discussed the changes in the structure and composition of companies that present weighty challenges for Product Management leaders. One of the most rigorous and daunting challenges stems from the vast variations in Product Management practices.

There has also been a serious drain of institutional knowledge and experience, especially in Product Management, as people move into and out of the organization. I recently talked to an executive who led a department of about 60 product managers. Due to an organizational realignment, a portion of his staff was picked up by leaders in other departments—and those product managers took every ounce of institutional knowledge with them! If a Product Management community had been deeply embedded in this firm, the "threads of continuity" brought about by the community could have helped accelerate the time required for recently acquired employees to get up to speed in their new departments.

In general, people participate in communities on a voluntary basis and often because of their level of interest, or even the time available to them. A knowledge-based Product Management community would be different because it would be directly supported by senior leaders. As such, it would exist to bind together the collective experience and tacit knowledge of its members: product managers and Product Management leaders. My recommendation is that senior leaders commit to this community for the long term, a point I will strongly reinforce in Chapter 9.

## THE ANCHORS OF THE PRODUCT MANAGEMENT COMMUNITY

Some of the subjects covered in this book talk to the configuration and function of Product Management. There are also topics that suggest some structured protocols to hire and cultivate product managers. These structural elements are required because they provide for a good foundation—*and a good foundation is important for the anchors of the Product Management community.*

On a recent business trip, I had to stop at a large shopping mall in Texas because I needed a battery for my watch. The size of the mall and the number of anchor tenants amazed me. The anchors were four large department stores, situated at the far ends of the mall. I had to leave my watch for an hour, so I strolled around the mall. Since I am not a shopper by nature, I observed the mall through a more objective lens, which made me feel more like a social anthropologist. The mall had a food court, a small parklike setting, and other "gathering" areas. There were some coffee shops with benches outside where people sat and talked. There was also a playground area for children. At the time, I was in the middle of writing this book, and I knew I would be writing about communities of practice. As I observed the mall in action, I realized how much my visit to that shopping mall influenced my ideas—and how it would contribute to some of the points I wanted to write about.

What I learned from the shopping mall validated some of the concepts I had in mind about the anchors for Product Management communities in any company. These anchors are discussed below.

1. **The Product Management community should have a purpose and a charter.**

   An association's charter serves to establish its mission and purpose. The interesting fact about a Product Management community is that it should be formalized in its purpose, yet somewhat informal in its execution. The exchange of knowledge and experience cannot be dictated and structured. The charter can be treated like a "certificate of enablement." It may also set some rules for leadership participation, for funding requests, or for handling other formalities. The charter should also be as flexible as the community itself, and it should be subject to change and modification as needed.

2. **The Product Management community requires leadership and guidance.**
One might believe that ultimately, the community of product managers ought to be self-motivated and self-driven. If you make this assumption, your community will not survive. Clubs of any sort, whether social or business, need leaders to start them and keep them going. By the same token, a Product Management executive should always be leading the way for the community because someone or some "body" (like the Product Management Governance Board discussed in Chapter 9) should be available for advisement, encouragement, and support. Leaders are the ones who must communicate the benefits from shared learning and understanding to community members. However, leaders cannot merely mouth words of support; they must also demonstrate their belief in these benefits in various ways, some of which are exemplified in this list of anchors. Also, community organizing should not be left to one person. A small core group of people should collectively govern the community and work together to plan events, shape discussions, and document the collective cognizance of the membership. The people in this group should serve staggered terms so that their own collective learning can be perpetuated.

3. **The Product Management community should provide destinations for product managers and other interested people.**
As the shopping mall exemplifies the concept of destination, so should the Product Management community. Many of the firms I work with have wide open plan offices. These have work areas, lounge areas, open kitchens, and many places where informal discussions can take place. The Product Management community, as I envision it, is not built around a conference room or an auditorium, even though these might be used from time to time. The idea is to encourage and inspire interactions.

4. **The Product Management community should have informal and formal events that have themes and activities that inspire structured and ad hoc interaction.**

   Continuing the discussion from the previous item, communities of people often need a reason to get together. All professional associations create events and activities for their members. The events are usually thematic and well planned. While it is highly desirable for the Product Management community to basically be self-guiding, some structure is needed. This means that specific events and activities should be planned far enough in advance to ensure that the product managers can schedule their time.

5. **The Product Management community requires resources and funding.**

   If senior leaders want to fortify the structure of Product Management and establish a community, that community will need money and other resources. This is an important investment with returns that may seem vague and may not materialize quickly. This can seem daunting if you have an organization with dozens or hundreds of product managers, especially when they are located in different geographic areas. However, I urge executives to take a wisely motivated leap of faith and support this endeavor for the long term. Leaders should recognize that foresight and direction of resources that build community become assets that will provide positive returns to the business.

6. **The Product Management community leadership must provide product managers with the perspective that the cornerstones of the community involve sharing, learning, and knowledge building.**

   Eventually, communities of practice do begin to flourish and have some self-directed behaviors. In one company, the director of Product Management gets her team of eight product managers together a couple of times a month for lunch. Each product manager is required to create a topic and then inspire a discussion among the team members. In my former corporate life, I brought product managers together on a monthly basis for product updates and shared learning. I also invited people from other functions from time to time to listen in. It's absolutely vital to keep in mind that you cannot hold these sessions via a conference call. Although it is fortunate that video conferencing is more prevalent and the quality is very good, unfortunately, it still engenders a certain formality and terseness that does not encourage side conversations and other types of sharing that naturally arise when people "hang out" together.

7. **The Product Management community should integrate the knowledge and understanding of professionals from adjacent disciplines to build broad perspectives.**

As communities evolve, they will become more dynamic. Topical discussions will inspire higher levels of curiosity. In such cases, leaders of the Product Management community should ensure that people from other functions or thought leaders from outside the company are brought in from time to time. This integration adds to the perspectives, builds other connective tissue, and encourages networking. If product managers are to learn to think more systemically, then their perspectives need to be broadened. In my earlier working days, our more insightful leaders would bring in outside speakers for half- or full-day events that would help us to learn about other disciplines or techniques. As a result, we grew in our vistas and performance. The point is that leaders who guide the community will also serve as role models for future action. I doubt that I would have been effective as a senior product leader if I had not had the benefit of participating in those coordinated events prior to my advancement.

8. **The Product Management community should utilize Reference Models and Product Management processes as topical guidelines.**

There is a delicate balance between the spark of inspiration for dynamic discourse and the situational use of models and processes. Because Product Management touches so many functions in the organization, it may be helpful for members to have some of these guidelines as topical reference points or simple reminders of important areas. The Product Management Life Cycle Model can serve as one of those references, and all of the guidelines will add to the product managers' core competencies, as mentioned elsewhere in this book.

9. **The Product Management community needs a portfolio of possible activities as a basic framework.**

   Referring to item 8 above, the Reference Model can serve as a helpful guide. Many senior leaders know of and use various types of events and activities to add to the portfolio. Here is a quick reference for those unfamiliar with these techniques:

   a.  Short interactive gatherings called "brown-bag" or "lunch-and-learn" sessions. You can run these at the start of a workday, during lunch time, or even at the end of the day. Have one individual prepare a topic for discussion from any source of interest to him or her, and have that person lead the discussion—but be prepared to facilitate if there are any gaps of silence. These sessions may last from 45 minutes to an hour. It's best to have people face one another instead of lined up at a lunchroom table.

   b.  All-hands meetings are effective in smaller organizations. They can be used where product managers from a product line or those who work in a specific location can gather from time to time. These can be showcase sessions during which a product manager reviews the outcome of a work activity or even a work-in-progress activity. In smaller environments of 10 or so people, all of the participants can talk about what they're doing. However, in larger organizations where there are many more product managers, structure and facilitation are called for. Some interesting topics could include these:

   (1) Use the findings from market research and derived insights as the focus for meetings. One or more presenters could conduct a discussion that identifies what they had set out to do, how they carried out their work, the situations they encountered, and what they learned. I once ran a session like this and asked the audience of 30 or so people: "If you saw what we think we saw, what would you have concluded?" That inspired a very long discussion.

   (2) Have product managers present their product strategy or road map to other product managers at least once a quarter.

   (3) Bring in R&D people to talk about new technologies or other areas in which they are working.

    (4)  Invite a university professor or an author to discuss recent research projects and findings.

c.  Recognition or "product manager appreciation" events can provide a great environment in which to showcase exemplary work. Public recognition can be highly motivating.

d.  Major off-site meetings should be held often enough for the broad product manager population to come together to share practices and successes. These require a tremendous amount of planning and a healthy checkbook. The communications company program described earlier in this chapter was a stellar event.

e.  During tough economic times, costs are under the microscope— but having a small group of people attend a professional association or industry event may be doable. When such a group of people attend these events, they should have an agenda and be required to prepare a report on key findings. Their findings can then be used during a subsequent all-hands meeting.

f.  Have a small group of cross-functional team members carry out a series of customer visits. Equip them with a structured visit plan, align roles and responsibilities, and set them on their journey. After they have returned and digested what they learned, ask them to make a presentation to the community.

g.  Periodically carry out some professional training in areas from which people might benefit, areas that are aligned with or are related to the core Product Management competencies. Make sure that, as with other activities, there is a way for people to share what they have learned with others in the community.

*Important note:* During these events, allow people ample time to "mingle" before and afterward. When they mingle beforehand, they don't know what's coming so they self-generate topics. When you give them time afterward, they have a chance to split off into smaller groups and carry on a host of random discussions—hopefully related to the topic at hand.

Summarizing the discussion this far, I have reviewed the foundational anchors that can be utilized to bring a Product Management community together and to help it take root in the organization.

## WHAT DOES COMMUNITY SUCCESS LOOK LIKE?

Although I advocate for this robust community and recommend senior leadership involvement and funding, the "business me" in my head tells me I must present some evidence for my contentions. It is also necessary to show that there will be tangible returns on the company's investment. This is not a "tale" of various companies' successes achieved from supporting communities. Rather, I am suggesting some ways to rate the gains from supporting communities as I have described. Therefore, here are a few recommendations that may serve to help you calculate and compute some critical success factors.

First, refer to the Product Manager Scorecard in Chapter 6. Look at the second page of the scorecard, where there is a list of product manager attributes and behaviors. Some of these are domain knowledge, technical knowledge, thought leadership, and customer relationships. You can use this list of attributes and make changes to it according to what areas are important for you. The rating scale is based on observed evidence. You can choose to assess product managers at a variety of levels that you believe will determine the degree to which community involvement is contributing to these attributes or behaviors. If you can, keep the scores and check the scorecards over time to look for correlations between improved effectiveness, decision making, and other relevant items.

Leaders can also set the agenda for the community. You can focus on topics or areas that require greater improvement. For example, if you are guiding a product manager in an applied-learning project (again, see Chapter 6), have that product manager work with others on the selected project. Upon completion, have the product manager facilitate an all-hands meeting to reveal what was done, how, and why—and then initiate a discussion about it, and perhaps even some debate. As a leader and a coach, you can do this one-on-one, or guide the product manager and a few peers into a working session to review the progress of the program and review what would be discussed at the upcoming all-hands meeting. The point is that you, as a leader who wants to see growth in a given competency, can guide the work of individual community members and inspire the knowledge sharing from those projects.

You may find that some people are reluctant to join in: they have another meeting, or they are just too busy. However, if you make the meetings mandatory, insist that people turn off their portable devices, and have them sign in, you will ensure maximum attendance and therefore exposure. You can also meet with individuals afterward, in a very informal or casual way. Ask open-ended questions to gauge the degree of engagement and mindfulness. For example, you can ask: "What did you think of the meeting today?" "Did you agree with their position?" "What would you have done?" As a leader who believes in community building and its results, this follow-up not only gives you a read on what people are taking away but it also allows you to get in on the discussion!

Documented evidence on centralized systems can be used to some extent. If a product manager wants to conduct an online presentation or meeting, using videos to record discussions or interactions can help. The presentation and the voiced interactions of all participants can be recorded. Managers can monitor the number of views and check in with others to determine the effectiveness of these programs. Video cameras are very inexpensive. Set one up in a conference room, and create a situation in which one product manager is being interviewed by others on his or her team with respect to a product strategy, an upcoming launch, or some key performance measures. A 20- or 30-minute video can be uploaded to the central Product Management community website for others in different regions to view.

Another area of evidence is where product managers establish a position of thought leadership. Writing articles, conducting research, and speaking at events are effective techniques and should be rewarded to encourage more of this behavior—if warranted, and as authorized.

Not all product managers have the interest or ability to serve as thought leaders. In a recent interview with 28 directors, senior directors, and vice presidents in a large multinational organization, I asked them what they thought about their roles as thought leaders. Only one of them acknowledged the importance of doing this work; but he then added that though it was a worthy cause, he didn't have any time for it. Generally speaking, I think this area deserves some additional discussion by senior executives about how it might contribute to efforts to build community while *positively* expanding the firm's exposure.

Leaders can set up any number of metrics, such as the number of meetings or presentations held or the number of website views by others. You can also use different types of surveys to check in with other stakeholders across the organization and then read the results to the leadership of the Product Management community.

Each organization's approach to success may differ in the execution, but it is possible to establish scorecards and measurements in order to check if certain methods work better than others, as well as to correlate the findings to impacts on the business.

## SUMMARY

The Product Management community of practice should be an ongoing element of any organizational strategy. In other areas unrelated to Product Management, communities of practice are catalyzed and perpetuated in a fluid, dynamic, unplanned manner. They are held together by their members' passionate interest in learning and sharing. The benefits of this type of approach cannot be disputed.

I acknowledge that setting up a community of practice is a complex challenge for senior leaders. Nevertheless, product managers are some of the most important knowledge workers in any organization. They usually work in hurried, high-pressure environments, and they are often scattered across many locations. Their day-to-day work lives are often unpredictable and stressful. So I reiterate that it is definitely worth it to confront the difficulties inherent in establishing communities of practice because they are needed and important.

Within the context I've provided in this chapter, a robust Product Management community *can* take root and thrive. While other types of information repositories can contribute to institutional efficiency, they cannot capture knowledge, logic, and lessons learned. That can happen only when product managers and other stakeholders talk to one another in both formal and informal sessions.

Leaders must recognize that when product managers share information and tacit knowledge, they build a neural network inside the organization. This knowledge network can contribute greatly to corporate success and competitiveness—if you have the stamina, patience, and budget to build it.

CHAPTER 8

# DESIGNING AND SPONSORING CROSS-FUNCTIONAL PRODUCT TEAMS

**EXECUTIVE SUMMARY**

- A cross-functional product team should be thought of as a "board of directors" for a product line and should be designed as a microcosm of the cross-functional senior executive team.
- Cross-functional product teams should be held accountable for the performance and contribution of the product or product line.
- Members of a cross-functional product team should dedicate their loyalty to the product team, not to the function they represent.

*No one can whistle a symphony; it takes an orchestra to play it.*
—REVEREND HALFORD E. LUCCOCK

Cross-functional teams are the norm, whether a company is organized by product lines, functions, or geographies. There is probably no other corporate structure that is as efficient at getting work done. However, there is a misnomer here, and I want to clarify and define some terms. The teams may be called cross-functional *product* teams, but they are usually organized and utilized as *project* teams. When it comes to product *development*—versus Product *Management*—the common practice is that people from other functions work together in various capacities as products are planned, developed, and launched. These are cross-functional *project* teams.

In cross-functional *project* teams, resources are dedicated to the team only for the duration of the project. When the project is completed, *the team is usually disbanded*, and the participants are assigned to other projects. This is the business-as-usual model for most people who work in today's companies. Despite any issues that emerge in terms of role alignment, responsibilities, and deliverables, this structure remains workable and relevant. But these teams should not be classified as *product* teams.

*Product teams are different.* They are microcosms of cross-functional executive leadership teams. The product team is in place for the life of the product. Their members are responsible for the performance of a product or product line. Product teams *don't disband because any one project is over.* The only reason a product team would be dissolved is if a product line is discontinued or withdrawn from the market. As an example of the longevity of a product team, some years ago, our AT&T Product Management task force benchmarked a military aircraft manufacturer. Those we interviewed told us the product team for one of the fighter jets was still in place after 30 years!

As is true for products and organizations, product teams need an end-state model. This chapter speaks to the design of the cross-functional product team as an engine that can support and propel the structure of Product Management.

However, before discussing the structure of the team and how it should be chartered, we need to examine some issues and sources of inefficiency in team performance. You are probably familiar with most of them, but a quick review can highlight some important areas of concern.

## SOURCES OF INEFFICIENCY

Patrick Lencioni, in his book *The Five Dysfunctions of a Team*, lists five areas of dysfunction: absence of trust, fear of conflict, lack of commitment, avoidance of accountability, and inattention to results. Beyond Lencioni's dysfunctions, there are four other issues that have been uncovered during the course of my company's research. These are listed below:

1.  Too often, team members say yes to everyone and act as if everything is OK and they can do everything they're asked to do. This happens because they don't possess the skill and know-how

to do all that was set forth. They're afraid of retribution if they say no, and they fear that management may think they aren't team players. In interviews with our company, some product managers have stated they are too anxious to push back and discuss the responsibilities outlined because they are afraid their employment will be jeopardized.

2.  People who work on teams are frequently challenged when it comes to the prioritization (or the reprioritization) of the many activities and tasks in their work. This may happen because there isn't enough data or the decision authority of the team leader is unclear.

3.  People who work on teams often misuse or misinterpret processes, or they simply don't pay attention to mandated processes. This may be in conflict with management directives, but the product managers feel that some of these processes add more layers of rigidity and are therefore too time-consuming, in the face of all the things they must do every day. Such lack of attention to processes can *expose the company to unnecessary market risks*.

4.  It's no surprise that there is much confusion about roles and responsibilities of team members. Often, people who work in different functions have to fill in for activities that should be done elsewhere. In my own experience and in my firm's organizational diagnostics, we have found that product managers often end up being the recipients of all the work that wasn't anticipated and planned for, or that was originally assigned to others. In plain words, product managers end up as the dumping ground of work that no one can or wants to do.

When we audit cross-functional team performance (regardless of its designation as "product" or "project" team) and explore some of the root causes for existing problems, we find many common elements. These include a lack of clarity in the following areas:

1.  Strategy and objectives
2.  Desired outcomes that are linked to the objectives

3. Explicitly defined roles of people in various business functions
4. Activities to be performed by people in those roles
5. Interdependencies, hand-offs, and synchronization of work between people in different functions
6. Decision-making authority
7. Rules for escalation and alerting management to problems
8. Consequences for not meeting objectives

I encounter one or more of these issues far more frequently than I would like to see. The motivation behind my mission is that we must find a viable way to reach a common understanding between executive leaders who delegate team participants and the team participants themselves.

Bruce Tuckman's stages of team development can serve as a good reference. The four stages are *forming, storming, norming,* and *performing.* When team members get to work together for some time and start to operate in the latter two stages, they begin to mesh in a way that seems to dispel some of the usual problems. The problem is that in most companies I work with, cross-functional teams tend to have higher rates of transition and team member turnover. This also applies to the teams' leadership. Because these conditions occur, the teams move back and forth across the stages of team development. The consequence is subpar performance, so that product quality may actually suffer.

## THE CROSS-FUNCTIONAL PRODUCT TEAM DEFINED

The cross-functional product team can be a remarkably effective work structure in any company. Think of it this way: The senior leadership team is a cross-functional entity in and of itself. That leadership team is accountable for optimizing and executing all aspects of the organization to fulfill the firm's strategic intent. Therefore, it must do the following:

1. Synchronize the efforts of all business functions, product groups, and geographic divisions.
2. Ensure that all groups are operating efficiently.
3. Warrant that the financial and business objectives are fulfilled.

4.   Provide for the appropriate level of governance consistent with the corporation's charter and other rules that may be required.

Picture this: What if the senior executive leadership team agreed to delegate and sponsor an empowered (and very capable) group of employees to be formed as a reflection of their own structure? What if the people on this team were assigned by their functional leaders to work together *and to be primarily loyal to the team, not to their function?* What if this team were held accountable for the performance of the product?

That is the idea behind the *cross-functional product team.* A cross-functional product team is a formally chartered and sponsored work group (think "self-contained community") composed of individuals from each of the different functions. This team reflects the characteristic of a mini-business or business-within-a-business. In a way, it operates like the board of directors for a product line. As envisioned, this is a highly functional business team that serves to integrate and orchestrate activities across business functions in a seamless manner in order to achieve the firm's strategic intent.

Many important benefits can accrue to the firm if this type of team is effectively deployed:

- It facilitates cross-team and cross-organization communication. Instead of disconnected pairwise conversations, everyone is brought into the same conversation.
- It facilitates dynamic market contacts and customer interactions that foster greater levels of market insight.
- It speeds decision making because the team's structure obviates the need to ask permission from executives. Therefore, it removes *some* corporate overheads.
- The team structure is dedicated to the product line's business, so the team can be flexible in adapting to changing situations, providing a degree of market agility and rapid response that might not otherwise be achieved in a standard matrix team.

In order for a cross-functional product team to function effectively, it should be chartered and sponsored based on these eight criteria:

1. A cross-functional product team needs to have a *delegated leader*. This would most likely be the product line manager or director. The most important requirement for these leaders is that they be sufficiently knowledgeable, experienced, and influential and that they have established credibility and good working relationships with their peers.

2. The senior leadership team agrees to designate a person from each individual business function to act as the representative of that function on the product team. Each team member is empowered with the authority to act on behalf of the business function he or she represents.

3. This team should be allowed a *considerable amount of sovereignty* for carrying out its work and contributing to the business impact of the product portfolio. It can achieve the desired results because its members are collectively accountable for those results. The team is also motivated because it is compensated for achieving those results.

4. The team should be virtually *self-governing*. The team's members should be able to clearly align their roles and purpose based on a common, agreed-upon set of objectives. Further, they should be able to comprehend and articulate the interdependencies between each other's function. This would ensure that their own organizations have the capabilities to meet a particular function's commitment to the team. However, despite its relative independence, the team members can only function properly if they are supported and sponsored by their leaders who work together on a Product Management Governance Board (see Chapter 9). This sponsorship is vital to the ongoing institutionalization of key practices and methods such that the organization, as a whole, can mature over time.

5. The cross-functional product team should, at a minimum, be *chartered to operate at the product line level*. It could also be organized at a level that consolidates similar product lines or a small portfolio. It may not be practical or feasible to charter a formal team like this for a single product. One reason is that possible conflicts might emerge in the utilization of other

functional resources. Another reason is that executives might not delegate complete accountability for the product's performance to a team at that level. If you were working in a start-up company with 10 employees and a single product, you would have what would be equivalent to a cross-functional product team.

6. The cross-functional product team is responsible for specific—and measurable—contributions to the firm. The metrics should be quite straightforward: revenue, gross margin, controllable costs and expenses, and market share. Key performance indicators (KPIs) specific to the product's position in the portfolio and in the market should be assigned by the senior leadership team.

7. The team members' compensation must be tied to agreed-upon performance indicators because of the level of risk and exposure they may undertake. In some companies where this structure is utilized, the team members receive tiered bonuses that are tied to achievement of revenue, profit, and market share targets. I have also seen instances where team members put a portion of their salary at risk (e.g., 10 or 20 percent). In these cases, the team members make back their money if they have met their performance targets. Furthermore, they can earn larger bonuses based on agreed-upon revenue and profit thresholds. Suffice it to say that common metrics and financial rewards can be powerful motivators.

8. The cross-functional product team *should stay together across the entire life cycle of all the products within their scope of accountability.* This is very important because (a) it allows the team to maintain a high degree of familiarity with the product line, and (b) it supports the cultivation of quality, long-lasting relationships between the team members. The longer that teams stay in place, the more efficiently and effectively they perform. This can be especially helpful when it comes to the allocation of investments across products within the line. Of course, as time goes on, there will be changes in team membership. From time to time, the senior leadership team and the members of the cross-functional product team should discuss succession plans for members of this team.

In some companies, the product manager is the person held accountable for the product's financial and market results. In such situations, the product manager has a small cadre of functional representatives that work on the team, but the loyalty of these functional representatives remains with their function. This kind of *informal product team* does not fit the eight criteria described above.

In order to avoid any potential conflicts, you might need to reconsider team nomenclature and make distinctions between casual references to a cross-functional product team and the "product line leadership team" that I refer to as the "cross-functional product team." How you name the entities is the option of your management, but keep in mind that consistency and common understanding of the definitions of the nomenclature are very important when referring to, and differentiating among, the teams in your company.

## ENABLING THE CROSS-FUNCTIONAL PRODUCT TEAM TO EARN EMPOWERMENT

There are some additional principles to be considered, aside from the preceding list of eight criteria. The additional principles are vital to the success of the product teams, and your leadership must pay attention to them as well.

Many authors and academics have written works dealing with keeping teams focused on the mission, establishing expectations for them, and providing clear guidelines to them. Those are all very important, but, in my opinion, *mere empowerment does not guarantee success*. The achievement of genuine success for cross-functional product teams requires an even more comprehensive approach. The team must *earn empowerment* through its actions and outcomes. Earned empowerment has a better chance of being fully realized if these suggestions are followed in establishing the teams:

- Select the right people.
- Delegate authority so the team can make decisions.
- Provide the ability to draw on, and direct resources.
- Link actions and outcomes with the goals set by the Product Management Governance Board.

- Furnish tools and systems to ensure that performance targets are met.

## SELECT THE RIGHT PEOPLE

Evaluate those who will be part of this team through the use of the same selection techniques used to hire or select product managers: interviews, demonstrated expertise in core competencies, credibility, and skills in communicating and engaging with others. In addition, they should have an excellent record, superior knowledge, and experience regarding their own functional discipline. When you appoint the product team *leader*, select someone with sufficient maturity and the depth and breadth of experience to lead a team of knowledgeable functional experts. To help you choose the best person to lead the team, use the Product Manager Scorecard located in Chapter 6. In *The Product Manager's Desk Reference*, the ideal composition of the team was suggested as follows:

- *Core team members*: These members are fully accountable for the business and financial results of the product line. For most organizations, a core team would include a *product team leader* plus five to eight other people who would originate from Finance, Marketing, Operations, Development (Engineering, IT, or other as relevant for your firm), Service, Supply Chain, and Sales.
- *Extended team members:* These individuals are appointed delegates from the core business functions who may play a vital role in communications to individual contributors or project work group members. They might also be involved in the direct supervision of "product projects" within their functions.
- *Advisory team members:* These participants are usually those who represent shared service functions and are engaged on an as-needed basis. These may include Legal, Regulatory, Compliance, Human Resources Management, Corporate Training, Facilities, Alliances, Intellectual Property, Field Operations, Process or Quality Improvement, and others who may be peripherally important in your firm or industry.

## DELEGATE AUTHORITY SO THE TEAM CAN MAKE DECISIONS

The delegation of authority enables the team members to fulfill the team's objectives by making their own decisions, with a minimum number of interventions by or escalations to senior leadership. Since this is a sensitive process, allocating empowerment will likely be a gradual process, with leaders keeping in mind that the team's credibility should be *earned* based on the types of decisions that are made and the outcomes produced. When team members do not have enough valid data on which to base their conclusions, their decisions may not be given the type of consideration required. This is why the use of relevant decision criteria is so important (as mentioned also in Chapter 6).

As I indicated earlier, the delegation of empowerment can be a challenge, especially in large, complex organizations. It is important for leaders to understand how a cross-functional product team makes decisions. Who is responsible to make the final decisions on important matters can have a profound impact on the performance of the team and the goals it achieves—and ultimately, the credibility they earn.

One last point on the topic of decisions may deserve some consideration. Some teams may find themselves with differing priorities, which can lead to team tension and conflict. Therefore, team members must be adequately coached and guided in order to work through these differences. In our research, we have found that many people who know these guidance techniques still find it difficult to facilitate a discussion when there are many individual "axes to grind." Senior leaders should be aware of problems like these and maintain an open channel of communication to make it acceptable to escalate to them (senior leaders) and to ask for help without fear.

## PROVIDE THE ABILITY TO DRAW ON AND DIRECT RESOURCES

Because of the autonomy sanctioned by the senior leadership team or the Product Management Governance Board, leaders on the cross-functional product team should be able to utilize and deploy resources that are consistent with objectives and aligned with key decisions. This can be a challenge for a newly established cross-functional product team, particularly if this work structure has not been utilized previously.

One of the ways that will allow the team to deal with this issue would be to create a "required resources and skills guideline." This would serve to document the process that the team (and others) could use to precisely iden-tify the capabilities they need, and for how long. The company should use some type of resource database or the talent management system to provide a comprehensive view of resource availability such that access to those (shared) resources can be made less complex. Another option would be that the cross-functional product team leaders engage their *extended* team members and have them review project profiles to identify important roles, responsibilities, and interdependencies. They should be able to judge whether the case for funds has been made, and further, whether those team members' recommendations should be given extra consideration and weight.

The Functional Support Plan (FSP) as identified in Chapter 2 of *The Product Manger's Desk Reference* can serve as a powerful planning tool in this regard. As defined, FSPs represent the *commitments by each business function to the cross-functional product team.* They also serve as a primary mechanism for communicating between the various functional organizations and the product team. These plans describe the activities to be completed and the deliverables, schedules (project plans), resources, and budgets. FSPs are used during the phases of new product development, as the product moves through the market, across the entire life cycle.

## LINK ACTIONS AND OUTCOMES WITH THE GOALS SET BY THE PRODUCT MANAGEMENT GOVERNANCE BOARD

The Governance Board will likely sponsor more than one cross-functional product team. Therefore, it's important that the board's goals be clearly understood by the people assigned or delegated to these product teams. This may include methods to manage product line performance, the support of communities of practice, use of supplied systems or data, or the proper utilization of the phase gate product development process. Not all of the members may work for the board, but the leader of the product team, in effect, does. Therefore, the leader of the product team must ensure that all participants are aligned and that outcomes are formally reported to the board.

## FURNISH TOOLS AND SYSTEMS TO ENSURE THAT PERFORMANCE TARGETS ARE MET

The best way to determine whether goals will be achieved is through actively managing the product's business and market performance. Therefore, the cross-functional product team needs a solid suite of data to guide its work. Timely financial data, market insights, and other key performance indicators should be made available on a constantly updated and consistent basis. These systems and tools should enable rapid analyses of performance-versus-plan and call attention to associated variances or anomalies. They should also support rapid responses and remedial action as required. In some cases, the chart of accounts in the general ledger may require some adjusting in order to provide the visible insights into the product's financial performance. Also, *be sure that the allocation formulas for overheads are as accurate as they can be.* Product lines may seem to have performed well prior to figuring in these allocations; however, if the allocation algorithms are not properly aligned, an audit may indicate that the products are unprofitable.

## ACHIEVING SUCCESS

Applying the idea of community building in Chapter 7, you can say a cross-functional product team is, in actuality, a small community composed of professionals from different functions who come together for the purpose of managing the product's business. Here are some additional recommendations to consider in order to successfully embed the structure of the cross-functional product team within in your firm:

1.  *Start small.* Start by creating one cross-functional product team—consider it a pilot program. This will help you to work through the protocols to establish this entity, monitor progress, maintain relationships, and review situations as they arise. I recommend "overcommunication" between the senior leadership team (or Product Management Governance Board) and the delegated members. It is better to err by communicating more, rather than less, and it is vital in setting the stage for success. As the senior leadership team (or the board) finds they have to let go of some of their accustomed decision making, they may not be totally comfortable with the experience. But since it is a *pilot program,* they should not feel too much has been taken away. The cross-functional product team members themselves will also encounter

challenges as they clamber for their footing and then begin to feel more comfortable in their new role.

2. *Take good notes.* It will be very helpful if the team utilizes the Product Master Plan as outlined in Chapter 2 of *The Product Manager's Desk Reference* for guidance. This is a vital, unifying plan that shows how to record everything related to the product or product line for which this team is responsible.

3. *Provide resources.* Before embarking on the program at all, the resources must be allotted and budgeted. The lack of sufficient resources may hobble the performance of the team. However, once the finances are in place, senior leaders will enable the cross-functional product team to effectively deploy resources.

4. *Set performance targets.* All team members must understand the objectives, their required contributions, and the rewards they'll receive for positive contributions to business results.

5. *Guide and coach.* The leaders involved should offer support and facilitation so that the team is given every chance to be successful. However, keep in mind that micromanagement is counterproductive.

6. *Use genetic splicing.* Once teams establish their credibility, consider the assignment of extended team members. This will allow others who work for the functional team leaders to learn from the team building process. It will also move things forward toward setting up the next team. Remember, since you need to build small victories over a period of time, it's not advisable to do a mass rollout of cross-functional product teams across the organization, even after you get the first one right. The reason this "go slow" approach is important is because this work structure takes time to deploy and to deliver results. Also, replication requires adequate, capable resources, and oversight— which may be in short supply in some organizations.

7. *Facilitate collective cognizance.* In Chapter 4, I suggested an approach to institutional learning that utilized this expression. The cross-functional product team can help foster ongoing improvements in knowledge and experience sharing to bring about the collective cognizance required to support team growth

and development. Also, you can use some of the techniques to
bring this about that I outlined in Chapter 7.

8.  *Be provocative.* This team may exhibit risk-averse behaviors in
    order to keep things moving along while avoiding the possibility
    of doing poorly. However, this pilot team exists to explore new
    opportunities and expand business, not to maintain the status
    quo. Attitudes toward risk in your own company's culture may
    also influence the team members. If warranted, it may be a good
    idea to push the team out of their comfort zones.

## VALIDATING THE TEAM'S DESIGN AND MONITORING THE TEAM'S PERFORMANCE

It's not enough to designate a pilot team and then watch for results. You
need to validate the criteria used to establish the team in the first place.
From time to time, the team's design should be tested against the original
set of criteria, as well as other measures of team performance. Consider
using a product team scorecard that would serve to evaluate some or all of
the following factors:

1.  The performance of the team leader
2.  The performance of the delegated core team members
3.  The effectiveness of the team's governance structure
4.  The degree of influence the team exerts to produce agreed-upon
    outcomes
5.  The actual business results they achieve
6.  The techniques they use to keep the sponsoring leadership team
    appraised
7.  The reported success of cross-team member interactions and
    collaboration
8.  The efficiency and speed with which they make good decisions
9.  The knowledge and experience they cultivate in people within the
    functions they represent
10. The team's effectiveness demonstrated by how they
    communicate, horizontally and vertically

11.   The degree to which they are recognized and respected by others in the organization

12.   The outcomes that derive from process improvements and the efficiencies they bring about (via task forces and study groups chartered by the cross-functional product team)

As the team progresses, your leadership team or the Product Management Governance Board will also develop suitable and reliable team monitoring tools. Further, as the team evolves, senior leadership may be alerted to other issues or challenges. The cross-functional product team, as an extension of the senior leadership team, becomes a microscope through which some of these issues may be observed and identified. For example, if the team makes poor decisions, it may signal that they are missing important insights. If the team does not pay enough attention to financial information, it may mean that their focus is on other urgent issues and they are therefore neglecting vital indicators. It may also mean that they do not have the analytical resources required to keep them informed. Another area to pay attention to is whether the team is focused on the product's business or on the team members' functional agendas. You will also want to make sure that the team provides timely reports, feedback, and other information required as evidence that the team is fulfilling its obligations.

## ESTABLISHING METHODS FOR ESCALATION AND PROBLEM RESOLUTION

The leadership team or Product Management Governance Board that charters and sponsors the cross-functional product team must have a way for difficult issues to be surfaced and communicated to senior leadership if all avenues for resolution are exhausted. The team charter may have some basic rules—for example, customer issues require immediate attention, as do competitive challenges, and major technical problems.

Unfortunately, it is impossible to plan for unforeseen events. Therefore, senior leaders and cross-functional product team leads should, in their routine reviews, establish some indicators to signal "problems ahead." Also, there needs to be a "hotline" to the sponsoring leadership team functional leader, or even to the CEO.

On the brighter side, as the product team members gain greater levels of experience and they handle (and document!) problem occurrences, precedents will accrue that will help them more effectively navigate the new problems they come across in uncharted waters.

## ACKNOWLEDGING DIFFERENCES

Many cross-functional product teams will likely have product lines that span many geographic areas in one country or multiple countries. Also, the team may be made up of people from various national and cultural origins. Therefore, team members will need to develop a healthy respect for each other's cultures, values, and norms. Recognizing the various aspects of diversity among cultures is one thing. Learning how to adapt can be quite a challenge.

Team members can be directed to check out articles, books, or information online to broaden their outlook. They should also check your company's guidelines (if they exist). Traveling to those areas with some degree of regularity is also important. Furthermore, it's not just about your team. If you have a geographically and culturally diverse team, chances are you have culturally diverse customers. Therefore, while providing guidance to their sponsored cross-functional product teams, senior leaders should establish the framework for the team to build awareness and knowledge of, and sensitivity to, people in different cultural environments.

Years ago, as I moved into higher levels of corporate management, I participated in a workshop called "Managing Cultural Diversity." Although I had some prior international experience, following the workshop, I felt further enriched. Better yet, years later, I found that what I had learned at the workshop stayed with me, and it was of great help when one of my clients asked me to conduct a workshop in China. Here's some of the "homework" we did in order to accommodate a different culture:

First, we met with several company people who were familiar with the participants in our workshop. They helped us devise the seating charts based on the criteria of language strength and product groups. We were careful to learn how to establish relationships at the outset of the program, based on cultural traditions and the human need to communicate, even with relative strangers. One of the things we did was to set up a large map of China in front of the room.

Then, at the start of the workshop, all participants introduced themselves, and they showed us the villages they came from on the map. They talked about their families and the local foods of their home regions. People whose English was less than perfect were helped by others so that they felt included. We established a close camaraderie that extended over the three days we were together. The introductions helped us adapt and work together more effectively. This story proves the point that cross-functional product team members should develop the skills needed to navigate an increasingly diverse and interesting business landscape.

## SUMMARY

The concept of the cross-functional team is not unfamiliar to companies. Such teams are used all the time, and we know they can be highly effective. However, running the business of the product requires a different level of governance. While senior leadership teams generally guide cross-functional groups to work on "product projects," they do not typically charter a cross-functional product team that operates as an autonomous business team.

The team structure defined in this chapter is logical and reasonable. The challenge is to have a cross-functional senior leadership team (or a Product Management Governance Board) that will charter and sponsor this work structure inside the organization. Smaller companies do this without even thinking about it. Consider a start-up firm or one that has moved to the next level after the start-up phase. In this model, the CEO serves as the "product line manager," and the rest of the people from the functions work collectively on behalf of the products. If such a structure works in this context, there should not be any reasons why it cannot be adapted to work in a larger, more complex enterprise.

We all know that there are politics and agendas, and those will probably never go away. However, when it can be posited that such a team might improve the bottom line, we might be able to convince forward-looking people to give it a chance. One way we can build organizational confidence is by trying this entrepreneurial approach in a limited manner. This team can be nurtured over time and "fed" with support and guidance from senior leaders. Once you get it right the first time, you can do it one more time—not with a big reorganization but just one more (and then perhaps another . . .). Go for the small victories, and revel in the success. Imagine how empowered people (in their own mini-businesses) will feel when they can strategize, plan, execute, and manage the products in their product lines—and deliver the results you demand. It's worth a try! And it just might work.

Steve Jobs once made a memorable comment. He said, "Let's make a dent in the universe." For me, innovation doesn't happen just by making cool products. Sometimes you have to innovate in the organization first before you see some of the cool innovations that may actually emerge from a properly chartered and sponsored cross-functional product team. Let's make a dent in the universe of the organization and build that team!

# CHAPTER 9

# EMBEDDING A GOVERNING MODEL FOR SUSTAINING PRODUCT MANAGEMENT

**EXECUTIVE SUMMARY**

- A vital Product Management Governance Board should be established by senior leadership and appointed to oversee the function of Product Management for as long as the firm is in business.
- An effective Product Management Governance Board works seamlessly with the senior leadership team to ensure that the function of Product Management survives for the long term.
- Under the guidance and leadership of a Product Management Governance Board, vital Product Management processes can be frequently examined and optimized.

*To be successful, you have to have your heart in your business, and your business in your heart.*

—THOMAS WATSON, SR.,
FORMER PRESIDENT OF IBM

When I was planning the content for this chapter on governance, I looked up *govern* in the dictionary. The verb *to govern* has its roots in the Latin *gubernare*, which means to steer or guide or "pilot a ship." The implication is that somebody or *some body* should be steering from a point or position of authority.

Most corporate business models include some form of governance.

Publicly traded companies are required by law to have some type of governing body—usually the board of directors. Corporate charters typically spell out the nature of the governing model and its protocols. In the same way that the board of directors serves to guide the company, so should a proper, chartered governing body guide the function of Product Management.

A firmly entrenched and chartered governing board for Product Management can help an organization achieve its broad business objectives through the following:

1. Focusing on high-performance products and product portfolios
2. Maintaining an able, knowledgeable staff of product managers
3. Enabling Product Management through effectively utilized processes
4. Supervising systems and tools used to monitor the performance of portfolios, people, and processes

As in any model where governance is required, bylaws, rules, and behaviors need to be identified and agreed upon. This can be achieved by precisely spelling out policies and procedures, processes and methods, protocols, and general rules of engagement. There are two additional key provisos to be considered when the board is established:

1. This board (and by extension, the bylaws and charter) should be flexible enough to adapt to situations or cases that arise over time. These cases and situations will create precedents that will add to or adjust the bylaws or charter so that successive leadership administrations do not have to reinvent the wheel (Chapter 1).
2. The formation of the board should be treated as an *ongoing transition*—not as a single change management initiative. Organizational change and development require the *gradual building* of specific competencies and capacities so that the initiative builds the best foundation that can achieve the envisioned end state. Refer to Chapter 2 so you can review the discussion of the Product Management Organization Master Plan and how it should serve as the repository in which the charter and bylaws for Product Management (and the Product Management Governance Board) are archived.

With this context in place, this chapter will focus on building a solid, durable framework for governing and sustaining Product Management: the Product Management Governance Board, or from now on, "the board."

## LEADERS NEEDED

Many of the recommendations in this book rely on some accepted "givens." The most important is that actions are catalyzed by leaders. About the time I started this book, my company did some research that looked at Product Management from the perspective of both leaders and product managers. What we found confirmed what we have encountered all along. There are many gaps between what *leaders say* and what *product managers see*. Without speaking to the actual details of the gaps, the bottom line is that product managers and their teams need clarity of purpose, and their teams look to leaders for guidance about this. Put another way, *product managers want to know what's expected, how they will be evaluated, and how their bosses will support and help them.*

To achieve this, a Product Management Governance Board is needed. Such a board should be sponsored by a cross-functional executive team as either an independent body or a subcommittee. For this board to be most effective, there are two important prerequisites:

1. Acknowledgment from the executive leadership team that an effective structure of Product Management is required for the company to be successful
2. A thorough and comprehensive understanding of Product Management

## WORKING IN DISHARMONY

According to Partick Lencioni, author of *The Five Dysfunctions of a Team*, and in referencing the works of other well-respected authors and academics, when cross-functional executive teams are *not* completely aligned, they don't act in harmony. Such lack of alignment results in unproductive behaviors like lack of trust, lack of accountability, or even role confusion. In turn, these behaviors have *trickle-down impacts* on the people who must work cross-functionally—namely, product managers and their teams.

Compounding the problem of disharmony among executives is that there are some Product Management executives who don't have broad enough Product Management experience. These leaders do not fully understand or appreciate the complexity of the role or the importance of the function. Since they do not perceive the value of Product Management to the firm, they cannot see why any change is needed. And as we all know, individuals do not want to lose control over their own domain. So if you have an executive team that doesn't "get" what Product Management is about and it's up to them to decide whether to shift the organization's focus to Product Management, they will not be in favor of the idea. As a result, nothing will happen except business as usual. This can be more of a challenge when there isn't a lot of pain and business is thought to be "OK." However, I believe this issue, and all others, can be addressed by considering an effective governance model for Product Management. Perhaps some minds can be changed if the benefits are spelled out.

## MISSING MOMENTUM

Despite many issues as mentioned in this book, in the past several years Product Management has had a profound impact on the corporate landscape. Nowadays, more and more senior product leaders are seated alongside other functional leaders at the executive-level "table" in a substantial number of companies. In the years before my recent observations and data collection, the majority of Product Management leaders reported to a Marketing executive, or in technology companies, to Product Development. In recent times, the situation has shifted: In the past couple of years, in about *half* the companies studied, Product Management reports to a CEO or general manager. This is especially true in larger business-to-business firms. About 25 percent of firms have Product Management reporting to a Marketing executive. The balance shows Product Management reporting to other functions, including Development, Operations, and Business Development.

In another interesting area, almost two-thirds of firms studied have now established governance boards for Product Management. However, in my research, 89.1 percent of respondents felt the board has had only mixed success. A large majority of participating executives felt this structure had not met expectations.

Factors said to contribute to *success* include these:

- Consistent executive support
- Positive and productive communication
- Good decisions
- Cross-member buy-in
- Clearly established roles
- Market orientation

Factors that detract from success include these:

- Unclear strategies
- Process confusion
- Executive turnover
- Too much financial focus
- Inability to make trade-offs
- Inadequate product manager staffing
- Functional department agendas

Another reason given for problems in governance (as cited frequently in this book) is the lack of an agreement on a common definition of Product Management, its function, and its purpose. Without a charter, purpose, clear goals, and executive support, any attempt at Product Management governance will be unsatisfactory.

There are a smaller number of successful companies who believe they deal effectively with some of the aspects of Product Management. In the 11 percent of firms who indicated that they had successful governing boards, the work of those boards focused mostly on *product development* decisions and on strategic product line planning. What's more disturbing is they said they *do not pay any attention to* product manager staff planning, product manager competency models, Product Management processes, or the provision of enabling systems and tools for product managers. If companies need to be more efficient and more profitable, this static state is less than acceptable. In my opinion, changes are urgently needed to establish a workable governance structure; one that will address the depth and breadth of *all* aspects of Product Management.

## GETTING READY TO GOVERN: THE INITIAL EVALUATION

In Chapter 2, I recommended that a Maturity Model be utilized to support the effective governance of Product Management. It was referred to as the Product Management Maturity Model-G (G stands for "Governance").

Getting ready to govern requires some preparation. You can start by doing this exercise as an *initial* evaluation of your organization's Product Management maturity level. Go to Figure 9.1, "Initial Evaluation of Product Management Maturity." The table has a main column, labeled at the top "Attributes for Product Management Governance." The next three columns have these headings across the top: "A, Current Usage"; "B, Desired Usage"; and "C, Gap."

- In the A column, use the scoring scale described below to indicate the degree of consistency or predictability of that particular attribute based on how this area is being used in your company.
- In the B column, indicate the level of usage that you will aspire to over the next 12 months.
- In the C column, identify the gap between what you have now and what you want (simple arithmetic).

Use the following point structure for this exercise:

- Very inconsistent and unpredictable: 25 points
- Inconsistent and somewhat unpredictable: 50 points
- Generally consistent and somewhat predictable: 75 points
- Very consistent and predictable: 100 points

When scoring, you might want to "aspire" to a score of 100 percent for all areas. However, I advise you to consider two other options: Either keep the same amounts across A and B, or just go up to the very next level under B. There is also a row in which to enter your total score. Add all your scores together for the total that will give you an overall snapshot of where your company is maturity-wise, where you want it to be as measured against the highest overall total, which is 1,000 points (100 as the best times 10 attributes).

## Figure 9.1 Initial Evaluation of Product Management Maturity

| | Attributes for Product Management Governance | A<br>Current<br>Level | B<br>Desired<br>Level | C<br>Gap<br>(A – B) |
|---|---|---|---|---|
| 1 | A committed group of leaders who work to fortify Product Management as a primary function in the company. This group also ensures that roles and responsibilities are aligned across the organization. | | | |
| 2 | A product portfolio council that rationalizes products, product lines, platforms, and technology investments. | | | |
| 3 | Creation and maintenance of all Product Management processes, procedures, and documents, which are continually evaluated and open to improvement and optimization. This includes the New Product Development (NPD) process for evaluating product investments and prioritizing NPD projects. | | | |
| 4 | Embedded cross-functional product teams that are accountable for producing positive financial and business contributions to the firm. | | | |
| 5 | Systems and structures that supply and/or house important market data, performance information, and relevant information for product managers and product teams to utilize in their work. | | | |
| 6 | Ongoing assessments and evaluations of product managers that help to guide staffing strategies and progression programs and that help to build core competencies across the product manager population. | | | |
| 7 | A chartered group to work on innovative initiatives, experimentation, and other exploration outside of mainstream Product Management activities. | | | |
| 8 | Routines and calendars for Product Management activities, plans, and other cyclical work items. | | | |
| 9 | Metrics and KPIs for evaluating overall Product Management organizational effectiveness. | | | |
| 10 | A vibrant knowledge-based community of product managers who learn and grow together. | | | |
| | Total score | | | |

Your completion of this initial evaluation is the starting point. Perhaps it may already have sparked some thoughts in your mind about your own organization. Whether that's true or not, as you read through the rest of the chapter, you may find that your perspective has changed—at least I hope so!

(Toward the end of this chapter there is another table [Figure 9.4], similar to the one used for the initial evaluation. With the insight gained from what you read in this chapter, that exercise [Figure 9.4] will help you establish some "go forward" objectives.)

## THE ORGANIZATIONAL STRUCTURE FOR THE PRODUCT MANAGEMENT GOVERNANCE BOARD

In Figure 9.1 you reviewed the 10 main attributes for Product Management governance, and you performed a "first pass" evaluation of your firm's Product Management maturity level. Now I'd like to turn your attention to the actual structure of the board. Refer to the "organization chart" shown in Figure 9.2. This depiction places the board at the top of the chart and shows the other areas for which the board is responsible. With this visualization, I'd like to take you through each area.

Mind you, many of these areas have been mentioned throughout the book. In such cases, I'll summarize the key points and refer you back to the appropriate chapters. In other instances, I'll speak more to the given area.

### 1. THE CHARTER FOR, AND MEMBERSHIP IN, THE PRODUCT MANAGEMENT GOVERNANCE BOARD

There are five main areas that executives should address to set up the board. These include:

- Executive sponsorship of the charter
- Membership
- The board leader
- Rules
- Connections

**Figure 9.2  Organization Chart for a Product Management Governance Board**

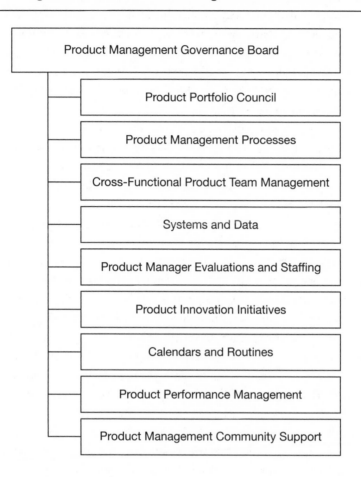

## Executive Sponsorship of the Charter

The board should be chartered or sponsored by the senior executive leadership team or executive cabinet of the company—either as a *subcommittee* or as an *independent council*. This charter establishes the articles that guide the conduct of members and establish the procedures, rules of operation, and other protocols that are typical to any governance body.

## Membership

The senior executive leadership team should appoint senior Product Management leaders as board members. They may also wish to appoint executives from other business functions so that there is a greater appreciation for Product Management across the organization. It is implicit that *the board should serve as the primary voice for Product Management processes, practices, procedures, policies, and systems.*

There may be variations in the composition of the board. Very complex organizations might require a central board with members from subsidiaries or business divisions. Other organizations might require membership from product line groups. It all depends on the size and makeup of the company.

From what I said above, it may seem that the board's leadership should be made up of Product Management leaders who are currently assigned to lead product organizations. However, the board will have many time-consuming responsibilities. In order to achieve its goals, I recommend that some of the board's Product Management leaders devote all their time and attention to it, by being employed in this capacity on a full-time basis.

Among the problems with staffing a board, membership transience can lead to a lack of attention to or inconsistency in the board's work. In many organizations with some type of Product Management board, most members do not possess sufficient bandwidth and depth of knowledge to do the work necessary to firmly entrench Product Management in the firm.

In my diagnostics, I have seen boards disintegrate for lack of attention, such as when members are pulled away for other important projects. There can be other problematic situations. After a major reorganization in the executive suite, some senior executives may not place a high value on Product Management, which means the board's efforts will most likely be suspended—as if "Product Management can wait." In my opinion, this is counterproductive for the company, the work already accomplished by the board, and the goal of moving Product Management forward. When there is a suspension or interruption in its functioning, the board's efforts may fail to restart, or the board may lose any momentum it had gained. Product Management cannot and should not have to wait. If this is to be a serious effort, *the Product Management Governance Board should survive for as long as the corporation is in business.*

### The Board Leader

As mentioned, board members should be appointed by the senior executive leadership team. Next the board members must appoint a leader of the Product Management Governance Board. This leader should carry an authoritative title and have demonstrated credibility with other leaders, peers, and subordinates. There should be rules established for this position, along with the general guidelines for appointment and service requirements of board members. All of these should be listed in the board's charter or bylaws. Each company, through its leaders, should establish and document minimum requirements for experience, maturity, and executive recommendations. This is important because board members will ultimately serve as leaders who may coordinate events, become process owners, community activists, and so on. To preserve and maintain continuity, board members should be required to serve a minimum amount of time, such as 12, 18, or 24 months, with, perhaps, a maximum of three or four years.

### Rules

As with most governance bodies, a set of rules or protocols should guide the board's operations, including those for meeting agendas, decision making, and other procedures that are necessary to ensure the board's smooth operation.

### Connections

Important linkages need to be established between the board and the senior executive leadership team. Ultimately, it is up to the senior executive leaders to figure out how they will deal with Product Management. However, if you've read this far, I'll make the assumption that you believe there is substance to the idea for the board.

Now, I'd like to offer you a visual perspective so that you can see how important the board can be and how its work can be linked to, or aligned with, the senior executive leadership team. This perspective is shown in Figure 9.3. As can be seen, the main work categories of the board are shown on the left, and the associated areas of work under the guidance of the senior executive leadership team are shown on the right. The items connected by arrows indicate areas where senior leaders might want to influence some of the programs and subcommittees of the Product Management Gover-

**Figure 9.3  Linkages between the Product Management Governance Board and the Senior Executive Leadership Team**

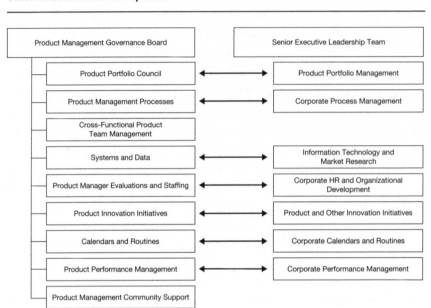

nance Board. The main point is this: Although the board should have a fair amount of autonomy, its activities must remain aligned with those of the senior executive leadership team.

## 2. PRODUCT PORTFOLIO COUNCIL

All companies should have a product portfolio council of some kind. In many firms, portfolio investments are directed by the senior executive leadership team. In my research for this book, I learned that a little over half of firms have a well-entrenched formalized portfolio review board, guided by a cross-functional senior leadership team. Very few firms have a portfolio council driven by a Product Management Governance Board. In firms that utilize a product portfolio council, its contribution is not fully visible or completely understood by product managers or product teams. One reason may be that the senior executive team does not have enough time, resources, or data to cover the depth and breadth of activity required to properly rationalize and balance product portfolios. For example, we've learned that less than 40 percent of companies *with* a portfolio council do *not* look across product lines to rationalize development and avoid duplication.

Without a doubt, the portfolio council should be made up of cross-functional leaders. However, if you want to improve the opportunity for the firm to expand its product portfolio performance, I would recommend that the portfolio council be led by (or strongly influenced by) a board member.

In some firms, it might be more efficient for the portfolio council to operate as a subcommittee, under the auspices of the board. This would mean the board would appoint a *portfolio subcommittee leader*. This subcommittee leader would work closely with senior executives to ensure that adequate time and effort were devoted to portfolio oversight of *all product investments*. Concomitantly, senior executives would therefore need to appoint various functional leaders to represent the senior leadership team in order to maintain portfolio oversight.

The main role of this subcommittee or council is to ensure that product investments are routinely balanced and rationalized so that product development efforts are strategically aligned and not duplicated elsewhere in the firm. The rationalization process would consider all products situated across their life cycles so that investments could include those in product platforms, technologies, and architectures utilized across all product lines.

Despite my own preference for the product portfolio council to operate under the auspices of the board, this type of structure may not align with the ideals of some senior leadership teams. Probably, this is because the portfolio council is generally cross-functional and so the senior leadership team might want to exercise a greater degree of control and oversight. It's not ideal, but I am not totally opposed to this, as long as all product lines are adequately represented and the board provides the proper perspective needed to optimize the product portfolio, either across the enterprise or within a given business division.

The establishment of the portfolio council is one thing, but the actual process of portfolio rationalization and optimization is easier said than done. For that reason, it is not always carried out correctly or even with enough frequency.

In dealing with this issue, the board has an opportunity to be an asset: It can ensure that the right data that concerns all products in all life cycle phases is made available for evaluation by the council. The Product Management Life Cycle Model offers the most useful reference because it allows products to be classified according to its main areas, which can then be evaluated according to the relevant criteria. These criteria might include strategic fit, market share, profitability, growth potential, organizational capacity, competitive position, and others (as needs dictate).

Because of the dynamic nature of product investments, there are several areas where the portfolio council's contribution to the board and to the executive leadership team will provide tremendous value. These include the following:

1. Reviewing Business Cases for *product projects*, whether they are for new investments or major enhancements. These reviews are driven out of the phase gate New Product Development (NPD) decision process.

2. Auditing the outcomes of prior Business Cases to ensure that the assumptions, forecasts, and anticipated contributions to the business are being fulfilled. By association, the portfolio council will also want to ensure that post-launch audits are part and parcel of the audits of Business Cases.

3. Evaluating the product portfolio of acquisition targets to ensure that new product lines can be strategically interwoven with the existing lines.

4. Prioritizing or reprioritizing the dynamic mix of incoming funding requests.

5. Determining which products or product lines should be discontinued based on the firm's portfolio strategy.

Overall, successful efforts and outcomes from this portfolio council will help the board gain greater levels of stature and credibility across the organization.

## 3. PRODUCT MANAGEMENT PROCESSES

Product Management activities are guided by many processes. The meta-level competencies discussed at various times throughout the book are closely related to all the major process groups. By the same token, just as a meta-level competency group is made up of many competencies, meta-level Product Management processes contain many subprocesses. I won't go into a detailed discussion about these meta-level Product Management processes. However, to establish the right context, I am referring to processes and subprocesses that achieve the following:

- Contribute to the development of market insights
- Enable strategies to be formulated
- Provide for efficient product planning and development
- Facilitate effective performance management

Unfortunately, many companies do not treat these Product Management processes with the degree of formality needed to *achieve consistent, predictable usage*. When there is a lack of focus on critical Product Management processes, it follows that there may be a lack of direction for product managers and others they work with. When they do not fully understand their roles and responsibilities, important work activities may not be adequately completed. The result is that either product managers have to complete the work of others, or others have to complete the work for which product managers are responsible. This can be a great challenge to the efficiency and product profitability. And you may find it problematic if your objective is to sustain Product Management for the long term.

Many firms actually have resorted to process-and-quality improvement functions that utilize Six Sigma and/or business process management techniques. These efforts are important as companies seek to fine-tune operations through greater efficiencies—all of which can impact the bottom line. Most of these formal techniques examine work flows and the activities of people across a variety of business functions to streamline work, improve communication, and speed decision making.

That's where the board can take a leadership role. The board's expertise can be leveraged to examine all relevant processes and to guide incremental improvements that will ultimately foster greater levels of cross-functional collaboration.

Therefore, I recommend that the board *own* all of the Product Management processes. Ownership involves the creation, maintenance, and continuous improvement of all Product Management processes, procedures, methods, and documents. *To achieve this, a capable process leader should be designated by the board.*

As with other board roles, there may be some cross-board and cross-organizational issues that the process leader must help to factor in, as the board becomes more firmly rooted in the organization. Some of these are listed below:

1.  Product Management processes may be included in the business processes that are periodically evaluated at the corporate level and driven by the senior executive leadership team. Therefore, the board's process leader should maintain close ties to the corporate process owners so that the board may benefit from work related to those corporate programs and avoid duplication of effort.

2.  One of the most visible Product Management processes, and one that most leaders are familiar with, is the phase gate New Product Development (NPD) process. As mentioned in other parts of this book, phase gate NPD processes are fairly ubiquitous in most organizations. However, the usage and administration of these processes are highly variable and inconsistent. This causes a couple of problems.

    The first is related to process misuse. The NPD process *should* be used to vet a dynamic pool of opportunities and make decisions about where to invest or not to invest. However, when all projects are treated in a similar manner, it becomes very difficult to distinguish between vastly different opportunities.

    This leads to the second issue. When all (or most) projects are put through the "process," the process itself becomes burdensome and unmanageable, causing excessive workloads for everyone involved. As an example: Process documentation might be misinterpreted. This would lead some employees to focus on submitting the required forms or being bogged down with other inconsequential details, instead of focusing more broadly on the other aspects of their work. The people who are supposed to use the process for rational decision making and efficient resource allocation feel discouraged by the rigid and "heavy-handed burdens." As a result, they become apathetic or disengaged: they may skip important "thought steps" that are actually needed to make better decisions. Many firms have abandoned the NPD process due to abject misuse, or under pressure from employees because it's seen as too rigid. To avoid these missteps, the board can play a major role in optimizing NPD process usage.

The first step in managing processes is to create *process libraries*. A process library is a documented collection of meta-processes and subprocesses, usually maintained on an internal and dedicated website. This allows the board to evaluate one meta-process at a time, which is important because it allows for the careful mapping out of each process and subprocess. Visual work flow tools and other techniques should be utilized to capture all process dimensions.

As the board begins to work more effectively with the senior leadership team and the team focuses more and more on improvement, small victories will begin to add up and accrue to the board.

### 4. EMBEDDED CROSS-FUNCTIONAL PRODUCT TEAMS

As described in more detail in Chapter 8, product teams operate as microcosms of cross-functional leadership teams. However, they should be guided by the rules and processes set forth by the board. Cross-functional product team members are responsible for the performance of a single product or product line. Product teams aren't disbanded because any project of theirs is over. The product team is responsible to deliver agreed-upon financial and other business contributions; it should also remain in place for the *life* of that product (or product line). There's only one reason a product team would be dissolved, and that is when the product or product line has been discontinued or withdrawn from the market. The board must:

- Devote enough attention to the efforts of the cross-functional product team so as to enable them to *synchronize the endeavors* of all concerned business functions, product groups, and geographic regions
- Inspire the appointed product team members to focus on essential market drivers and to be sensitive to the overall business environment to bring about a common focus across

the concerned organizational constituencies for the product or
product line

To ensure that the embedded structure of the cross-functional product
team can survive for the long term, the board appoints people to work on
these product teams. The board then makes sure to align these appoint-
ments with the senior leadership team so that everyone in senior leadership,
including board members, knows who the important players are on these
high-performance teams. To refresh your understanding, or if you skipped
over Chapter 8, a review of its contents might be in order.

## 5. DATA, SYSTEMS, AND TOOLS

Every company collects a diverse set of data from a number of sources. Some
firms do have formal structures for data collection and presentation, and
some do not. As with many corporate functions, there is a vast amount of
variability in these efforts. This irregularity of effort results in intermittently
positive or negative impacts on the effectiveness of Product Management.
When product managers have good data, their decisions tend to be superior;
when they do *not* have good data, their decisions tend to be suboptimal.

Therefore, it should be the board's responsibility to the cross-functional
product teams and to the product manager population to ensure that a constant stream of relevant data is made available and accessible. All product
managers should be guided by data and information from which they can
derive insights and make decisions. Without necessary data and other indicators, it is virtually impossible to run the products' business with any degree
of precision. Further, just as the senior leadership teams are able to examine
all aspects of the firm's performance, so should cross-functional product
teams be enabled to do so: This, of course, applies equally to the board.

Data comes in many forms. There are sets of data that come directly
from embedded corporate systems. These sets include data related to plans
and outcomes of the business functions which include, among others: Supply Chain, Operations, Sales, Production, Development, and Service. They
are also linked to explicit processes that are used to guide these functions.

Product managers should routinely examine a host of data elements
that include the following:

1.  Key performance indicators (KPIs) to evaluate each function's contribution to the product's success.
2.  Important figures and reports from financial systems that include budgets, forecasts, and other allocations. These outcomes can and should be compared to original plans so that variances can be analyzed and addressed.
3.  The suite of important market data that needs to be planned for, captured, organized, and analyzed. This includes customer research, industry analysis, competitor information, and competitive product evaluations.

Admittedly, it's easier to identify the data elements than it is to set up the programs and protocols to ensure that these data elements are available on an ongoing basis. Therefore, the board must ascertain that adequate resources are dedicated across the functions so that these evaluations can be made. That is one of the advantages of having a board.

In some well-run firms, the marketing department organizes data collection efforts and maintains a shared-services group so that product managers can make requests and collaborate on important research projects. In other organizations, this work is very widely distributed. Research projects are often carried out at the request of a corporate manager without including or even considering the needs of product managers. I have personally seen situations in which outcomes of independently chartered research projects were not shared with others who would greatly benefit from such knowledge.

In one example, a large bank engaged a firm to carry out brand recognition research and customer preference studies and to collect market share data. During my discovery sessions with product managers, they had no idea that these research projects had been decided on, much less that they were underway! Such information would have been of tremendous help to them. Who knows what was missed because research findings were not made available to the product managers? Product managers in every company can benefit significantly from corporate research—but only if they are aware of its existence.

It is to any company's great advantage to make sure that adequate investment is directed to data collection, analysis, and dissemination. Doing so will contribute greatly to improved insights, shared perspectives, and strategic alignment, for the leaders and, particularly, for the product teams. As they receive this data, product teams should keep in mind the Product Master Plan with its centralized repository for all things "product." The board can generate a variety of tools to house templates, process documents, sales and marketing material, and so on for active use and for storage in the web library. There are an infinite number of such technologies and techniques available now, which will continue to grow exponentially. However, only if they are utilized and applied assiduously will they benefit the firm and its Product Management community.

## 6. ONGOING EVALUATIONS OF PRODUCT MANAGERS

Good product managers should be considered treasured assets in the company. I dedicated Chapters 5 and 6 in this book to staffing strategies and the cultivation of product managers. I felt that by doing so, I was making an imperative statement to senior leaders about the importance of the Product Management role because it can have such a positive impact on the company. In this brief section, I will recap the most important points covered in those chapters.

The board must make sure that the staff includes enough of the right product managers with the right skills and experience to discharge their responsibilities well. It is clear to me that leaders and managers don't dedicate enough time and effort to the evaluation and management of product managers. To restate an important fact, *more than two-thirds of companies do not have formal hierarchies and progression plans for product managers.* Unfortunately, in a number of firms, evaluations are rarely carried out; and if they do take place, they are carried out in an unstructured manner, and they are not well documented or shared.

It should be noted that product managers are promoted mainly when their contribution to business results is confirmed and they have demonstrated superior ability to influence and guide others. Therefore, it is essential that Product Management be positively situated in the firm. Aside from being able to retain your best people, it is necessary to ensure that product managers, as a population, are treated as corporate leaders of the future—that is, as a pool of potential talent that, if cultivated, promises great achievement.

A few years ago, I did an evaluation of more than 60 product managers for a company. Five years later, other leaders in that very same firm contacted me to carry out an evaluation and assessment of their current population of about 100 product managers. Believe it or not, the *current* leadership team had no knowledge or record of the initial evaluation! Most of the *original* leadership team was no longer there, and there didn't seem to be any documentation from the past.

After we produced the initial report, we reviewed it with the leadership team. At that point, we found that only about half the original product managers were still on the staff. We helped the company reconstruct some of the evaluations and analyze the contributions of those product managers who were still there. The outcome of the new evaluation was that the organization's overall scores were significantly lower after the five-year period. The reasons for the lower scores were not only rapid growth and several acquisitions, but also a lack of focus on Product Management. When advancement and growth result in the loss of potential, it is logical that changing how things are done will offer improvement. That is why, in this book (and in my work), I advocate so strongly for improved hiring and evaluation practices, the encouragement of communities, and governance by a chartered board.

Ongoing competency and maturity assessments must be carried out by the board; they must also ensure that product managers are segmented based on potential and developmental needs. The board will need to evaluate other areas too, including the need for domain expertise and the level of interaction required with others.

Carrying out a program of ongoing, consistently employed evaluative activity will result in more focused efforts to cultivate product managers and those they work with (as discussed in Chapter 5). In Chapter 6, I provided a unique tool to help with this goal—the *Product Manager Scorecard*. This instrument captures and delineates all evaluative activity and applies it to focused developmental programs. Continued evaluations will provide enough periodic snapshots so that the board can better direct its investments in human capital toward product managers. High-performing product managers will be the jewels in the crown—some of the most vital assets in the firm's investment portfolio.

## 7. INITIATIVES TO CATALYZE PRODUCT INNOVATION

From my vantage point, in fact from any corporate vantage point, the topic of innovation has been and will continue to be the major imperative in all aspects of business. In basic terms, conducting business is about making profits from selling products or services. Conducting *really* profitable business is about raising sales levels, elevating the firm's reputation, and outselling the competition. If you do not have a pipeline of innovative, creative, new and/or enhanced products and services in the future, what will you be able to offer as markets evolve?

Barely a day goes by without the word *innovation* being mentioned in business news broadcasts, articles, and research studies. Virtually every media report about commerce begins with overused phrases that add up to "Doing business in today's marketplace is complex, and the only way forward is to innovate."

Investors "fall in love" with companies that break fresh ground or change to a new or different business model. The public constantly goes for the latest tech gadgets, new fads in music, fashion, and autos. Those most often discussed include a company that changed its distribution model for music or another company that came up with a new search engine wrapped in a good advertising model.

What I (and others) admire most about these firms is they *invest* huge amounts of money in pure or basic *research initiatives*. When I was with Bell Laboratories, I was filled with awe each time I passed the labs and saw the company's scientists and technologists at work, experimenting and tinkering. I recall an executive's words from an interview, wherein he stated that Bell Labs didn't focus on products; instead, it focused on technologies or techniques that might not even materialize for decades.

It may seem a stretch to ask that, in addition to its other responsibilities, the board oversee some of the innovative work being done in the company. The problem is that a focus on innovation does not guarantee positive outcomes. In my research, I found that approximately 40 percent of companies have established separate innovation groups to hunt for radical or game-changing innovations. However, several firms discontinued these groups because they failed to come up with anything radical or different. On the other hand, I found that among companies with well-run Product Management Governance Boards, about two-thirds of their leaders *do* believe their board should encourage innovative initiatives. In my interviews with these firms, they did not discuss their successes or failures so it is difficult to gauge their success.

It can be difficult for product managers to feel innovative, creative, or inventive when they are on their day-to-day work cycles. Therefore, it can be a challenge for the board to take on this daunting role (to inspire innovative thoughts and creativity) that may not produce favorable outcomes, especially in a risk-averse environment.

For companies who are open to the idea of adding innovative thinking to the job descriptions of their Product Management communities, there are some important aspects that should probably be examined. I'm not talking about making major changes to the status quo or expecting the immediate production of radical innovations. What I *am* talking about is that there are realistic steps the board can use toward embedding these capabilities within the firm. For instance, in Chapter 7, I discussed the benefits of building a knowledge-based community of practice for Product Management. Such a community can enhance creativity, deepen understanding, and sharpen collective problem solving. As another "baby step" toward encouraging more imaginative thinking, I also listed some ideas that could be used to engender a more "aware" population of product managers and cross-functional product team members. These might include efforts to improve market insight and business understanding. It's hard to ask product managers and others to come up with creative ideas if they don't even know how to derive market insights.

I believe the board members can play a role as "cultural influencers" who can *guide* people to think creatively rather than enjoining them to do so. Furthermore, nourishing innovative mindsets for leaders and product managers will be encouraged by the positive attitudes of the board members.

One company I studied was actually *obsessive* about customer research. The company employed over 200 professionals who were psychologists, anthropologists, and sociologists. These people worked in small teams *outside* of the company walls, and they studied how people lived their daily lives. As a result, this company came up with interesting, innovative products, based on what the customer researchers observed about human behavior.

When I tell other companies about these customer researchers, their usual defense for not having staff members dedicated to customer research is that they don't have money for these types of "adventures."

However, picture this: What if the board worked with the senior executive leaders to generate some ideas that would move product managers toward thinking more creatively?

For just one example: Suppose the board created some small roving cross-functional teams. The teams would be assigned to visit customers with enough frequency that their collective cognizance and sensitivity to nuance would be increased. They might grow *less reactive* to customer requests and grow *more proactive* about solving big-picture customer problems within a given market segment. It may not be a big step to go from innovating solutions to customer problems and to innovating improvements to existing products. New ideas might become more possible as another step in their growth.

To translate this train of thought for greater simplicity: There are a variety of incremental steps that can be taken by the board to instigate techniques that might inspire creativity, inventiveness, and, therefore, greater levels of innovation.

## 8. CALENDARS, CYCLES, AND ROUTINES

Every organization follows a regular annual cycle that includes processes to assemble budgets and plans for the subsequent year. Whatever the basis for the schedule (calendar year or fiscal year), the process usually starts in the middle of the preceding year and is completed later in the current year. People in different functions understand the routine and generally allow ample time for the completion of tasks so that corporate timelines can be met.

However, many people find themselves caught by surprise when an important due date looms and they are not ready. I recommend the use of calendars to help teams maintain schedules and meet all the due dates in the business cycle. You can try to depend on people with all of their fallibilities—or you can opt for the more reliable and accurate use of calendars. Aside from noting actual due dates, calendars can provide advance notifications of dates to remind people of important upcoming events.

The board can help fulfill its charter through the establishment of a series of routine activities that should be planned out—*scheduled and calendared*—throughout the year. With these routines formalized, product managers and the board can predict and project their work schedules. Furthermore, maintaining a schedule can help smooth out the bumps that occur from unplanned or unexpected demands.

This recommendation may be a challenge to those who are unfamiliar with or uncomfortable with such a degree of structure. Unfortunately, I have seen (as I am sure you have) the undesirable outcomes that arise from the lack of up-to-date information. Had work been *adequately planned*, things might not have slipped up when an urgent request had to be met.

It would be foolish to try to convince people that if they entered all their scheduled work into a calendar, the unplanned or urgent requests would stop or those that still occurred would be taken care of with no sweat. But using a calendar does reduce the number and severity of those events, and it can therefore help people meet cyclic events and dates as well as plan ahead for their work year.

As an example (mentioned at another point in the book), I indicated that market summaries should be prepared and updated on a periodic basis. These updates would be captured as "stories" about customers, industry changes, and competitive shifts. If a market story is to be updated quarterly (on the schedule), then data collection activities to support the story will need to be scheduled. These activities might include conducting a given number of customer interviews each month, making a number of customer visits, and taking competitive snapshots. If the market story can be updated because the necessary data gathering is scheduled, the job of a product manager will be made easier.

For one example of a benefit: Every time a product line review is held, product managers and others won't be taken offline for a number of days to prepare the presentation. If a Business Case is prepared and updated regularly, a time-consuming research effort won't have to be undertaken every time the current status needs to be validated.

Starting a calendar may be a small step, but such steps accumulate and grow into larger-scale efficiencies.

It's important to note that for calendars to work effectively, they should be based on and take into consideration a variety of factors, including the product life cycle state, market maturity, and market velocity.

There is usually a cyclic rhythm as to when product life events occur, and it helps to be reminded that they are coming up. Firms with fast-evolving products and services will certainly require intense discipline whereas firms with products and services that remain active for longer periods of time will need less draconian systems. The routines that are placed in calendars can include a host of activities. Many can be aligned with the product life cycle, and some can be aligned with corporate edicts. Other items might be scheduled as reminders to update or validate documents and other data storage repositories.

The board's role in this is to stimulate the calendaring and scheduling efforts, especially in the following areas:

- Product line reviews and strategic updates (including product line scorecards)
- Competitive product analyses
- Competitor analyses
- Industry profiles
- Updates to market segmentation models
- Target customer-need profiles
- Periodic (e.g., monthly) cross-functional product team updates
- Launch plans
- Development reviews
- Document update and refresh activities
- Examination of and adjustments to templates and tools
- Retest and/or validate value propositions
- Retest and/or validate product positioning
- Win-loss audits
- Post-launch audits
- Business Case audits

Which items may make it into the program schedule and which do not will depend on the needs of a particular business and the people who will be affected. The board should appoint a leader to start the gradual steps that will grow this stabilizing practice for Product Management, where every day brings the unexpected.

## 9. PRODUCT PERFORMANCE MANAGEMENT

There is nothing more important for a business than knowing where you are and how you got there. This certainly extends to product and portfolio performance. Therefore, one of the board's primary roles is to ensure that product performance management practices are front and center.

Management of product and portfolio performance is crucial to validating strategies and to ensuring that the product's business is kept on the right track. It also plays a vital role in a company making optimal decisions about future directions. I have discussed, several times, the need for up-to-date data and the systems required to provide that data. As I have also said, it's absolutely crucial that product managers be held responsible for the examination of a host of measurements, metrics, and indicators—all of which are interconnected.

Senior leaders certainly review financials and other performance indicators as they review corporate or business line results. However, some of their monthly reviews may not cover *in sufficient depth* the issues related to individual product performance. When this happens, senior leaders may make suboptimal decisions because they have less information than they should have.

Individual contributor product managers often do not review financial and other performance information. One reason is because this data is not always available to them. Another reason is that many company financial systems do not provide product-level financial statements. In other cases, product managers do not exhibit any interest or strong motivation to find out about their product's financial and other business indicators.

Additional research has revealed that people who come into Product Management from technical disciplines, operations, or related functions do not have a natural affinity for financial or other performance data. This may not be true in every instance, but it is something to look into within your own firm.

Even when that data is available, many product managers do not spend enough time and effort in evaluating and analyzing variances. They may be too busy, or they don't know how to understand or utilize the material, or they view it as just another burden they don't need. *The point is that financial information and other market data are vital to the proper performance of their jobs.*

As described in items 3 and 8 above, a variety of methods should be overseen by the board to ensure that product managers and product teams are analyzing data and providing readouts on a continuous basis. The core idea is to get everyone into the "numbers game" to ensure that every product, regardless of its life cycle status, is evaluated as frequently as needed.

With that information in hand, optimal options and decisions can be made quickly and easily—and well. The board's job (and it is very important in this case) is to ensure that this performance orientation is universally embedded throughout the Product Management structure.

## 10. KNOWLEDGE-BASED PRODUCT MANAGEMENT COMMUNITIES OF PRACTICE

Chapter 7 was devoted to this topic. The concept is that a community of product managers offers an optimal way to maximize the performance of the Product Management function. Therefore, the community of practice should be sponsored and supported by the board. By having members of the Product Management community share what they've learned through presentations, stories, and other documentation, the community of practice helps to stimulate learning and greater breadth of scope. (It even brings out the creative spark that can lead to innovation!)

Although a community can meet in video conferences and online forums, I advocate strongly for person-to-person contacts because people are wired to be social and such contacts can be more productive. A community also needs a designated, dedicated website where standard Product Management documentation can be kept (e.g., templates, tools, brand information, marketing guides and style sheets), updated, and managed as active or archived documents.

Part of the board's responsibility in community building is to encourage its formation and cultivate an environment that reflects the mission and values of the organization. This should not be taken lightly. A collaborative culture can and should be encouraged and nurtured and ultimately rewarded. The basics of team building and leadership include behavioral attributes such as acting with integrity, "doing right" by customers, giving clear communication, helping one another, improving core competencies, striving for innovative ideas, and always looking to improve a process or a method.

It will be through the board's direct observable actions that these behaviors can be instilled in the Product Management community. This also puts key leadership team members, such as the CEO, general manager, or the chief marketing officer, in positions of being role models for those in the community to observe and, hopefully, emulate. There are many more benefits to such a community, but those have been covered more completely in Chapter 7. The bottom line is that the board should be the source for the origin of this valuable community, as well as its nurturer.

## RESOLVING PROBLEMS AS ESCALATED BY THE PRODUCT TEAMS

Another area of responsibility of the board is to address and resolve problems that are escalated from the product teams. In order to achieve this stature, the rules for escalation must be established so that the product team members know the conditions under which escalation is warranted. Usually some kind of external event, project jeopardy, or customer issue will require a leadership team intervention.

Note, however, that some thresholds should be established so that the product team can maintain its autonomy, which means that whenever possible, most issues should be resolved by the product team. This is important because you want to *cultivate an environment of collaborative problem solving and decision making.*

In the event that there are any blurred lines between urgent and less than urgent, the product team leader should ask the team to think through the issue and come up with some options for action. If the team needs help in this area, you may wish to engage the services of a consultant or coach to help the team through the process. These lessons are an important part of the team's earned empowerment.

With a good set of tools, the team will know exactly what to communicate in terms of the severity of the problem, what specifically to ask for in the escalation, *when* action is needed, and *why.* As with all lessons in the team's evolution, leaders should allow time for post-event analyses and continued coaching.

## THE IMPORTANCE OF MENTORING

Earlier in my career, while working in a large company, I was assigned to a *mentor.* My mentor was an executive who worked in another area of the company. When I found out that I would have a mentor, I wasn't sure what to think of the idea and how to make good use of it. At times, I found it awkward because I didn't know what the rules were.

Over time, I became somewhat more comfortable and a relationship formed. Although it was like an arranged marriage, I knew I could reach out to him when I needed to. I now understand and value how I benefited from my experience of having a mentor; he was there for me not only when I asked for help but also, and more important, when I had to navigate through corporate politics.

Though I had a formal mentor at one point, I had many other mentors along my entire career journey. Some of those who helped me did so for short periods; others for longer periods. I also found that my learning relationships were enhanced when I also brought something to the table. Give and take was better than just take. In the end, I learned that when mentoring involves two-way interactions, they are the most rewarding.

The board can serve as a facilitator to the Product Management community by providing some guidelines for how mentoring should work. It would not be a hard-and-fast model, but it would be important because most people do not understand the dynamics and protocols. The board could also undertake a mentoring program for Product Management. It would be a "good fit" for the board's purposes. How and how well it would work would be up to the board, the willingness of staff members to participate, and the corporate culture in which they work.

## CRITICAL SUCCESS FACTORS IN PRODUCT MANAGEMENT GOVERNANCE AND YOUR GO-FORWARD PLAN

The foundation of any maturity model is based on the degree to which stability and predictability are effectively embedded in the organization's practices, methods, protocols, routines, and work structures. When an organization is committed to a sustainable, long-term structure of Product Management, it is because its leaders are dedicated to fine-tuning each and every aspect of the governance model.

Governance of Product Management will most certainly add a layer of complexity to your organization. There is a lot the board must pay attention to. Therefore, it's always important to remember that the *upside potential*— the overarching value proposition—can serve as a foundation for *competitive advantage* beyond anyone's individual paradigm. However, the structure of the governance effort is based on senior leadership's comprehensive knowledge of how it is all supposed to work, both at a macro-level and at a fairly granular level. Success can be achieved, but the level of commitment is significant to the outcome.

Now, based on what you've read in this chapter or in this book, I'm going to ask you to take a look at the table in Figure 9.4. This is an enhanced version of the table in Figure 9.1. However, it is now modified because two columns have been added. I suggest that you reevaluate your current *and* your desired future state (next 12 months, subsequent 12 months, and so on) and prioritize the areas where you would like to focus your efforts. You may find that you can tackle only one area, or you might feel able to take on more than one area.

How far you wish to go is entirely up to you and your senior executive leadership team. However, I urge you to keep in mind that this is a *very long-term program*. It will also require a commitment of human and financial resources that may be difficult to marshal and maintain. Or you and some other leaders may find that dealing with this whole routine is just too complex.

At a certain point, you may want to quit. Everyone is saying, "That's enough,"—possibly echoing what's in your own mind. Again, I urge you to not stop your efforts. Always remember: Take *baby steps*. Start out small; taking one little step at a time allows you to grow and improve at a gradual and comfortable pace.

## SUMMARY

One of the lessons I've learned over the years is that people will go to extraordinary lengths when they believe in a cause or have a common purpose. This thought can be extended to Product Management and to its sustenance.

A sponsored Product Management Governance Board can serve as a powerful anchor for the function of Product Management and for the community of product managers. It can also serve as the *voice of Product Management to the senior executive leadership team*. The charter places the board at the heart of the organization, as it assumes the role of steward for Product Management. Its goal is to make sure the function of Product Management can survive for the long term, beyond reorganizations and other structural changes.

## Figure 9.4  Enhanced Evaluation of Product Management Maturity

| | Attributes for Product Management Governance | A Current Level | B Desired Level | C Gap (A − B) | D Priority (High, Medium, Low) | E Action Steps |
|---|---|---|---|---|---|---|
| 1 | A committed group of leaders who work to fortify Product Management as a primary function in the company. This group also ensures that roles and responsibilities are aligned across the organization. | | | | | |
| 2 | A product portfolio council that rationalizes products, product lines, platforms, and technology investments. | | | | | |
| 3 | Creation and maintenance of all Product Management processes, procedures, and documents, which are continually evaluated and open to improvement and optimization. This includes the New Product Development (NPD) process for evaluating product investments and prioritizing NPD projects. | | | | | |
| 4 | Embedded cross-functional product teams that are accountable for producing positive financial and business contributions to the firm. | | | | | |
| 5 | Systems and structures that supply and/or house important market data, performance information, and relevant information for product managers and product teams to utilize in their work. | | | | | |
| 6 | Ongoing assessments and evaluations of product managers that help to guide staffing strategies and progression programs and that help to build core competencies across the product manager population. | | | | | |
| 7 | A chartered group to work on innovative initiatives, experimentation, and other exploration outside of mainstream Product Management activities. | | | | | |
| 8 | Routines and calendars for Product Management activities, plans, and other cyclical work items. | | | | | |
| 9 | Metrics and KPIs for evaluating overall Product Management organizational effectiveness. | | | | | |
| 10 | A vibrant knowledge-based community of product managers who learn and grow together. | | | | | |
| | Total score | | | | | |

Some might feel that the board structure recommended in this chapter is just too much, especially in this era of scarce resources, pared-down staff and budgets, and the ever-increasing need for corporate agility. To be clear, I'm not advocating for a board to administer a set of processes that add weight and rigidity to the organization. However, Product Management governance as called for in this chapter can actually have a very powerful impact on the corporation's performance for the long term. Here's why:

- It establishes a level of transparency that allows others to see the positive impacts of Product Management.
- It gives product managers a chance to gain a better foothold in the organization.
- It enhances or reinforces efforts by the executive leadership team to build greater levels of business and market focus across the entire enterprise.

My last suggestion in this summary is simple: Stay the course. At times, the board's work may seem overwhelming. It can be difficult to maintain the level of effort because companies and product managers are always being pulled in so many directions. I advise patience and perseverance because excellent Product Management is worth working for.

*Case Study IV*

## SPOTLIGHT ON PRODUCT MANAGEMENT EXCELLENCE

# JETBLUE AIRWAYS

*By Rachel McCarthy, Director of Product Development*

At JetBlue, our success has been enhanced by the collaborative efforts of an empowered cross-functional product team. This story demonstrates how JetBlue used this team in the race for "internet access at altitude."

When JetBlue first took to the skies in 2000, it was the first airline to offer customers individual seat-back televisions with live programming. It was a game changer. By the end of JetBlue's first decade of operations, most U.S.-based airlines had introduced live, personalized television on at least a portion of their fleets.

In 2007, a JetBlue aircraft called BetaBlue was the very first commercial airliner to offer e-mail, shopping, and instant messaging services in flight. The product, which delivered narrowband connectivity from a number of ground stations to the aircraft, was designed and implemented by LiveTV, a wholly owned subsidiary of JetBlue. Three years later, the company joked, "BetaBlue is STILL the only JetBlue aircraft with in-flight e-mail, IM, and shopping."

For JetBlue, launching BetaBlue was a proof of concept that was developed by the product team and LiveTV. The team's intention had been all along to outfit the rest of the fleet (then numbering around 120 aircraft) with the technology or later generations of the product that would offer greater connectivity. However, after careful market and technical analysis, the product team recommended an adjusted strategy to take a *wait-and-see position*.

When I joined JetBlue in 2009 as director of product development, the airline was on the brink of signing a contract to install BetaBlue's technology on 20 more aircraft.

As I began my work, the highly functioning product team enabled me to ramp up quickly. I didn't know a lot about the technology behind in-flight connectivity, but I knew our product wouldn't scale. Our product, while innovative for the industry and groundbreaking at the time, had already been lapped by several technical generations, and consumer appetite for greater connectivity had already doubled or tripled.

Stopping a product line is one thing. Reversing course on a strategy is quite another, especially if you're the new kid on the block. As a new member of the JetBlue team, I found the culture of our company and an enthusiastic and innovative cross-functional product team highly receptive to reconsidering the course.

I raised a few questions to test the waters, to see if this was a team committed to full steam ahead, damn the cost, or if this was a culture in which the best idea won. Immediately, the team was receptive to finding the right way forward. It seems ages ago, but in 2009, making these product team decisions took a combination of psychic ability and faith that the public's needs would continue to evolve—and evolve rapidly.

LiveTV, JetBlue's subsidiary and developer of BetaBlue's product, agreed. "Our focus was on creating the right product for the industry—not just for JetBlue, because our clients span all airline brands," said Mike Moeller, vice president of sales for LiveTV. "That gave us the right motivation to retrench, reconsider, and start over." The product teams from JetBlue and LiveTV evaluated the current off-the-shelf solutions to see if they could be made better. We established as one of the program goals to create a product that could be used by most customers onboard without degradation of speed. We discovered that a huge investment would yield only a fractional improvement in bandwidth. We reached a point after a year that the only viable solution deemed appropriate by the product team was to go create a new product.

Eyes turned to ViaSat, a high-tech digital communications company that had built its company on providing communications support for military and privately owned aircraft. ViaSat had revolutionized the digital communications space through Ku- and Ka-Band satellite technology, and it was on the brink of taking connectivity to the next level.

Bill Sullivan, the director for strategy and business development for mobile broadband at ViaSat, indicated that we could amp up the bandwidth and serve over 10 times as many aircraft.

That speed would meet our criteria for accessibility for everyone onboard, and it would truly allow us to leapfrog our competitors. As the product team's strategic recommendations resonated across the enterprise: "Sometimes it pays to wait." ViaSat agreed to provide the hardware and infrastructure for the end product, and LiveTV signed on to provide installation and maintenance support. JetBlue signed on as launch customer, with the understanding that the product would be marketed to the industry as a whole.

While the investigatory and development phase had its own challenges, the JetBlue product team encountered quite another, unique challenge internally.

The product team learned that JetBlue's crew members were losing faith in our cutting-edge brand and culture. We had always been the first, the best, the latest, and the freshest at whatever we put our minds to, but launching in-flight connectivity so publicly in 2007 had led to high expectations from our crew members and customers—expectations that we couldn't meet and didn't manage.

Before the ViaSat announcement was released in September 2010, the product team found themselves tap-dancing when asked about the airline's "experience" strategy. We couldn't tip our hand to the competition that we were building something better, but we had to communicate something to our crew members in order to get them excited about the future and to have them understand the timeline around building this new product.

The internal communications strategy focused its messaging on "smart" choices being more important than "fast."

Externally, the buzz started building, tempered somewhat by the long lead time before implementation. We announced a product that wouldn't see the light of day for 12 to 18 months. The product team felt it was important to reclaim the innovation space but not set market expectations so high that we would let our customers and crew members down.

The contribution of the cross-functional product team at JetBlue played a vital role. The team had established a level of credibility with stakeholders across the company. Its role was pivotal, in the validation of the strategy and in the detailed planning. The role extended to the hundreds of line-item tasks associated with the launch of this industry-defining product. Some of the big-ticket items included the following:

- Developing the appropriate antennae for both the A320 and E190 that could be integrated under the radome and work in conjunction with our existing systems (i.e., DIRECTV)
- Obtaining certification from the U.S. Federal Aviation Administration (FAA) for the new system for both fleet types
- Developing the customer portal experience—designing a portal that customers would want to visit

With three partners in three different states across the United States, the team decided that regular team meetings (both on the phone and in person) were a necessity. The project timeline would be managed in phases: ViaSat would control Phase I, the building and launching of the satellite; Phase II would be controlled by LiveTV, to enable installation and certification with the FAA and onboard JetBlue's aircraft; and Phase III would be controlled by JetBlue with support from LiveTV, and it would include the deployment and marketing to customers.

The role of the product team at JetBlue serves as the glue for the organization for developing the customer experience. The team knows, as with all plans, there will be adjustments due to unanticipated events. However, the team accepts the risks and is devoted to the product's success because of several factors. Among the most important of these is a high degree of communication because of the collective commitment we have for the business. The team is always keeping an eye on the goal—to offer great products to our customer that will meet their current needs and that will scale to meet those needs that they haven't yet envisioned.

# EPILOGUE

In the Prologue, I described the path I traveled to get to the point where it seemed important—if not urgent—to write this book. I wanted to focus a brighter spotlight on Product Management to give this function greater recognition and respect.

However, as many other authors have also found, what was in my mind's eye when I started out was not exactly what ended up in the finished product. One thought leads to another. A continuous stream of data inspires new thoughts. Revisions become the norm. As I reviewed what I wrote, reread, and rewrote, the book became an "addiction." I didn't want the process to end. It was as if I was having an ongoing conversation with my audience, and I wanted to continue to explain my rationale and share other examples. Then, an epiphany—James Joyce again! It dawned on me that the reason I felt this almost obsessive need to continue was because *I care* so deeply and passionately about each and every topic, and I wanted to be sure I got your attention, with the hope of making you a believer.

As human beings, when we carry out a task at work or we do something we feel is constructive, we want and need some sort of validation. Did we do a good job? Did we make the customer happy? Could we have done better? In other words, I don't know if I hit the mark. As I came to the conclusion of my work on this book, I realized my human limitations.

What I am left with is hope—hope that you, as product leaders, aspiring product leaders, or business executives, will adopt some of recommendations and suggestions mentioned in this book.

I would like to share with you some final thoughts to keep in mind.

If you can secure a relevant *context* for Product Management, you will know the road you've already traveled and where you are now. If you and your cross-functional colleagues can *clarify* the purpose, fit, and function of Product Management, then you will know the direction to take. If you can find a way to *select* product managers and *improve* their capabilities, then you will more effectively *cultivate* their talent. And if you can *build* a community, *form* the team, and *govern* Product Management, then you can bring about the *continuity* required to sustain Product Management. And when Product Management is effectively governed and sustained, executives and leaders will be able to:

1.  Go forward without reinventing the wheel
2.  Build an organizational strategy that includes Product Management
3.  Get everyone into the Product Management sandbox
4.  Assemble the pieces of the Product Management puzzle
5.  Clarify the role of the product manager to improve staffing strategies
6.  Cultivate and shape product managers
7.  Build a knowledge-based Product Management community of practice
8.  Design and sponsor effective cross-functional product teams
9.  Embed a Product Management Governance Board that will enhance both the company and Product Management

And so it goes.

As you can see, these final thoughts reflect the modules and chapters of this book. It is my hope that this journey we have taken together will equip you with the thoughts, ideas, and action plans necessary to raise the bar so that Product Management can assume its rightful role in the organization and that everyone in every company around the world will have a common understanding of Product Management.

I also hope you'll want to continue the conversation with members of the Product Management Executive Board (www.productmanagement-execboard.com) to raise our collective cognizance as a knowledge-based community of senior executives and managers.

I am deeply grateful to you for investing your time and energy in reading through this book. I hope that you refer to it as often as you need to and that others in your universe will benefit from what it has to offer.

# BIBLIOGRAPHY

Allen, David. *Getting Things Done: The Art of Stress-Free Productivity*. New York: Penguin, 2001.

Blanchard, Kenneth H. *Empowerment Takes More Than a Minute*. San Francisco: Berrett-Koehler Publishers, 2001.

Bossidy, Larry, and Ram Charan with Charles Burck. *Execution: The Discipline of Getting Things Done*. London: Random House, 2002.

Cohen, Allen, and David L. Bradford. *Influence without Authority*. Hoboken, N.J.: Wiley, 2005.

Collins, Jim. *Good to Great: Why Some Companies Make the Leap . . . and Others Don't*. New York: HarperBusiness, 2001.

Curtis, Bill, William E. Hefley, and Sally Miller. *People CMM: A Framework for Human Capital Management*, 2d ed. Boston: Pearson Education, 2010.

Drucker, Peter F. *The Practice of Management*. New York: Harper & Row, 1954.

———. *On the Profession of Management*. Boston: Harvard Business Review Book (a collection of articles from 1963–2003).

———. "The Effective Decision." In *Harvard Business Review on Decision Making*. Boston: Harvard Business School Press, 2001, pp. 1–20.

Galbraith, Jay, Diane Downey, and Amy Kates. *Designing Dynamic Organizations*. New York: AMACOM, 2002.

Kanaga, Kim, and Michael E. Kossler. *How to Form a Team: Five Keys to High Performance*. Greensboro, N.C.: Center for Creative Leadership, 2004.

Katzenbach, Jon R., and Douglas K. Smith. *The Wisdom of Teams: Creating the High-Performance Organization*. Boston: Harvard Business School Press, 1993.

Lencioni, Patrick. *The Five Dysfunctions of a Team*. San Francisco: Jossey-Bass, 2002.

Nonaka, Ikujiro, and Hirotaka Takeuchi. *The Knowledge-Creating Company*. New York: Oxford University Press, 1995.

Pfeffer, Jeffrey, and Robert I. Sutton. *The Knowing-Doing Gap: How Smart Companies Turn Knowledge into Action*. Boston: Harvard Business School Press, 2000.

Senge, Peter. *The Fifth Discipline*. New York: Doubleday, 1990.

Senge, Peter, Art Kleiner, Charlotte Roberts, Richard Ross, and Brian Smith. *The Fifth Discipline Fieldbook*. New York: Doubleday, 1994.

# INDEX

Academic programs, 172
Accountability:
    avoidance of, 200, 219
    building shared, 130
    of cross-functional product teams,
        204, 205
Action plan, unified, 29
Analysis paralysis, 129
Applied learning projects, 170, 196
Appraisal, 30–33
Apprentices, 151–153
AT&T, 120
Audit:
    Business Case, 230
    cross-functional teams, 201–202

Baker Hughes, 107
Belief-based responses, 49
Bell Laboratories, 238
BetaBlue, 250
Bipolar statistical range, 49
Brand management, 18
Bundling strategy, 112
Business Case, 54, 75, 128
    audit, 230
    New Product Planning process and, 91
    reviewing, 230
Business model, 89
    changes to, 32
    evolution of, 36

Calendars, 101
    governance board, 240–242
    maintaining scheduling, 240
Campus recruiting, 141

Capability Maturity Model Integration
    (CMMI), Level 3, 29–30
Caplan, Janet, 185
Case studies, 13
    FedEx Services, 175–179
    JetBlue Airways, 250–253
    TD Canada Trust, 111–115
    Thomas & Betts Corporation,
        61–66
Clarity, 9–10, 54
    New Product Development
        process, 92
    of product manager role, 10, 121
    of responsibility, 22, 28–29
    role, 15, 18, 28–29, 94, 118, 182
    in teams, 201–202
CMMI (see Capability Maturity Model
    Integration)
Coaching, 153, 163
    cross-functional product teams, 211
Collective cognizance, 85, 92
    benefits of, 93
    in cross-functional product teams,
        211–212
Collins, Jim, 10, 148
Commitment:
    to cross-functional product
        teams, 209
    to Product Management, 32
Communication:
    in cross-functional product teams,
        210–211
    improving, 101
    nonthreatening channels of, 155
    Product Master Plan to foster, 42

Communication (*continued*):
  in reorganizations, 27
  staffing strategy team policies on, 124
Community, 11, 25
  activities, 192
  all-hands meetings, 194
  anchors of, 190–195
  benefits of, 244
  brown-bag sessions, 194
  challenges, 198
  charter, 190–191
  cornerstones, 192
  cross-functional product teams
    and, 210
  cultivation of, 244
  defining, 187–188
  documented evidence on, 197
  examples of, 187–188
  formal events, 192
  framework portfolios, 194–195
  funding, 192
  governance board supporting, 244
  guidance, 191
  guidelines for, 193
  informal events, 192
  knowledge building, 192
  knowledge exchange in, 189
  leaders, 191
  learning, 192
  off-site meetings, 195
  purpose of, 190–191
  Reference Models in, 193
  sharing, 192
  structures, 186–187
  success, 196–198
  support, 191
  themes, 192
  threads of continuity in, 189
  value from, 187, 188–189
  voluntary, 188, 189
Competency:
  clusters, 47, 57

  core, 125–130
  defined, 43
  governance board requiring gradual
    building of, 218
  groupings, 45, 124
  meta-level, 45, 57
  New Product Planning relying on, 90
  product performance as
    nonnegotiable, 165
  rating scale, 47
  staffing strategy, 124–125
Competency assessments, 28, 42,
    46–49, 57, 156
  frequency of, 133
  ongoing, 237
  scores, 135
  in staffing strategy, 143
Competency gaps:
  common understanding of, 51–52
  evaluating, 49–52, 59
Competency Model, 42, 43–52, 59
  agreement on, 8
  to assess product line, 44
  to build core capabilities, 44
  consistency of, 132
  defined, 43
  groupings, 45
  product managers assessed with, 44
  purposes of, 44
  reference point of, 45
  staffing strategy and, 124–125
  work flows defined by, 44
Competitive advantage, 127, 246
Competitive positioning, 47
  critical thinking and, 48
  strategic planning and, 48
Competitive product analysis, 47
Competitor analysis, 47
Competitor monitoring, 168
Conflict, fear of, 200
Consistency, 36
  of Competency Model, 132

in governance board, 226
in interviews, 141–142
New Product Development and, 232
in Product Management, 8, 37
of Reference Model, 132
Context, 7–9, 15–16
Continuity, 11, 181–183
defined, 182
New Product Development, 77–78
Corporate culture, 22
adopting new, 80
Corporate Darwinism, 69–70, 79
Crafting effective strategies, 127–128
Creative process, 90
Credibility, 169, 176
building, 153
through decisions, 165
of leaders, 227
Critical thinking, 48
Cross-functional guidance, 38
Cross-functional participation, 81
Cross-functional product teams, 11–12
accountability, 204, 205
advisory members, 207
authority, 204, 208
autonomy of, 245
basic rules, 213
being provocative, 212
benefits of, 203
as business-within-a-business, 203
challenges for, 213
charter, 203–205, 213
coaching, 211
collective cognizance in, 211–212
commitments to, 209
communication in, 210–211
community and, 210
compensation for, 204, 205
conflicts in, 204–205, 208
core members, 207
criteria, 203–205
culturally diverse, 214

decisions, 208
defined, 202–206
design validation, 212–213
directing resources, 208–209
duration of, 200, 234
duties of, 202–203
earning empowerment, 206–210
embedded in governance board,
233–234
escalation methods, 213–214
establishment suggestions, 206–207
exposure of, 205
extended members, 207
furnishing systems to, 209–210
furnishing tools to, 209–210
geographically diverse, 214
governance board resolving
problems in, 245
guidance for, 211
ideal composition of, 207
at JetBlue, 252–253
lack of alignment in, 219–220
leader of, 204, 207
meeting performance targets,
209–210, 211
membership changes, 205
metrics, 205
motivation for, 204
performance monitoring,
212–213
priorities of, 208
problem resolution, 213–214
providing resources for, 211
purpose of, 12
required resources, 208–209
required skills, 208–209
responsibility of, 205, 234
role confusion in, 219
scorecard, 212–213
selecting right people for, 207
selection techniques, 207
as self-governing, 204

Cross-functional product teams
  (*continued*):
  sovereignty of, 204
  sponsor based on, 203–205
  starting small, 210–211
  success of, 210–212
  synchronization of, 234
  written works on, 206
Cross-functional project teams, 11
  disbanding, 200
  resources dedicated to, 199–200
Cross-functional teams, 161, 182–183, 199
  audit of, 201–202
  challenges to, 201
  dysfunction in, 200
  exposure to different situations
    through, 161–162
  forming, 202
  inefficiency in, 200–202
  lack of clarity in, 201–202
  prioritization of, 201
  role confusion, 201
  staffing strategy, 123
Cross-geographic learning, 107
Cross-organizational impacts, 24
Cross-product councils, 106
Cross-product strategies, 113
Cultivation, 10–11, 117–118
  of community, 244
  defined, 148
  guidelines, 118
  of leaders, 168
  of product managers, 87
Cultural adaptation, 107
Cultural influencers, 239
Customer visit plan document, 55
Customer visit process, 53–56, 138
  high-level work flow for, 55
Customers:
  culturally diverse, 214
  exposure degree, 134
  meeting needs of only external, 177

  monitoring, 168
  product managers connecting
    with, 24

Darwin, Charles, 69
Decisions:
  combining options for, 166
  by cross-functional product
    teams, 208
  decision matrix for, 143–144, 166
  empowerment through, 165
  fact-based, 165–167
  improving, 143–144
  morphological boxes for, 166
  New Product Development and
    making, 91, 92
  New Product Planning gates, 91
  staffing strategy team rules for,
    123–124
  techniques to make, 166
  translating information sources
    into, 129
Deming work activity cycle model, 130
Design for Six Sigma (DFSS), 78
Developmental projects, 170
  combining, 173
  guidelines for, 173
DFSS (*see* Design for Six Sigma)
Discovery process, 90
Domain:
  familiarity, 137
  knowledge, 196
  understanding, 23
Domain expertise, 23, 24
  determining need for, 137–138
Drucker, Peter, 122, 188

Education improvement programs, 52
Electronic repositories, 11, 186–187
Employee reports, 170
End state:
  describing, 18

organizational strategy, 31
Engineering, 73
Experience:
  activities for, 172–173
  benefits of, 169
  of cross-functional product
    teams, 220
  drain, 189
  past, 135
  years of, 136
Experiential scale, 50
Exploration process, 90

FedEx Services, 175–179
  foundation of, 179
  overview, 175–176
*The Fifth Discipline* (Senge), 85
Finance, 28
Financial indicators, 171
Financial knowledge, 171
Financial statements, 243
FIRO-B personality test, 135
*The Five Dysfunctions of a Team*
    (Lencioni), 200, 219
Ford Motor Company, 37
Foundation:
  building stable, 40–41
  FedEx, 179
  organization and, 87–88
FSP (*see* Functional Support Plan)
Functional misalignments, 89
Functional Support Plan (FSP), 209
Function-oriented structure, 105
Funding requests, 230

Geneen, Harold S., 83
General Motors, 107
Geography-oriented structure, 106–107
Goethe, Johann Wolfgang von, 147
*Good to Great* (Collins), 10, 148
Governance board, 12, 31–32, 76, 79, 128,
    182, 204

attributes for, 222–224
autonomy, 228
behaviors of, 218
bylaws, 218
charter, 218, 225
community support from, 244
connections with, 227–228
contributing to success, 221
data management of, 234–236
detracting from success, 221
disintegration of, 226
embedded cross-functional product
    teams in, 233–234
flexibility of, 218
goals of, 209
inconsistency of, 226
innovation initiatives, 237–240
justification for, 183
key provisos, 218
leaders, 227
linking actions to goals of, 209
membership, 226
membership conduct, 225
mentoring guidelines, 246
organization chart for, 225
prerequisites for, 219
Product Management definitions
    and, 221
product manager evaluations by,
    236–238
product performance and, 242–243
product portfolio and, 242–243
product portfolio councils and,
    228–230
requirements for, 218
requiring gradual building of
    competencies, 218
resolving team problems, 245
role of, 242
rules, 218, 225, 227
sponsoring, 219, 225
success from, 246–247

Governance board (*continued*):
  in transition, 218
  transparency established from, 249
  visual representation, 228
Grove, Andrew, 104

Hierarchy, 149, 236–237
Hiring (*see* Staffing)
History, forgetting, 2, 84
Hybrid managers, 94
Hybrid structure, 107–108

Inattention to results, 200
Industry data, 168
Information Technology, 73
Innovation, 244
  discontinuing, 239
  encouraging, 239
  governance board initiatives for,
    237–240
  investing in, 238
  job descriptions and, 239
Insource-Outsource Model, 4
Institutional learning, 85
Interconnected systemic interfaces, 24
Internships, 172
Interpersonal skills, 136
Interrelationships, 138–139
Interviews, 52
  consistency in, 141–142
  improving procedures for, 140–143
  open-ended situational questions in,
    142
  paradigms, 132
  protocols, 140–143
  question sequences, 141
  records of, 142
  standardizing, 141
  styles, 141
Investors, 238

Jackson, Andrew, 17

JetBlue Airways, 250–253
  cross-functional product teams at,
    252–253
Job:
  levels, 152–154
  requirement standards, 117
  rotation, 172
  titles, 6, 70, 117
Job descriptions, 125
  general outline, 139–140
  innovation and, 239
  rewriting, 139–140
  universal, 139
  validating, 139–140
Jobs, Steve, 216
Journeymen, 151, 153–154
Joyce, James, 169, 255

Keirsey Temperament Sorter, 135
Kelley, Robert, 185
Key performance indicators (KPIs), 235
  availability of, 164
  monitoring, 96–97, 164
  visually prominent, 167
Knowledge drain, 189

Launch:
  analysis post, 95
  delayed, 128
  effective, 128
  improving, 25
Launch Plan, 75, 93
  formal assembly of, 95
  New Product Planning process and,
    91
  overlooking, 94, 95
Leaders, 219
  abilities, 136–137
  communication of, 26–27
  community, 191
  correctly staffing, 94
  credibility of, 227

of cross-functional product teams, 204, 207
cultivating, 168
expectations, 70
external resources for, 168
as generalists, 114
of governance board, 227
identifying potential, 168
influence of, 167–168
informal opinions of, 150
initiatives made or broken by, 79
leaving mark, 77
process, 232
reorganizations described by, 18
respect for, 27, 31
at TD Canada Trust, 113–114
testing, 169
variety of, 130
Lencioni, Patrick, 200, 219
Likert scale, 49
LiveTV, 250, 251
Lombardi, Vince, 69
Luccock, Halford E., 199

Machiavelli, 36, 119
"Managing Cultural Diversity," 214–215
Market:
acceptance, 107
experts, 168
insight library, 138
pay scales, 138
research, 96
segment management, 18
segmentation model, 47
summaries, 241
Market insights, developing, 28, 47, 126–127
ongoing research for, 126
Marketing:
Product Management differentiated from, 62
responsibility of, 28

Marketing mix, 127–128
Masters, 151, 154
Maturity:
product, 133, 156
product portfolio, 156
progression plans and, 154–157
Maturity evaluations, 57, 59, 183
enhanced, 246–247
example, 58
frequency of, 58
initial, 222, 223
ongoing, 237
rating scale, 57
scoring, 156, 222
statements, 57–58
Maturity Model, 56–58, 222
defining, 56
dimensions of, 56
purpose of, 56
(*See also* Capability Maturity Model Integration; Product Management Maturity Model, Product Manager Population)
Mentors, 154, 246
benefits of, 246
governance board and, 246
Mergers, 80
Mission statement, 12–13
Moeller, Mike, 251
Motivation, 204
Myers-Briggs Type Indicator, 135

Natural selection, 69
Need profiles, 72
New Product Development (NPD):
administration of, 232
clarifying, 92
data elements in, 91, 92
as decision-making tool, 91, 92
inconsistency in, 232
incorrect use of, 78
misusing, 92

New Product Development (NPD)
(*continued*):
phase gates, 78
process continuity, 77–78
subphases of, 93
as task management tool, 91
New Product Introduction (NPI), 45,
75, 93–95
New Product Planning (NPP), 45, 75,
90–93
Business Cases and, 91
concept phase of, 91
creative process and, 90
data produced from, 94
decision gates, 91
definition phase of, 91
discovery process and, 90
exploration process and, 90
feasibility phase of, 91
Launch Plans and, 91
outcome of, 92
Product Requirements Documents
and, 91
relying on core competencies of
people, 90
NPD (*see* New Product Development)
NPI (*see* New Product Introduction)
NPP (*see* New Product Planning)

Onboarding, 145–146
Online forums, 244
Operational audit, 33
Operational control systems, 96
Operations, 73
Organization, 3
challenges, 53
company direction and, 52–53
design considerations, 52–56, 59
diagnostic projects, 28
disconnects in, 70–71
elements of, 54
end state, 31

foundational elements of, 87–88
governance board chart, 225
influential people and, 109
as living system, 84–85
longevity, 87
master plan for, 41–43
nonnegotiables for, 109–110
outcomes, 53
overarching strategy linking to, 31
Product Management as backbone
of, 40
recognizing each process in, 109
Reference Model for alignment of,
88–90
searching for, 84
strategy for, 8–9
at TD Canada Trust, 113–114
vision for, 20–22
(*See also* Reorganizations)
Organizational amnesia, 37
Organizational Development, 19, 77
Organizational efficiency, 162
Organizational gaps, 8
Organizational indigestion, 110
Organizational interactivity, 85
Organizational learning, 85–86
facilitating, 85
Organizational silos, 4–5, 9

Paradigms, changing, 38–39
PDCA (*see* Plan-Do-Check-Act)
Peer referral network, 171
Peer review council, 142
Performance Management, 28
Personal vision, 12–13
Personality profile tools, 135
Perspectives, changing, 38–39
Plan-Do-Check-Act (PDCA), 130
Platform committees, 106
PLMs (*see* Product line managers)
PLPM (*see* Post-Launch Product
Management)

PMEB (*see* Product Management Executive Board)

PMLCM (*see* Product Management Life Cycle Model)

PMMM-G (*see* Product Management Maturity Model, Governance)

PMMM-P (*see* Product Management Maturity Model, Product Manager Population)

Population assessment, 131–133, 155–156

Post-Launch Product Management (PLPM), 45–46, 75, 95–96

PRDs (*see* Product Requirements Documents)

Predictability, 36

Prioritization:
  of cross-functional product teams, 208
  product managers, 47–48
  of teams, 201

Process diagrams, 162

Process library, 138, 162, 233

Product:
  category management, 18
  Competency Model to assess, 44
  complexity, 133, 134
  differentiating, 26
  expectations, 5
  extraordinary, 76
  familiarity, 137
  financial data, 164
  groupings, 105
  increasing quality, 25
  late delivery of, 163
  life cycle process, 71, 134, 241
  maturity, 133, 156
  narrowly defined requirements for, 177
  ownership, 70–71
  reversing course on, 251
  strategic reviews of, 169
  technology, 134

Product development, 81, 93
  approach to Product Management, 97–99
  financial impact of, 99
  oversight of, 94
  vortex of, 94

Product line managers (PLMs), 23

Product Management:
  as backbone of organization, 40
  chartering, 86–87
  codified, 40
  commitment to, 32
  common characteristics of, 4–5, 101
  consistency in, 8, 37
  defined, 6, 75, 81
  defined by governance board, 221
  development-centric approach to, 97–99
  embedding, 22
  function of, 1, 7, 80
  as genetic material, 75
  as horizontal function, 31, 39
  impact of, 220
  importance of, 2–3, 19
  integration challenges, 3
  interconnected systems of, 75–76
  involving everyone in, 80–82
  just-in-time, 96
  long-term, 78–82
  main players in, 6
  Marketing differentiated from, 62
  misunderstandings about, 4
  purpose of, 80
  reinventing, 19
  reorganizations impacting, 22–24
  responsibility of, 28
  role in, 75
  at Thomas & Betts, 61–63
  transformational framework for, 19
  typical incorporation of, 39
  universal approach to, 8, 17, 35
  varied interpretations of, 67, 76–77

Product Management (*continued*):
  weak areas in, 4–5
Product Management Council of
    Executives, 25
Product Management Executive Board
    (PMEB), 256
Product Management Leadership
    Summit, 25
Product Management Life Cycle Model
    (PMLCM), 45, 46, 88, 90, 102,
    109, 230
  Areas of Work, 45, 75, 89
  implementation of, 76
  modified, 108
Product Management Maturity
    Model, Governance (PMMM-G),
    57, 222
Product Management Maturity Model,
    Product Manager Population
    (PMMM-P), 57, 155
Product Management Mind Map,
    88–89
  reality accurately represented in, 92
Product manager, 6
  background of, 135
  classifications, 149
  Competency Models to assess, 44
  cultivation of, 87
  customer connections with, 24
  earnings drivers and, 112
  at FedEx, 176–179
  governance board evaluations of,
    236–238
  inequality of, 133–137
  managers of, 163–164
  prioritizing work, 47–48
  promotion of, 237
  reorganizations reducing, 103
  role clarity of, 10, 121
  skills of, 81
  as stop-off job, 122
  at TD Canada Trust, 111–112
  testing, 169

Product Manager Scorecard, 10, 57, 118,
    125, 156, 170, 237
  example, 158–159
  rating scales, 196
Product Master Plan, 41, 59, 86, 145
  building blocks of, 42
  to establish precedents, 42
  to foster communication, 42
  items to include in, 42
  to minimize confusion, 42
  outline, 43
  properly maintaining, 41
  purposes of, 41
  tracking, 42
  updating, 42
Product performance:
  being conscientious about, 164–165
  governance board and, 242–243
  monitoring, 129
  as nonnegotiable competency, 165
Product performance analysis, 48–49
  financial, 50, 70
Product portfolio:
  categories, 156
  Competency Model to assess
    managers of, 44
  composition of, 30
  evaluating, 230
  governance board and, 242–243
  managing, 129
  maturity, 156
  monitoring, 129
  optimization, 229–230
  rationalization group, 72
  rationalization of, 229–230
  robust process in, 24
Product portfolio council, 24
  contributions of, 230
  governance board and, 228–230
  membership of, 229
  role of, 229
Product Requirements Documents
    (PRDs), 91

Product Strategy, 75
Product-oriented structure, 105–106
Progression plans, 149–150, 236–237
   criteria, 149–150
   maturity and, 154–157
Project management, 4, 38–39, 130

Quality and Productivity group, 77

Reference Model, 45–46, 59, 75, 83
   agreement on, 8
   common definition of, 9
   in communities, 193
   consistency of, 132
   for organizational alignment,
      88–90
   overwhelming people, 30
"Release train" approach, 99
Reorganizations, 29–30
   communication in, 27
   detrimental impacts of, 2
   domino effects of, 2
   dysfunctional, 18
   evaluating, 8
   failed, 86–87
   frequency of, 15
   geographical, 71–72
   leaders describing, 18
   length of, 21
   measurements, 29–30
   milestones, 29–30
   multiphase, 25
   phases of, 21
   Product Management impacted by,
      22–24
   promises in, 17
   prompting, 20–22
   reasons for, 104
   reducing product managers in, 103
   resistance to, 32
   static effects of, 2
   theoretical constructs of, 22
   time allotted for, 24–26, 29

   timeline, 31
   understanding, 24
   unexpected problems in, 22
   unsatisfactory reactions to, 27
   (*See also* Organization)
Reorganizations, past:
   appraising, 19–30
   assessment of, 17
   basic questions about, 20
   justifications for, 15
   (*See also* History, forgetting)
Resource database, 209
Respect:
   for CEO, 29
   for leaders, 27, 31
Responsibility:
   clarity of, 22, 28–29
   of cross-functional product teams,
      205, 234
   of Finance, 28
   of Marketing, 28
   of Product Management, 28
Role:
   defining, 22
   designation, 53
   of governance board, 242
   interdependencies, 53
   in Product Management, 75
   of product portfolio council, 229
   of salespeople, 55
Role alignment, disparities in, 100
Role clarity, 18, 28–29, 94, 118, 182
   lack of, 15
   of product manager, 10, 121
Role confusion, 52, 70
   in teams, 201, 219
Root-cause analyses, 162–164

Sales:
   resistance, 143
   training plan, 95
Saying yes to everything, 200–201
Second opinions, 52

Segmentation, 133–137
  market model, 47
Self-evaluation, 50–51
  rating scale, 51
Self-learners, 154
Seneca, 173
Senge, Peter, 85
Sequent Learning Networks, 4
Shaping, defined, 148
Shopping malls, 190
Situational profiles, 160
Skills:
  cross-functional product teams
    required, 208–209
  improvement programs, 52
  interpersonal, 136
  product manager, 81
  soft, 136
  suites, 156
  work management, 130
Socialization, 145–146
Software Engineering Institute, 30
Staffing:
  challenges, 117
  consistency in, 119
  leaders correctly, 94
  model, 88, 92
  procedures, 150–151
Staffing strategy, 10, 122–124
  adjustments to, 137
  competencies, 124–125
  competency assessments in, 143
  Competency Model and, 124–125
  defining agreed-upon set of goals, 123
  defining sequence of events and
    activities, 123
  effective, 125
  guidelines, 123–124
  improving, 118
  meta-process for, 131–144
  reference point, 124–125
  steps, 131–144

Staffing strategy team, 123
  communication policies, 124
  cross-functional, 123
  decision rules for, 123–124
Strategic Planning, 28, 168–169
  competitive positioning and, 48
Strategic profiling, 99
Structure, 3, 102–104
  bias in, 102–103
  community, 186–187
  correct, 102
  function-oriented, 105
  geography-oriented, 106–107
  hybrid, 107–108
  in matrixed mode, 105
  product-oriented, 105–106
  reasons for current, 102
  statistics, 104
  Thomas & Betts, 64
  types of, 104–108
Sullivan, Bill, 251–252
Supervisors, 154
Synthesizing, 169
Systemic awareness, 86
  defined, 85

Talent management system, 209
Targeted development programs,
  169–173
TD Canada Trust, 111–115
  easy principle at, 113
  leadership at, 113–114
  organization at, 113–114
  product manager at, 111–112
  Senior Executive Operating
    Committee for, 114
  talent development at, 115
Technical knowledge, 196
  determining need for, 137–138
Thomas & Betts Corporation, 61–66
  overview, 61
  Product Management at, 61–63